'Fifty Finest'

A Tribute to England's Test Cricket History

by

Andrew Bee

Fifty Finest — A Tribute to England's Test Cricket History
was first published in 2010 on behalf of the author
by
BRIDGE BOOKS
61 Park Avenue
WREXHAM
LL12 7AW

© 2010 Andrew Bee
© 2010 typesetting and design Bridge Books

All Rights Reserved.
No part of this publication may be reproduced,
stored in a retrieval system, or transmitted
in any form or by any means, electronic,
mechanical, photocopying, recording or
otherwise, without the prior permission
of the Copyright holder.

A CIP entry for this book is available from the British Library

ISBN 978-1-84494-066-0

Cover illustration and illustration on page 259 by Sara Bee

Printed and bound by
MPG Biddles Ltd
King's Lynn
Norfolk

Contents

Introduction	4
Of Trott and Broad	7
Those that did not make the grade	9
Fifty Finest	41
Statistical analysis	269
Bibliography	271

Introduction

This book is, in fact, dedicated to my father, Bob Bee. His quite obsessive love for English cricket, not one-day rubbish but proper cricket, knows no bounds.

Once upon a time I waded into a cold, hidden north-facing mountain pool in the Cambrian Mountains and my older brother Nicholas splashed me, quite deliberately. My father, clearly angry gave me a thump to the shoulder, certainly firm enough to know my screaming, even as a nine-year-old, was an act of unwarranted, inappropriate behaviour. My father administered corporal punishment – hard, but not too hard. What nonsense. A little later on my father apologised. David Steele had just been dismissed for 50 in his first innings against Lillee and Thompson, and my dad was still seething. I was a victim of circumstance.

Also this book is dedicated to my mother, Martha, for her excellent levels of tolerance at my father's obsession. It is dedicated to my lovely wife Claudia who encouraged me to 'get on with your book!' on many occasions late into the night. Perhaps she was trying to tell me something. To my brother Nicholas for offering a different perspective as well as for editing the book, to my sister Sara for her excellent art work, and to my children Harry and Suzanna.

This has not been a sole enterprise, a labour of love perhaps but I have asked many august people to comment on their favourite innings. A few favourites crop up for example Basil d'Oliveira's 158 at the Oval in 1968, mentioned by both Derek Barnard of the Cricket Society and Joe Davies, headmaster of Haileybury. Brian Close's 70, battered and bruised, against Hall and Griffith was put forward by Andrew Hutchinson. Colin Milburn's 139 in Pakistan – just before his career shattering car crash – was mentioned by Bob Carr, housemaster at Sutton Valence, but though a Milburn century pro-vided high entertainment with those lavish hooks against the quicks, none of his cameos gate crash this party.

My memory stretches back only as far as Lord's 1975. For the vast majority of innings I have had to rely on first-hand accounts from

Wisden as well as the mountain of cricket books covering entire shelves in my parents' TV room. Identifying innings that could break into the top 50 was a time consuming business exploring every test match.

From my own memories over the past 35 years, and my father's dating back to Bradman's 1948 series, we steadily drafted a list of unforgettable knocks. Certainly those played in the nineteenth century by Shrewsbury, Grace, Stoddart, A. G. Steele and Ranjitsinji rely – but for the most brief information – almost exclusively on the annual edition of *Wisden* dating back to 1864. Fortunately my father has collected the entire series to provide a most fortunate bank of detail on any colossal innings.

Statistically over 100 of England's finest innings have been assessed on many criteria – see the end of the book.

Enjoy the book. As the list unfolded before me, a point remains. The list continually evolved as more evidence came to light. Analysing *Wisden* for mentions of the chanceless innings led to the list finally becoming rooted only after the last word was read and the list agonised over one final time. You will note, for instance, several of the innings ranked between 51 and 60 written to the same depth as those in the top 50. This is because, until the last criterian had been statistically incorporated, the situation facing the batsman and the job he had to perform, these innings had made the top 50. My advice is to leave the temptation of finding out the greatest knock to the last pages. Hence the book will read more like an epic story through English Cricket in a mix-match of scenes à la the film *Pulp Fiction*.

I've lived the last 35 years as one of England Cricket's most passionate fans. I have lived through all of the finest knocks in my middle-aged life. I judge innings ultimately by the mark they made on me at the time. I tweaked the analysis until I felt the list was right.

I passed the list onto my father, arguably England Cricket's number-one fan. He can compare his gut reaction to Compton's finest innings with Botham's. He has lived through them, tasted the wine in their aftermath and now fondly remembers them through pages in *Wisden*. English fans have this strange habit of remembering exactly where they were when these innings happened. Where were you when Boycott got his 191 at Headingley in 1977?

I was in Norfolk at my grandparent's house. That day we had swum in the River Waveney. I remember it being a warm and sunny day with a gentle breeze. I was with my cousins who had recently been traumatised by their mother's untimely death from breast cancer. We rushed back to my grandparent's colour TV to watch the on drive off Greg Chappell and subsequent crowd reaction. I remember Giles, my nine-year-old cousin, smiling for the first time in six weeks. Over all it was a very fine day indeed.

E. W. Swanton would not be drawn into a comparison of cricketers from different ages, certainly not averages because as Swanton intimated, comparing cricketers from different eras is like comparing military battles through time – techniques and conditions change, they evolve. From 1884 to 1885 for instance, Webber states that team innings in first-class cricket suddenly increased by about 50. One can infer that conditions for better pitches improved, also that batting techniques thanks to the incomparable W. G. Grace shifted the odds in favour of the batsmen. Would anyone today take over 100 test wickets at just over 10 like George Lohmann? All the more reason to include heroic innings from the 1880s! Thankfully this author's statistical calculations bare that in mind. Today though, bowlers have no balls and wides counted against them and bowl on flat covered tracks; bowlers in the new millenium have a higher runs per wicket average than those before the new millenium. This downplays recent innings in the statistical analysis. Perhaps there is scope in a future book to consider the contributions of both innings a batsman plays in a test match. Poor Alec Stewart played two thunderous innings against Walsh and Ambrose in their prime at Barbados, both centuries. Possibly one or both would get into the top 100 ever played though neither – considered purely on its own – warrants a top 60 place.

At any rate, enjoy the book. The innings are spread evenly throughout the generations despite the plethora of test cricket in modern times, so weighted slightly in favour of past times but then they did have to face fast bowling on dodgy tracks with a clothe hat for protection!

Ready? Here we go then ...

Of Trott and Broad

Parents' house, TV Room, Lichfield Avenue, Morning Session, 28 August 2010.

The most fabulous hour unfolds as record after record tumbles. The Ames/Allen stand from '31 shatters as we sit down. Father cheers every run, singles to leg, no balls, boundary leg byes then a sweeping Broad cover drive off Mohammad Asif reduces the septuagenarian to a giggling fit. Rubbing his hands with glee, now fully replenished from the light, kipper salad, father strolls across the carpet whilst recalling the Gooch/Gower stand from 1985, such is the gay abandon in which runs are being harvested. 'More like the Knott/Boycott one for me' I reply, recalling a similar shared well-being 33-years earlier. We lose transmission and father's face becomes furious, a short fuse, and he fires off a four letter tirade at the TV; soon we realise he's sat on the remote and after a few frantic heart-stopping moments we locate the remote and press the required buttons.

The 400 arrives, then the 300 stand, followed by an urgent call from wife Claudia to return home. Kiss Mum, shake hands firmly with father and I am out on the road, glued to Test Match Special. Somewhere near Chartham, driving through country roads, I listen as Wahab Riaz loses his line and Broad crashes a back-foot cut through extra cover; the world test record eighth wicket stand of 313 is broken. It feels like I am floating on a million bubbles of champagne. 'Absolutely brilliant' purrs Geoffrey Boycott, 'this kid can bat.'

Then it dawns on me. My publisher has sent the copy of this very book to the printers and already it is out of date. When Broad falls for 169 in desperately anticlimactic fashion, following a 'review to the third umpire, hot spot and hawk-eye', I know my readers would demand to know where in the pantheon of great England test-match innings, Broad's and Trott's now stand.

For the record the tall, lanky, left-handed Broad scored the highest ever innings by an England number nine, crushing the previous highest by 47 runs; indeed the 24-year-old came within a single boundary of the world record. He made 169 in a little over six hours, entering the arena when England stared down the barrel of another ignominious collapse. The subsequent cover drives, illuminated in sunlight, deserve statue status in the centre of Broad's home town; folk will look on in 100 years, brows furrowed in astonishment. It was not a chanceless innings and Broad arrived in the 39th over with the clouds lifted and venom spent from the attack. It would land at number 38 in the all-time rankings if the book began its journey again, between innings from Alec Stewart and David Gower.

The right-handed, more compact Jonathan Trott was not out overnight on the rain ruined first day, and weathered the twisting Mohammad Amir tornado that swept down Cook, Peitersen, Collingwood and Morgan in the first 20 minutes of day two. Standing mainly at the non-striker's end, Trott survived then found a willing ally in Prior, but the wicket-keeper perished soon after lunch and when Swann edged to slip, England had plummeted to 102–7. Broad caught the eye with the quality of his stroke-play, but Trott was rarely troubled, a rock, an accumulator and a dissipater of Pakistan morale. His 184 is ranked number 32, sandwiched between a gladiatorial Robin Smith rearguard and a barnstorming Botham assault – that warm.

In the evening, news broke of allegations involving 'spot fixing'. Mohammad Asif and Mohammad Amir both no-balled deliberately to satisfy a betting syndicate, to fuel the pockets of the corrupt. Apparently three no-balls were delivered, two early on in England's innings, one from 18-year-old Amir overstepping by a good foot. The aftermath left a foul taste and severed, albeit temporarily, the harmonica tremor of pleasure normally felt from so superb a fight-back.

Trott faced one of the deliberate no balls from Amir, a sharp rising missile that he struggled to play down on the leg side – hardly the friendliest no ball. That apart, Trott and Broad's innings deserve due accolades; 332 for the eighth wicket is the seventh-highest stand in all of England's test cricket history, an astonishing achievement and the only world record test stand from an England pair. The 28 August 2010 stands as a very proud day for English cricket and long may it be remembered.

Those that did not quite make the grade

Innings Ranked Number 60
Rhodes' 179 at Melbourne in 1912

Opponents: Australia
At stake: Ashes
Bowling attack: Cotter, Kelleway, Armstrong, Matthews, Hordern, Minnett, Ransford. 28.22 runs per wicket.
Pitch: Fair
Game situation: Australia had been dismissed for 191 after England had won the toss and inserted them. England led by two tests to one. This was the fourth test in a 5 test series.

There had been some headaches back in England, searching around for the ideal opening partner for Jack Hobbs. There were a number of contenders: S. P. Kinneir of Warwickshire, Leicestershire had C. B. J. Wood, Kent had H. T. W. Hardinge and there were also F. L. Fane, George Gunn, Tom Hayward and P. F. Warner.

Instead, England gambled on the legendary all-rounder Wilfred Rhodes. Not only was Rhodes on his way to an all-time world record of 4,187 wickets as a slow left-arm bowler – unlikely ever to be broken – but also he scored a small matter of 58 hundreds, and only 17 other batsmen in the history of the game have scored more than his 39,802 runs.

Rhodes's batting began at number 11 both for Yorkshire and England. He rose up the ranks with a thorough defence and a tenacious reputation. In only his second test as opener, Rhodes put on a stand of 159 and, in the fifth test, 221, with Jack Hobbs in South Africa in 1909/10. Therefore despite the attentions of a wealth of County openers, England opted for their star spin bowler to perform the job.

The six-week voyage to Australia gave the cricketers time to acquaint themselves with their team mates. Some wiled away the hours reading or playing bridge, others, including the enthusiastic Rhodes, played deck cricket to hone their skills. At this time, the autumn of 1911, Scott began his ill-fated expedition to Antarctica. By the time the tour finished, Scott, along with two other explorers, would lie frozen in their tent.

Australia could justifiably be considered the world champions at the time. They had beaten South Africa 4-1 the previous summer at home and England in the last two Ashes series – 2–1 in England in 1909 and 4–1 on home turf in 1907/08. England, having lost the first test, had seized the initiative by winning the second and third tests thanks to some awesome batting by Jack Hobbs, in youthful 32-year-old mould. S. F. Barnes, statistically recognised as the greatest bowler of all time, spearheaded the England attack with F. R. Foster.

Controversially, for the first test Barnes didn't open with Foster, the captain, J. W. H. T. Douglas, chose himself instead. Barnes didn't like it and openly sulked.

On inspection of the fourth test wicket, just having soaked up a thunderstorm, Douglas consulted Plum Warner, the official captain for the tour. Warner, stricken by a serious illness which was to remove him from featuring in all five test matches, advised 'Better talk to Wilfred'.

Rhodes, flattered by the complement, sank a toe then a thumb into the pitch. With a highly analytical facial expression, not dissimilar to a wine connoisseur assessing a vintage, Rhodes announced that England should 'put 'em in.' Warner, struck by the out-of-box suggestion, replied that as a policy inserting the opposition had never previously succeeded.

'Well' replied Rhodes, 'there must be a first time.' Sure enough, Foster and Barnes shot them out for 191.

Hobbs and Rhodes strode out to bat content in the knowledge that Australia, inserted against history, were bundled so cheaply. Rhodes the bowler had only delivered a couple of wicketless, but economical overs. There was no doubt though that his bold assessment of the pitch and momentous advice that morning, relieved and inspired Rhodes even before he faced a delivery.

At 34, Rhodes was at the peak of his career. After missing the first test, he had replaced Kinneir at the top of the order and so far had scored three 50s in four innings, the last one a 'Not out' to guide England to a seven-wicket victory.

Australia's bowling attack consisted of Albert Cotter, similar in style to Jeff Thomson, and the fast, medium swerve of Charles Kelleway. The giant Warwick Armstrong was first change, a large all rounder who bowled accurate line and length off an unfeasibly long run up. T. J. Matthews provided leg breaks in a brief but successful career.

The rest of the bowling was provided by two doctors: H.V. Hordern (who's googlies had won the first test), and R. B. Minnett, a seamer with a windmill flow of arms who released accurate medium pacers.

Hobbs and Rhodes had the knack of stealing singles and although vastly different characters, they shared a half-magical understanding of running between the wickets, a mixture of daring and safety. Always it seemed runs ticked over without sufficient pressure building.

Rhodes played the percentage game. His favoured strokes included the off drive played by leaning into the ball. Hobbs of course was the master batsman, the true great who had all the mainstream scoring shots, so it was for the entire duration of the partnership Hobbs always ahead.

It must have been dispiriting for the Australians, as first the hundred partnership came up, then the hundred and fifty. The Aussies saw the openers race passed the previous Ashes record opening partnership (185 between Hayward and Jackson in 1899) and on to a first innings lead, still no wicket down. Both batsmen struck centuries, Hobbs first, then the openers eclipsed their own English record first innings partnership of 221 against South Africa. On they batted until eventually Rhodes too reached his century, his first for England.

Hobbs came close to exceeding his own record score at the time of 187 in the last test, before edging Hordern to Carter the keeper. The pair batted for only 268 minutes, a little under $4^1/2$ hours, scoring comfortably in excess of a run a minute. The partnership realised 323 runs and was to remain an England first-innings record for another 36 years, until broken by Hutton and Washbrook in late 1948.

Rhodes continued on with a century partnership for the second wicket with the eccentric George Gunn for company. At 425 for 1, with a first innings lead of 234, Rhodes succumbed with a fine edge to the keeper off Minnett's slightly comical windmill action. His 179 was England's third highest test score in the 34-year history of the game behind Hobb's 187 and R. E. Foster's 287.

England regained the Ashes as they compiled 589, a new record total in tests, before dismissing Australia again for under 200, this time 173. England were hugely indebted to their finest opening pair of bowlers possibly of all time.

S. F. Barnes and F. R. Foster took 66 wickets between them in the series. Neither were express paced but their styles complemented each other. Foster was left arm over whilst Barnes was the archetypal right arm, fast medium with metronomic accuracy.

In fact no other test side came close to emulating England's feats. At this point in history, right through to the Great War, England was without doubt the greatest cricket nation on the planet. Then war on the Western Front rather threw a spanner in the works and no test cricket was played until December 1920.

Interestingly just six weeks after this famous partnership, a large cruise liner set sail for New York. It never made it, on her maiden voyage the *Titanic* struck an ice berg.

As for Wilfred Rhodes, he lived on to become one of England's longest-lived cricketers. Right to the end, although sight deserted him, Wilfred could be seen supporting his beloved Yorkshire, surrounded by friends and former cricketers. He died peacefully, aged 96, in 1973.

No one is ever likely to break his haul of 4,187 first-class wickets. He must have been some all-rounder to be included in this book. Less distinguished to look at than W. G., Wilfred Rhodes remains comparable to the great man nonetheless.

Australia 191 (Minnett 56, Barnes 5-74, Foster 4-77).
England 589 (Rhodes 179, Hobbs 178, Gunn 75, Woolley 56, F. R. Foster 50, Hordern 3-137).
Australia 173 (J. W. H. T. Douglas 5-46).
ENGLAND WON BY AN INNINGS AND 225 RUNS.

Innings Ranked Number 59
Strauss's 161 at Lord's in 2009

Opponents: Australia
At stake: Ashes
Bowling attack: Johnson, Hilfenhaus, Siddle, Hauritz, Clarke: 30.00 (estimated)
Pitch: Good
Game situation: England won the toss and Strauss elected to bat under fine conditions.

During the first test at Cardiff – just five days earlier – England had clawed their way out of a deep abyss but only by the breath of Monty Panesar's bat. He and number 10 James Anderson held on for 69 balls to defy Ponting's Australians. For most of the last day, and certainly all but the last five minutes of play, England could so easily have lost by an innings. That was Sunday, it was now the following Friday.

Lord's had seen six draws from the last seven first-class games and the Australians had not lost a test at there since 1934. What chance for Strauss and England? Escape with another draw and hope the pendulum swings later in the series? All of England hoped and prayed for the miracle turnaround.

It was believed the pitch would have more in it for the seamers than Cardiff so Strauss made only one change. He said good-bye to hero Monty Panesar (1–115 at Cardiff) and hello to Graham Onions, the Durham seamer who enjoyed slicing through the West Indies at Lord's nine weeks earlier with match figures of 7 for 92. Ricky Ponting left his team as it was in Cardiff, unchanged, for although England had escaped, his team had comfortably outperformed them.

And so it came to pass that on the 16th day of July in the year of our Lord 2009, England captain Andrew Strauss called correctly and, on winning the toss, elected to bat first under glorious conditions and on a plum wicket.

Ben Hilfenhaus, right-arm fast medium and broad as an ox, began proceedings by running in and bowling a steady maiden to Strauss. Strauss had enjoyed magnificent tours to India (252 at 84.00) and the

West Indies (541 at 67.62) during the winter, but his 103 runs from three home tests so far this season needed improving.

The compact left-hander sported a blue helmet with the three lions emblazoned on the front. Gloves, pads, inner and outer thigh pads, of medium build, short brown hair beginning to thin – this 32-year-old was in his absolute prime! Clothes a very fresh white, the married family man looked the model of professionalism, almost as though a city slicker had just changed out of his suit for the day.

Mitchell Johnson, a new world star that had shattered South Africa in the winter with both bat and ball, now ran in from the Pavilion End. All bustling speed and aggression the finely tuned young athlete released a rapid leg stump half-volley from his swift left-arm over style, to which Alistair Cook, England's taller, leaner and younger left-hand opener nonchalantly clipped to the mid-wicket boundary for four. Lord's erupted as the England journey began.

Whilst Hilfenhaus, unshaven, commanded the greatest respect from the Nursery End, Johnson bowled a wide long hop outside Strauss's off stump which purred across the well manicured out field to the point boundary. Next ball, Johnson tried the Yorker but Strauss clipped the offending full toss to midwicket for another four. In amongst the early skirmishes, Haddin let through two sets of four byes.

Seeing Johnson lose his stride with the Lord's slope, Ponting switched him to the Nursery End, whereupon Cook cut the first two balls for four. Poor Johnson endured a torrid first hour and England reached 50 in the thirteenth over without loss. The onslaught showed no signs of abating as Peter Siddle too found the slope confusing and just could not keep a tight line consistently enough. Two of Siddle's rockets took the edge along the ground through the slips for a couple more boundaries in the deserted third man region. At the other end Johnson spilt 53 runs from his first eight overs as England galloped off to take control.

Hilfenhaus still caused problems, now running in from the Pavilion End and Strauss edged behind only to be dropped off a no-ball. It was not Australia's day. None of their four bowlers had ever bowled at Lord's before, a telling statistic as Cook reached 50 from just 73 balls.

Ponting removed Johnson and falling short of options brought Nathan Hauritz the orthodox off spinner on at the Nursery End. Strauss, seeking to dominate, swept Hauritz behind and in front of square for two boundaries. Ponting brought on Marcus North – another orthodox off spinner but in the team as a batsman - and Haddin let through another four byes. By lunch, Cook had dominated with 67 to his name whilst Strauss could be highly satisfied with his 47. In 29 overs England had rocketed to 126 for no wicket, including no fewer than 22 boundaries.

That afternoon Cook stormed ahead with a couple of furious pulls off Johnson that scorched the earth. Strauss took on Hilfenhaus stoically and remained run-less for the first 20 minutes. Then against Hauritz, Strauss danced down the wicket and clobbered the ball on the half volley – it flew inches off the ground whilst Hauritz stuck out a despairing hand. The ball knocked the top joint out of place on the bowler's middle finger of his right hand. The batsmen scampered through for three. For the rest of the innings Ponting had no specialist spinner. Hauritz departed the field of play but not before vomiting on the pristine playing surface.

In desperation the Australian skipper placed a sweeper on the point boundary to the part time off spin of Marcus North. North bowled wide outside the off stump and leaked a steady four singles an over. Siddle too leaked runs at the same rate.

Both Strauss and Cook took their partnership beyond the 182 achieved by Hobbs and Sutcliffe at the ground in 1926, this 83-year-old record evaporated away in the extravagance of Johnson's waywardness, the Australian inexperience and the injury to Hauritz.

Ponting returned to Johnson who now bore the look of a school boy flogged by a Victorian school master. It was the 48th over and England had raced to 192, a run rate of exactly four an over. Still Johnson was errant and Cook helped himself to another boundary. Ponting chewed vigorously down on his gum, worry lines etched across his forehead.

Then, out of the blue, Johnson managed to bowl a blinder which swung in and left Cook palpably in front for 95. The appreciative crowd clapped him all the way to the Pavilion. In came Ravi Bopara, who had enjoyed feasting on West Indian bowlers earlier in the season, and immediately took 10 off a Johnson over to calm the nerves; Bopara looked serene and English hearts were raised as he cruised to 18, including four boundaries, but then Hilfenhaus trapped him in front, another promising Bopara innings nipped in the bud.

When Pietersen arrived at the crease Strauss stood with a smug smile on 90 not out. Ponting moved himself from mid-wicket to mid-on knowing Pietersen's penchant for stealing a fast, furious single to get off the mark. Pietersen played the ball to Ponting, but declined the single. Ponting, noticing Strauss out of his ground, hurled at the stumps, missed and gave away four runs. A cheer roared around Lord's. Pietersen lived dangerously though, especially against Hilfenaus in the over before tea. Indeed, in that over, Pietersen batted as though punch drunk; twice he almost handled the ball before fending off Hilfenhaus's last delivery to a vacant leg gully – fortunate.

In the same over, Strauss (on 97) cut behind square and the ball raced towards the boundary. The tall substitute, Andrew Macdonald, lunged towards the ball and just managed to stop it from rolling over the rope. Pietersen, running to the danger end, called for the third run despite a significant Achilles-heel issue and made his ground to the delight of the capacity crowd. Strauss waved his bat in the air and soaked up the applause. This was his fourth century at Lord's in the space of five years. It was important now for Strauss to emulate the Australian skipper and make a big hundred. England went into tea sitting pretty on 255 for 2.

Post tea, the Australian bowlers at last hit their straps with Siddle extracting an edge from the showman and Pietersen's cameo 32 from 42 ended up in Haddin's gloves. Collingwood, another hero from Cardiff with his monolithic 74 on the final day, started to play some shots and together with the increasingly comfortable Strauss took the total beyond 300.

By now Strauss had mastered all of the bowlers, being particularly grateful when they ventured onto his pads. With Clarke called on to bowl slow left arm before the second new ball, Ponting prayed for some control to rest his seamers. Suddenly, Collingwood danced down the track and mistimed the ball to the extent that it lobbed over to mid-on, a truly awful shot. Now it was Strauss's turn to be annoyed.

Johnson at the other end began to find some reverse swing and took out Matthew Prior, bowled from a break back, and Andrew Flintoff, edging to slip. England had slumped to 333 for 6 with the initiative gone. Stuart Broad kept his head to the close and faced down 16 deliveries, whilst Strauss took a couple from a yorker then spanked a couple of resounding boundaries to finish the day on a lordly 161 not out. England finished on 354–6 and set her sites on 450.

Hilfenhaus started proceedings on the second day with Ponting reasoning that at least this chap could bowl a searching line from the off. Strauss left the first ball outside his off stump, but did so to the second which swung back in and bowled him, an ignominious end to a grand innings during the course of which the England skipper passed the 5,000 career run barrier.

Strauss had scored 52 from 49 Johnson deliveries, seemingly thrashing the much-trumpeted spearhead at will. Almost three quarters of Strauss's runs came square of the wicket on either side. There was a beautiful on drive and three clips to fine leg, all of which beat the rope. Helped for a long time by the front runner, Alistair Cook, Strauss nonetheless had seen off the first new ball, then the reverse swing as it aged, followed in the last hour of play by the second new ball. Broad and Swann soon followed to leave England somewhat teetering on 378 for 9 with the Australians warming to parity.

There followed a high-octane last-ditch stand between numbers 10 and 11, Anderson and Onions. The two tailenders crashed out at any width on offer to add a stinging 47 runs for the last wicket. England reached 425.

Immediately the Australians were under the cosh as Andrew Flintoff, pumped up on his designated last-ever Lord's test, ran in on that dodgy knee from the Pavilion End to re-write history. Hughes fell to Anderson and Ponting, LBW, was given out caught behind with the help of the third umpire. Needless to say, Ponting walked off furious at the injustice of it all. 11 for 2 became 152 for 8, and the Australians squeezed passed the 200 mark to finish on 215: Anderson 4 for 55; Onions 3 for 41; Broad 2 for 78 and Flintoff 1 for 27. Of the pick was Flintoff for a hostile spell which brought the wicket of Mike Hussey. This classy batsman, with an average of over 50, let a ball go through at 95.1 mph. It clipped the off-stump bail.

England chose not to enforce the follow on but batted again. The idea was to push the first innings lead of 210 up beyond the 500 mark and allow two days to bowl the Australians out. That said, Strauss and Cook both scored brisk 30s, then Bopara and Pietersen shored up the innings with a partnerhip of 73 but both fell before Prior, in particular, with 61 not out from only 42 balls, a 54 from Collingwood and a rapid 30 not out from Flintoff allowed Strauss to set the imposing total of 521 in two days.

England began well. The policy of opening with Flintoff paid dividends with both Hughes and Katich perishing in controversial circumstances. Though Katich sliced to gully, Flintoff was over the line, although umpire Koertzen failed to notice. Hughes edged to

Strauss at slip who caught the ball with fingers on the ground. Broad and Swann removed three further wickets, and the inevitable Australian fightback started at 128 for 5 when Brad Haddin joined Michael Clarke. Together these two fine right handers batted with great ease to soothe Ponting's nerves and lower his blood pressure.

For once Strauss fretted as his bowlers looked haggard. During the last 47 overs of the day, curtailed by 12 overs due to bad light, Clarke and Haddin added a daunting 185 to take Australia to within 209 of what would be a famous victory. The second new ball was only six overs old when Anderson bowled an exceptional, if unrewarded, first over of the day, on day five. Flintoff ran in once more from the Pavilion End and started from the very off to get lift and bounce. Haddin, rushed into playing back to a lifter, edged Flintoff to Collingwood at second slip who gratefully accepted the chance.

It was not over yet though as Johnson began to drive and pull with relish. Michael Clarke continued to look comfortable so Strauss replaced Anderson with Swann. Second ball Clarke, on 136, danced down the wicket in a show of dominance but yorked himself.

From then on the end was in site as Flintoff roared in one more final time from the Lord's Pavilion End. Gathering momentum with every step, Flintoff unleashed the fastest sustained spell of in excess of 90 mph seen from an Englishman for a long time. Each well-directed missile asked searching questions of the batsmen's reaction times, technique and courage.

Hauritz was bowled playing no shot, then, after being no-balled against Siddle, Flintoff ran in off a shortened run and bowled a full inswinger which shattered the stumps. Flintoff sank to his knees and the crowd rose to him. Swann bowled Johnson and England had won their first test against Australia at Lord's for 76 years, and only their second since 1899.

There are occasions when noble batting performances are overshadowed by quite exceptional bowling. For instance the fourth test of the 2004/05 South African test series, where Hoggard's 7 for 109 overshadowed even Trescothick's blistering 180. Likewise, history will recall Flintoff as the man of the match here for his winning spell, the greatest fast bowling by an Englishman since Devon Malcolm's 9 for 57, not statistically but for the sheer brute force inflicted by a wounded legend on his last opportunity at the centre of cricket.

Ultimately of course England won the series 2–1 despite Australia scoring eight centuries to England's two. As Strauss neatly put it at the

Oval: 'When we were bad we were very bad but when we were good we were just good enough!'
England 425 (Strauss 161, Cook 95, Hilfenhaus 4-103, Johnson 3-132).
Australia 215 (Hussey 51, Anderson 4-55, Onions 3-41).
England 311-6 declared (Prior 61, Collingwood 54, Hauritz 3-80).
Australia 406 (Clarke 136, Haddin 80, Johnson 63, Flintoff 5-92, Swann 4-87).
ENGLAND WON BY 115 RUNS

Innings Ranked Number 58
Hammond's 251 at Sydney in 1928

Opponents: Australia
At stake: Ashes won by England in 1926
Bowling attack: Nothling, Grimmett, Ironmonger, Blackie, Hendry, Ryder, Kippax: Runs per wicket bowling average 39.46
Pitch: Fine
Game situation: England 51 for 1 in reply to Australia's first innings of 253.

At the time, Britain was the heaviest smoking nation on the planet. Although pipe use and cigars were in decline, there was a sudden rise in cigarette smoking, especially among women. It was estimated that the British smoked an average of almost $3^1/2$ lbs of tobacco per person per year. Indeed Hammond enjoyed a smoke.

Returning to cricket, England had won the first test with arguably the strongest batting line up in history. George Geary won the nod ahead of Phil Mead for the second test, despite Mead scoring 73 in the second innings of the Brisbane opener. Australia, one nil down in the series after the first test defeat by a gargantuan 675 runs, won the toss and elected to bat. They, in search of a stronger bowling unit, decided to drop Don Bradman after the 20-year-old's modest scores of 18 and 1 on his debut and selected instead another Don, Don Blackie, to make his debut at the age of 46. Blackie bowled medium-paced off breaks to augment the spin department, together with Clarrie Grimmett, the leg break specialist, and the heavily built 'Dainty' Ironmonger who bowled left arm. Australia lacked quality pace so their selectors planned to spin England out.

Larwood and Geary reduced Australia to 253 all out by sharing eight wickets between them. Hobbs and Sutcliffe opened England's account and appeared to be set for yet another significant stand. Then Ironmonger came on first change to dismiss Sutcliffe, caught by Hendry, for eleven, in a Hobbs dominated stand of 37.

Hammond arrived at the crease to partner the greatest ever batsman, scorer of most first-class and test hundreds, most first-class runs and most test runs, Jack Hobbs. In the next 461 minutes of playing time Hammond, hitherto little known amongst Australians would knock Hobbs off top spot.

Hobbs dominated for a while, but edged Grimmett to Oldfield for 40 with the score on 65. Still the game was in the balance. An 83 run partnership with the serious-minded Jardine took the score to 148 for 3 before Jardine was run out. In came Elias Hendren, the chirpy cockney fresh from 169 and 45 from the first test. Hendren batted almost in a comical manner. A stout man of scrum-half build, Hendren began nervously in a low, squat stance before settling down to the spinners.

Hammond and Hendren put on 145 to take England into a commanding lead. Hendren fell at 293 caught by Richardson off Blackie, to give the 46 year old his first test wicket. On Hammond batted with steady partnerships. Chapman played a typical cameo of 20 trying to keep up with Hammond before offering a catch to Ryder to give Blackie his second wicket. Then Larwood elevated to number 7, played his part in a 91 partnership, to make 43. George Geary helped himself to some loose deliveries drawn from a tired, thrashed attack.

Finally, at 496 and beginning to bat in the bloated manner of a Christmas feaster, Hammond played across to a straight delivery from Ironmonger, for 251 authoritative runs.

This knock moved the Sydney 'Hill', then a grass bank for cheap priced tickets – and among the most partisan supporters in the Southern Hemisphere – into admiration. 'Bloody good for a Pom' they remarked, but actually an innings full of charm.

Hammond scorched the covers with 30 fours so reducing the need to run. His off driving, both from the front and back foot, touched the heavens. This meant the bowlers tired sooner. On those occasions when the bowlers strayed to leg, Hammond guided the ball down to fine leg. He batted as though providing an exhibition. He minded not that drives went to fielders for dots, he saw it as practice. Hammond knew the value of building a long innings. He knew that three hours graft were required at test level to achieve the same in one hour of a testimonial game. This innings was seven-and-a-half-hours long.

This tour saw Hammond emerge as an international star and become, along with Hobbs and Sutcliffe, a household name in Britain. He hit the balls the way they came, with timing and power. He accumulated through waiting for the bad ball, then clicked through the gears to become, during this series, the greatest attacking batsman in the world. Right now Hammond was the undisputed champion, taking the crown at last from the 46-year-old Jack Hobbs. He was 25 and possessed an impressive athlete's physique, strong and handsome and was to experience an avalanche of female attention.

The Australians made a better fist of things in the second innings, scoring 397. They were indebted to centuries from Woodfull and Hendry and 79 from Ryder. It was not enough and Chapman, England's skipper, opened the England reply with his tail-enders. Geary and Tate were dismissed before the 16 runs required to give a comprehensive England win by eight wickets.

Hammond piled on the runs in a manner no Englishman has ever managed for a five-test series. Consider the scores, they show an English batsman at a height no other has reached: 44 and 28, 251, 200 and run out 32, 119 not out and 177, 38 and 16. In total 905 runs at 100.56.

By the final test, when Hammond's scores were modest, England lost by five wickets in an eight-day game, despite the 46-year-old Hobbs scoring 142 and 65. Not only had the Australians teased Hammond into playing the square cut, so sacrificing his wicket in both innings, they had also introduced a new force that was to smother English hopes and bowlers' hearts for two decades. Don Bradman emerged from the token Australian victory with 123 and not out 37.

Hammond's reign at the top was short lived, all records trumped in 1930 by 'boy' Bradman.

Australia 253 (Woodfull 68, Geary 5-35, Larwood 3–77)
England 636 (Hammond 251, Hendren 74, Geary 66, Blackie 4–148)
Australia 397 (Hendry 112, Woodfull 111, Ryder 79, Tate 4–99)
England 16–2
ENGLAND WON BY 8 WICKETS

Innings Ranked Number 57
Willey's 100 not out at the Oval in 1980

Opponents: West Indies
At stake: Dignity.
Bowling attack: Holding, Garner, Croft, Marshall
Pitch: Fine
Game situation: Desperate, England needing to bat out time for a draw.

The summer of 1980 saw troubled times for England. By July the country appeared to be plunging into recession with 40,000 losing jobs every month.

Willey's knock was played during the Moscow Olympics and at around this time Coe, Ovett and Wells won the 800m, 1,500m and 100m races to collect golds.

English cricket had a more than decent side at the time. Willis and Botham were in their prime and the batting department was dominated by a 40-year-old Yorkshireman by the name of Geoffrey Boycott. For company, he had talented but youthful twenty-somethings for company; most notably the Three Gs: Gooch, Gower and Gatting.

This was the time of the great West Indian pace quartet, an era defined by West Indian teams with brutally talented batsmen and ruthlessly hostile quick bowling, of a sustained intensity unmatched at any previous time in history. The quartet would normally be made up of 3 or 4 of the following: Andy Roberts, Michael Holding, Joel Garner, Colin Croft, Malcolm Marshall, Curtley Ambrose and Courtney Walsh. Waiting on the sidelines were bowlers serving in the County Championship as hostile as Wayne Daniel, Sylvester Clarke, Patrick Patterson and later on Ian Bishop. During the era stretching from Colin Cowdrey to Michael Vaughan the West Indies either had the most lethal attack in the world or one that would square up favourably against any on the planet.

The attack in 1980 was nasty enough. Funnily enough though,

unlike in the scorched summer of 1976, the 1980 team had to contend with a wetter, windier summer with many days of test cricket washed away.

England had lost the first test by the narrow margin of two wickets in a low scoring contest. Almost ten hours of rain saved England in the second test where they were still 116 runs behind with eight wickets left.

The third test once again saw a dismal first innings performance by England, dismissed by tea on day one for 150. West Indies in turn took a first innings lead of 110. England's second innings lasted over 140 overs and they finished 281 ahead with Peter Willey on 62 not out at the close; some consolation from a hitherto one-sided contest.

It was during the fourth test that England at last produced their best display, but it took a heroic effort from a strong, strong man to ward off defeat and emerge ahead. Peter Willey could reputedly beat Ian Botham in an arm wrestle. His batting defied belief. The stance became one of the most talked about cricket topics of the decade stretching from 1976 to 1986. It was simply horrendous, horribly open so that his chest faced the bowlers. Unlike Chanderpaul, who moves from an open stance to the normal side-on stance as the bowler releases the ball, Willey remained chest on throughout.

Willey's favourite shots were obviously square of the wicket, he was a great cutter and a powerful driver through the off-side. His first-class batting average for a career (30.9) is mediocre compared to the greats, as was his overall test average of 26.9. However, against the fastest attacks, the sort that really tested the mettle of batsmen, Peter Willey was indisputably one of England's finest of his generation. It was said that at the first sign of gunsmoke the selectors called for Willey.

England took a first innings lead of 105 over the West Indies thanks to 50s from Gooch (83), Boycott (53) and Rose (50). Useful contributions from a young Mike Gatting (48), Peter Willey (34) and John Emburey (24) took the score to 370.

In reply, West Indies collapsed to 105 for 5 before recovering to 265 all out. Dilley took four with a couple apiece to Botham and Emburey. Poor Botham had the captaincy issued to him following a typically remarkable all-round performance in the Bombay Golden Jubilee Test: 114, 6–58 and 7–48. Since then, his form at the peak of his career faded to that of a mortal, indeed he was barely worth his place in the team. Though today Sir Ian Botham stands tall on all aspects of the game, particularly in finding talent (he was the first to call for the inclusion of Jones and Harmisan into the England team), selecting the raw 24-year-old as captain was probably the worst post-war error of judgement by the England Cricket management team.

England's second innings started bleakly. With just two on the board Holding pinned Gooch in front for a duck. Boycott shell-shocked when a Colin Croft bumper cut the 40-year-old above his right eye in the first innings, edged Croft behind for five. Holding then bowled Wayne Larkins, like Peter Willey from Northampton-shire, to bring in John Emburey for nightwatchman duties, but Emburey edged a Croft lifter to slip to leave England reeling on 18–4. Gatting took a single before the close, 20–4.

The next day, a gutsy stand from Brian Rose, the Somerset left hander, and Mike Gatting stemmed the tide for an hour. Then a devastating spell from the 6ft 8in Barbadian Joel Garner removed Gatting caught behind (15), Botham caught at slip (4) and Rose LBW (41). In amongst this carnage stood Peter Willey, entering the arena at 67 for 6 with the fall of Botham.

On 84 Knott fell, LBW to whispering death Mike Holding. England were 92–9 with the fall of Dilley, also to Holding. This was unrelenting pace. In a little under a session of play England had capitulated to pace of quite extraordinary quality. Consider the attack on the day. Has there ever been a more hostile quartet of fast bowlers than Holding, Croft, Garner and Marshall? No.

Absolutely fed up and with no interest in the Moscow Olympics running at the time, my father and I retreated to a cold mountain pool for a swim, hidden away from tourists in the Cambrian Mountains of mid-Wales. We left my brother Nicholas, an avid West Indies fan, 'because they play the better cricket' to the television set and the prospect of being ground down by the nagging from his mother and grand-mother.

Usually the sight of England's spearhead Bob Willis approaching the wicket with his pads on signalled the dying embers of the innings. I distinctly remembered the site of a thunderbolt thundering into Willis's pads leaving Tony Greig stranded on 76 at the other end, and England losing by 55 runs in the closest of tests against the all conquering West Indies of 1976. By a sheer coincidence I watched both test matches in the same holiday house, Y Fron ,Tregaron. I left to save myself the chance of witnessing grim history repeat itself.

England were a mere 197 runs ahead when the last pair, Willey and

Willis came together at 2.09 pm. There was still 151 minutes and a further 20 overs of the day's play, so plenty of time for the West Indies to chase, and take an unassailable 2–0 lead in the series. Taking blows on the body both batsmen strived for survival. Fielders were brought in like vultures to crowd the bat of Willis. Willey at the other end hammered any delivery off target to push the total upwards.

For an hour or so Lloyd fired his best shots, juggling the bowling attack around and chivvying his team along. Then, as misfortune would have it, whilst fielding he pulled a leg muscle and went on to take no further part in the series. Hobbling off to seek medical attention Lloyd handed over to Richards. Onwards through the afternoon session Willey and Willis continued on to close down the time and ensure a draw

Eventually as a last throw of the dice, Viv Richards seeking to give the fast bowlers a rest brought himself on and genuine part timer Alvin Kallicharran. Willey's 100 came just before the declaration and in the last 20 overs. England finished 314 runs ahead with still one wicket intact.

Had there been an extra day could England have bowled the West Indies out and won? I suspect so. Despite a line up comprising Greenidge, Haynes, Richards, Lloyd (now injured) and Kallicharran the West Indies batting only really succeeded once all summer, in the first innings at Lord's. For the rest of the series the West Indies totalled a mediocre 245 to 308. England's bowling, if not batting, had proper depth: Willis, Botham, Dilley, Hendrick, Old, Lever, Underwood and Emburey all selected at various times.

The batting was the problem. That winter England had to face the West Indies again, on harder wickets in a hotter Caribbean climate. Peter Willey remained one of the foremost batsmen in that series. In fact Willey was just one of only four batsmen to score over 32 in any innings in the series, Gooch, Boycott and Gower being the others.

Peter Willey never cemented a place in the England team following an average of 47.87 in the West Indies. Occasionally he would be picked when the going got tough. Recalled at the age of 37 for the first test of the 1985/6 series, Willey faced Marshall, Garner, Patterson and Walsh. In an England total of 152, Willey chiselled out 71 courageous runs. He played his last test scoring 44 and 42 against New Zealand in 1986.

Both Willey and Willis excelled in later life. Peter Willey at the time of writing (2009) is an international umpire whilst big Bob is a successful cricket analyst for Skysports. Their bold last-wicket stand realised 117 runs and lasted 171 minutes. In over 100 years of test cricket, it was only one of three last-wicket century stands for England. Against an attack unrivalled for its hostility in all of history, Peter Willey's knock deserves its place.

England 370 (Gooch 83, Boycott 53, Rose 50, Croft 3–97)
West Indies 265 (Bacchus 61, Dilley 4–57)
England 209–9 (Willey 100*, Willis 24*) Holding 4–79, Garner 3–23)
MATCH DRAWN

Innings Ranked Number 56
Hussain's 94 at Headingley in 1998

Opponents: South Africa
At stake: Series set at 1–1 with this the final test.
Bowling attack: Donald, Pollack, Ntini, Kallis, McMillan, Cullinan, Cronje: 25.2
Pitch: Lively.
Game situation: South Africa took a slender lead of 22 on the 1st innings in a low scoring ecounter, 230 against 252. Hussain came in first wicket down with Atherton LBW for just 2, 1–2.

The South Africa series of 1998 provided the first instance of England winning a five test series on home soil since Gower's victorious 1985 side. This was a series marred with umpiring controversy and there was no doubt in South Africa's eyes that decisions on the whole went against them. After rain ruined the outcome of the first test at Edgbaston, England succumbed to Donald, Pollock and Kallis to lose by 10 wickets at Lord's in the second test. The third test saw an impres-sive England rearguard with Alec Stewart's masterful 164 and Croft and Fraser's holding out for 31 balls at the end. South Africa point to the last ball call for LBW from Donald but Angus Fraser survived the over and the shout. England's triumvirate of seamers came to the party for the fourth test with Fraser collecting ten, Gough five and Cork four wickets to win a thrilling contest with England required to score 247 to win. Thanks to Atherton's 98 not out, England won.

Now the scene was set up for the grand finale, not at the Oval for once but Headingley, Darren Gough country.

This was a pulsating match from start to finish with each side holding the honours for a short time before relinquishing control, a match which saw Gough, Fraser and Cork – and a medium-paced twenty-year-old called Andrew Flintoff – line up against Donald, Pollock, Ntini and Kallis – a great bowling line up.

England won the toss but threw away the advantage set by Mark Butcher's maiden test century and slumped from 181–3 to 230 all out. This was a bowler friendly surface according to Mike Atherton. Nasser Hussain displayed barnacle qualities yet scored only nine in 47 deliveries and over 68 minutes, excruciatingly slow and reminiscent of Boycott. For the third time in succession Angus Fraser took five wickets as South Africa scrambled the slender lead of 22.

The test match witnessed some of the nastiest sledging ever dished out, especially to Butcher and Atherton as they started the second innings. Neither side willing to give, it was full-on, intense test cricket which made for riveting viewing on the TV screens up and down the country. They survived at the close of the second day with the score on 2–0.

Hussain waited padded up at the start of the third day and wondered how long it would be before he was required. Donald opened his account by striking Atherton in front first ball and Hussain entered the fray with England still 20 runs behind South Africa and now without their sheet anchor. Again he showed his game plan of solid, watchful defence and an imperturbable concentration.

It is claimed that Butcher batted better for his 37 than when compiling his first innings century, such was the ruthless menace from Donald and Pollock who gave nothing in a furious display backed up by Ntini and Kallis. When Butcher fell, England had a lead of 59.

Stewart came in and upped the tempo with his usual flair. Wicket-keeping again in this match, Stewart was to average 34 as a wicket-keeper batsman but 46 as a specialist. Time and again England called on Stewart to occupy both roles, knowing this took the edge from his concentration with bat in hand. Nonetheless runs flowed freely when Donald returned for a second spell. Too good to last, Stewart edged Pollock behind for a delightful cameo of 35. An interruption for bad light affected Ramprakash rather than Hussain. Despite surviving a close call before the break, the second new ball pinned a full swinging Pollock delivery into Ramprakash's pads for a valuable 25. At the close of the third day, where ball had dominated bat, conditions hostile, situation crucial, Nasser Hussain remained undefeated, carrying England's hopes, on 84 with his side on a healthy 206 – 4, 182 runs ahead.

The swingometer swung back dramatically towards the South Africans at the start of day four in another monumental day of test cricket. With so much at stake, Donald and Pollock, armed with an almost new ball, tore into the England batting. Nightwatchman Salisbury feathered a lifter from Pollock to Boucher then three overs later Hick drove a slower delivery from Donald to extra cover, gone for one, completely deceived. Flintoff fell edging behind at the end of the over. England had slumped to 201–7. Runs now came at the price of gold, Cork and Hussain eeked out a vital 22 in 10 overs.

As Hussain prepared to face his 341st delivery spread over 428 minutes from Pollock, what must he have been thinking? I've got to get more runs for the team. I've got to keep getting my head down, build a total, set them 300, come on.

Pollock, one of the finest proponents of the fast medium swing propelled a slower ball of full length. Hussain, dormant for most of the morning, sprang onto the front foot and flowed through with his much practised off drive. Deceived by the subtle variation, Hussain drove uppishly to mid off to end a great innings of immense dedication to the cause, in a disappointingly soft manner. England were 229 for 8 soon to be 240 all out.

As he walked off Hussain did not hear the crowds and allegedly tears filled his eyes – not so much from failing to score a century but he felt that England hadn't quite got enough, that so much effort and nervous energy from so many would amount to the same sorry England, defeated again. Head drooped down facing the ground, bat trailing behind him, Hussain walked off to a standing ovation, oblivious to the fact.

He needn't have worried. South Africa set just 218, sank to 27–5, Gough three to Fraser's two. Another twist though as Rhodes and McMillan added 117 and on the final, sell-out day England needed to take the final two wickets before South Africa scrambled the last 34 runs.

In the end, Donald edged Fraser and Gough slammed a 90 mph missile into poor Ntini's pads. England had won by 23 runs to seal the series.

Hussain's last three centuries had all ended in an England defeat. As it turned out his concentration at the most telling time, against hostile high-quality pace bowling on a wicket of increasingly unpredictable bounce, was the difference between the sides. Mark Butcher received the man of the match award for his first innings century and that purposeful, attractive 37 in the second. However, the pitch deteriorated and the South African pace attack steamed in with even greater hostility in the second innings. *Wisden* described Donald and Pollack as 'tearing at the innings like lions fighting over a fresh kill.'

Such was the growing intensity of international cricket that, less than six years later, only Flintoff remained in the England team, and then only when fit.

It is quite astonishing that, with Thorpe injured, all of England's batting line up in 1998 ended up with test averages of under 40, yet 10 years later all of England's top six do. This is evidence of how unplayable and top-tier bowling attacks were back in the 1990s. Consider the following: Australia – Warne and McGrath; Pakistan – Wasim Akram and Waqar Younis; South Africa – Donald and Pollock; West Indies – Ambrose and Walsh; Sri Lanka – Muralitharan. No wonder.

Such high hopes were soon dashed. England lost the Ashes in Australia 4–1 in 1998/99, then perished against the underrated New Zealanders at home in 1999. Rated bottom of the world championship, something needed to change.

Against South Africa a young Yorkshire batsman, Michael Vaughan went out to face Donald and Pollock and soon the score was 2–4. Welcome to test cricket! England lost that test and the series too, but green shoots of recovery, though slow growing, would emerge triumphantly in the not too distant future.

Hussain as captain, along with coach Duncan Fletcher, over the next few years built up a much more difficult to beat England team.

England 230 (Butcher 116, Ntini 4–72, Donald 3–44, Pollack 3–51).
South Africa 252 (Cronjé 57, Fraser 5–42, Gough 3–58).
England 240 (Hussain 94, Pollock 5–53, Donald 5–71).
South Africa 195 (Rhodes 85, McMillan 54, Gough 6–42, Fraser 3–50).
ENGLAND WON BY 23 RUNS.

Innings Ranked Number 55
W. G. Graces' 170 at the Oval in 1886

Opponents: Australia
At stake: Dead game, England are already 2–0 up in the three test series.
Bowling attack: Giffen, Garrett, Palmer, Bruce, Spofforth, Evans, Trumble.
Average runs per wicket: 25.6
Pitch: Fine
Game situation: England won the toss and A. G. Steel, the England captain, elected to bat first.

W. G. Grace's highest innings came in $4^1/2$ hours against a worthy attack which included F. R. Spofforth. He hit 24 fours and completely dominated a stand of 170 with the limpet W. H. Scotton, 34, before eventually falling caught by Blackham off Spofforth for 170. So masterful was the champion on 12 August 1886 compared with his peers, that the score when he fell was only 216.

The Australian team was weak compared to their previous teams as the the threat from the demon bowler Fred Spofforth started to wane. England's bowling, especially by 5ft $10^1/2$ins George Lohmann, the right-arm round bowler from Surrey, was altogether too much for Australia as his match aggregate of 12–104 demonstrated.

England 434 (W. G. Grace 170, W. W. Read 94, Briggs 53, Spofforth 4–65, Garrett, 3–88).
Australia 68 (Lohmann 7–36, Briggs 3–28) and 149 (Lohmann 5–68, Briggs 3–30).
ENGLAND WON BY AN INNINGS AND 217 RUNS.

Innings Ranked Number 54
Hobbs' 178 at Melbourne in 1912

Opponents: Australia
At stake: Ashes
Bowling attack: Cotter, Kelleway, Armstrong, Matthews, Hordern, Minnett, Ransford: Average runs per wicket 28.22.
Pitch: Soft.
Game situation: England won the toss and elected to insert Australia. Hobbs and Rhodes opened for England that afternoon after dismissing Australia for 191.

At the start of the series Australia were firm favourites. They had just defeated South Africa 4–1 a year earlier. England had lost to both South Africa and Australia in the previous occasions and the first test defeat hinted that nothing much had changed. S. F. Barnes had a poor test and England defeated by 146 runs. In the second test, England came back strongly with hundreds from J. W. Hearne and Hobbs. Hobbs scoring the winning runs, an undefeated 126 out of 219–2.

Outscoring partners was typical of the young pre-War Hobbs, a slightly built 5ft 9^1/2ins athlete with an amazing eye honed from practice in isolation – throwing a tennis ball at a wall and using a stump as a bat a technique also used by Bradman. Some, such as Percy Fender, say Hobbs was better on bad wickets than even the great Australian. At any rate, read the authors of the time, and a strong body of opinion points to Hobbs as the finest England batsman ever. He reached 197 centuries and scored 98 after the age of 40. He started the game late, and did not make his first-class debut until he was 22. By a historical quirk of fate, opposing Hobbs on that first class debut was none other than the great W. G. Grace, then aged 57. I digress.

England had taken the lead in the third test, the score now 2–1 ahead, thanks once again to Jack Hobbs with 187. Could Australia recover or would England steam-roller over the Australians and regain the Ashes?

It rained for two or three days before the test but was sunny at the start of play on the first day. The Melbourne Cricket Ground was yet to develop into the grand stadium of today. The scoreboard stood beyond the deep mid wicket with cricketers' names emblazoned on wooden placards. Here the crowd sat in rows of ten on one side and twenty on the other. Mature trees provided the scenery beyond giving the air of leafy suburbia, another world, another game. England won the toss and elected, with Wilfred Rhodes's advice, to bowl first. The plan did not seem to work initially as Barnes and Foster bowled erratically, too short and wide, and were picked off with relish by Hordern and Kelleway. Fifty came without a wicket but after lunch Barnes and Foster fired properly and tore through the openers, Bardsley, and the old guard of Hill and Trumper. Australia were bundled out with 40 minutes of play remaining.

So it was that Hobbs and Rhodes walked out of the thronged pavilion into the evening sunshine, both of similar height, wearing peaked caps. Hobbs was slighter of build, Rhodes the stocky one. Immediately the pair set about the Australian quicks, stealing singles with apparent abandon. Rhodes leaned nicely into his drives whilst Hobbs soon brought out his famous square cut. At the close the score stood ominously at 54–0.

Next day the heavy roller flattened the wicket and the sun baked the pitch into a flat track perfect for a couple of bullies. Hobb's strokes flowed all round the wicket with a slight preference square on the off side. He batted with almost indiscriminate ease. He gave one proper chance, a stumping just after completing his hundred. The stand proved a record for the first wicket against Australia that is still unbeaten today. Both were at their performance peaks. After stroking 22 boundaries Hobbs turned Hordern's googley off his body to be caught at short square leg, 323–1.

Hobbs scored 662 runs over the five test series at an average of 82. England regained the Ashes with a convincing 4–1 win and remained world champions until the outbreak of the First World War in 1914. Although Hobbs was the finest batsman of the time in the world, England were also fortunate to have statistically ranked, the greatest ever bowler in S. F. Barnes and such stars as the left-handed Frank Woolley, as well as the bowler with the highest number of first-class wickets ever, the slow left-arm all-rounder Wilfred Rhodes.

Australia 191 (Minnett 56, Barnes 5–74, Foster 4–77).
England 589 (Rhodes 179, Hobbs 178, Gunn 75, Woolley 56, F. R. Foster 50, Hordern 3–137).

Australia 173 (J. W. H. T. Douglas 5–46).
ENGLAND WON BY AN INNINGS AND 225 RUNS.

Innings Ranked Number 53
Tom Graveney's 165 at the Oval in 1966

Opponents: West Indies
At stake: Pride; England had already lost the series by losing 3 of the previous 4 tests.
Bowling attack: Hall, Griffith, Sobers, Holford, Gibbs, Hunte: average runs per wicket: 32.77
Pitch: Fine
Situation: West Indies scored 268 after winning the toss. Graveney entered when England were 72–2.

Graveney's 165 lit up a depressing summer for England who were being systematically thrashed by the West Indies. The series stood at 3–0 to the West Indies after the first four tests.

Although England restricted the West Indies to 268, despite a thrilling 81 from Sobers and a Kanhai century, that total looked good when England had slumped to 166–7. Then Graveney and J. T. Murray put on an astonishing 217 at almost a run a minute for the eighth wicket. When Graveney fell at 399–9, England were ahead by 131, and his job of resurrecting English cricket had been completed.

Higgs and Snow then pushed the total up beyond 500 with a stand of 128 for the last wicket, just two short of the record set by Foster and Rhodes back in 1903. The West Indies subsided for a second time around and England won by an innings and 34 runs to salvage some much needed pride.

West Indies 268 (Kanhai 104, Sobers 81, Barber 3–49).
England 527 (Graveney 165, Murray 112, Higgs 63, Snow 59*).
West Indies 225 (Nurse 70, Butcher 60, Snow 3–40).
ENGLAND WON BY AN INNINGS AND 34 RUNS.

Innings Ranked Number 52
Shrewsbury's 105* at Melbourne in 1885

Opponents: Australia
At stake: Ashes: In the first ever five-test series, England won the first two, then Australia won the next two. The final test at Melbourne would decide the fate of the Ashes.
Bowling attack: Giffen, Bruce, Spofforth, Trumble, Garrett, McShane, Jones, Horan: average runs per wicket: 25.16
Pitch: Fine
Situation: England are 97–3 in response to Australia's below-par 163.

Shrewsbury's first hundred was the first to be scored by an England captain in a test match. Batting sensibly and showing impermeable defense, Shrewsbury put on stands of 115 with Billy Barnes, a further 68 with J. M. Read (who retired ill) and Flowers, and 49 for the last wicket with wicket-keeper J. Hunter.

England's first innings lead amounted to 223; Australia capitulated in the second innings for 125 and England won by an innings and 98 runs, so winning the series 3–2.

Australia 163 (Spofforth 50, Ulyett 4–52, Peel 3–28).
England 386 (Shrewsbury 105*, Barnes 74, Bates 61, Bruce 3–99).
Australia 125 (Attewell 3–24, Ulyett 3–25, Flowers 3–34).
ENGLAND WON BY AN INNINGS AND 98 RUNS.

Innings Ranked Number 51
Hutton's 202 not out at the Oval in 1950

Opponents: West Indies
At stake: Losing a series for the first time at home against the West Indies.
Bowling attack: Jones, Worrell, Ramadhin, Valentine, Gomez, Goddard: average runs per wicket: 30.83
Pitch: Fine.

The West Indies had grown in test stature rather quickly in the years immediately after the Second World War. England arrogantly sent a second-string side to the Caribbean in early 1948, shorn of the services of Hutton (initially), Washbrook, Edrich and Compton – the four great batsmen now all in their prime and far superior to any other batsman in England. Also missing was the spearhead Alec Bedser, the only pace bowler with any potency in the land, and Doug Wright – surely the nation's top spinner with 19 South African wickets the previous summer. England's batsmen were found wanting at various times in the series against Johnson, Goddard and Ferguson. Moreover the West Indies batting line up was now something to be feared and three youngsters filled the upper-middle order: Weekes, Walcott and Worrell – the famous 3 Ws.

The eagerly anticipated 1950 home series attracted large crowds now mixed with hundreds of recent Caribbean migrants. This served to fuel intense national pride in the visitors. This summer was the first to go four tests between the teams, evidence of England's growing respect.

Old Trafford, scene of the first test, provided England with a welcome win by 202 runs on a crumbling track that suited the spinners. England chose three, Hollies, Laker and Berry. Though Laker disappointed with just a single wicket in the match, Berry with nine and Hollies with eight wickets, justified the selectors' hunch.

England's batting failed to impress in the absence of both Cyril Washbrook and Denis Compton. Extraordinarily, Alf Valentine and Sonny Ramadhin, the West Indian spinners had played barely a handful of first-class games yet shared fifteen of the England wickets.

Lord's and Trent Bridge were lost heavily and crowds witnessed a tectonic shift in the power of world cricket. The West Indies proved too good to get out and just seemed to be growing in stature innings after innings. Hundreds were scored by Rae, Walcott, Weekes and a superb 261 by Worrell, a record-breaking score at Trent Bridge. This was fast becoming a disastrous summer for England, out gunned in the batting stakes and out spun in the bowling department. Thirty wickets had been captured by Valentine and Ramadhin and there seemed no answer to the wiles of these whipper-snappers.

Washbrook, returning from injury in the second test, showed at least some heartening defiance with 114 at Lord's and 102 at Trent Bridge. Hutton had not fired properly in the first two tests and withdrew with injury on the morning of the third test. That meant England had to fight a test without the services of Hutton, Edrich and Compton.

So for the fourth and final test, England needed to win to level the series otherwise her cricketers would always assume the mantle of allowing a relatively new nation to beat them in a series for the first time. Not good. Hutton returned from injury and so too the much awaited Denis Compton, but unfit for purpose this time were Edrich, Washbrook, Evans the keeper and Parkhouse – in other words the three England batsmen who had so far scored most runs against Valentine and Ramadhin that summer.

The England team now assembled at the Oval chopped and changed according to who was fit until, with Bailey reporting fit on the morning, the final selection was: Hutton, Simpson, Sheppard (debut, shrewd move thought Arlott), Compton, Dewes (fortunate) Bailey, Brown (captain), McIntyre (WK on debut), followed by Bedser, Hilton (debut, slow left armer, surprise selection) and Wright.

The West Indies duly won the toss and posted their second successive total in excess of 500. Rae took a second hundred in the series and Worrell feasted once again for 138, following his 261. Doug Wright bowling brisk leg breaks took an honest 5 for 141 in 53 overs.

With 65 minutes left of day two, Hutton and Simpson opened England's account with the target to bat out time and pick up any available gift. In the event, the pair saw through to the close with no significant turn, though Simpson was dropped at short leg off Valentine who proceeded to draw Hutton forward on middle and off and beat the outside edge. Valentine spun the ball more and at greater pace than any equivalent England player.

Day three began with the two in earnest occupation, slow and gritty against some trying swings from Worrell and Jones, each bowling a leg stump line and defensive fielders squeezing out the possibility of too many scampered singles. It was intense and neither batsmen broke their morning shackles. The crowd grew impatient and it was felt that these two had to break through and up the scoring rate. Soon the spin twins would return when the shine was gone.

Half an hour after the start, Goddard switched first to Valentine and an attacking silly mid off, then Ramadhin with a short leg and slip. Now runs were doubly hard to come by. After the first 100 minutes, including the previous evening, Simpson had but 15 to his name and even Hutton only 23.

One could tell from Hutton's almost scientific enquiry of the pitch, prodding it, and the general weather conditions (fine) that he was in for the long haul. Simpson stroked and ran a three off Ramadhin coming from the Pavilion End but that took him down to Valentine where upon Simpson played out eleven maidens on the trot; dire stuff. Simpson was in obvious distress and smote Valentine straight to Jones on the leg side to end the torture. The score stood at 73–1, Simpson gone for a painstaking 30.

The boyish-looking Shepherd came in at three on debut and on the back of some sublime shots in county cricket, a real touch player yet at once he faced one of the most hostile overs from Valentine which he managed, through luck and class, to survive. Hutton came down mid wicket for conferences with Sheppard and imparted his wisdom, so re-assuring for the youngster.

Sheppard did more than survive when he stepped back and cut Valentine for four. The 100 came up in 175 minutes and Hutton played both spinners with growing confidence. Simpson retreated into his shell somewhat in the run up to lunch but at least Hutton faced the final over from Ramadhin before lunch. Here he blocked the first four balls then punched a firm on drive that appeared to be past mid on until an outstretched dive from Gomez saved a two or very probably a three. Sheppard faced the last ball, a straight one that straightened further with the off break and try as Sheppard might to defend the ball, his bat got stuck clipping the pad on route down from a high backlift and his stumps shattered. Just on the stroke of lunch, England were now 120–2.

Out came the last truly great pair of England batsmen, defined as those that gathered their first-class and test runs to averages both in excess of 50. No one in the 50 years after have achieved such a feat and England's batting looked more manly as Hutton and Compton walked out – both in their 30s with weather-worn anxious brows sporting deep furrows. Hutton wore a peaked cap as he always did, Compton hatless, hair combed over.

At once Compton seemed all at sea against Ramadhin and survived a confident appeal for LBW yet he had faced the likes of Valentine before the war. It took seventeen balls before Compton swept a single to start his account, amid an audible relief from the crowd.

Both grew more sure of themselves by the minute and though the scoring was far from electrifying, 47 was added in the first hour after lunch. Compton grew in confidence against Ramadhin and cuffed a couple of fours off consecutive balls. This took him to 20 whilst Hutton had scored 27 in the same time.

The 103rd over saw Goddard take the new ball and Hutton on 96 at the time hit the first ball from Jones to the fence to record his century. Worrell from the far end contained both batsmen, but they now fed from Jones's wayward thunderbolts and punched five fours in four overs. Gomez replaced Worrell and Compton took seven from the over before playing out a maiden to Goddard which phased him not one jot. The 100 partnership had arrived and the crowd appreciated the master craftsmen of their time.

Hutton turned Gomez's first ball of his second over to just behind square and set off for a single. Stollmeyer raced in with unexpected speed, Hutton stopped and recovered his ground whilst Compton kept running towards him. Now both at the batsman's end, Stollmeyer calmly set the tone on the series by throwing back to Gomez and though Compton made an attempt, he was out by 15 yards and the game as well as the series evaporated away at that precise point. Compton had made 44, his first test innings coming back from injury. England were 229–3. Compton's return had been the symbol of hope and now it was gone.

John Arlott wrote:

> I think I have never reacted with so much emotion to an event in a cricket match ... once again, for an hour and a half, English batting had flowered.

Dewes replaced Compton almost unnoticed. The crowd felt he was lucky to be picked. Hutton hit the next ball for two with the crowd still very much in deep disappointed conversation, smoldering from the Compton runout, although it was not clear who was to blame.

At any rate tea came with Dewes still intact on four with Hutton, 136. Rain delayed the restart by an hour. Soon after Dewes fell edging Valentine to Worrell at slip, but Bailey batted through with Hutton to take England to 282-4. Hutton remained undefeated on 160, the solitary factor that kept England in the game.

Rain overnight dampened the pitch, but the heavy roller ironed out the cracks and for a while the pitch behaved calmly both towards Ramadhin and Valentine. Ten minutes later, Goddard placed himself on for Ramadhin and brought paceman Jones back on Valentine's end. Hutton duly smote Jones for four and soon he was replaced with Valentine brought back. Now the wicket started misbehaving. It had dried and become scuffed. Goddard in particular bowled his fast off breaks and generated vast angles and considerable bounce. Hutton played equally well by confronting a spell of such awkward intensity and danger by revealing his drop-wristed technique. Bailey sensing time to accelerate and hang the consequences hit a three then a four before edging a ball onto his pads which flew to Weekes at short leg.

Freddie Brown, the 40-year-old veteran captain, at once staked his intent for quick runs but edged to slip. McIntyre caught the disease, struck a four off Valentine before gifting a gentle return catch. England had slumped to 321-7.

Bedser seemed outclassed against Valentine, but a single from Hutton off Goddard brought him down to the more threatening end. He did not last, LBW for 0. England were now 322-8 and still 32 away from the follow on.

Hilton mixed cross-batted aggression with straight-batted defence and reached three in a stand of four before Goddard cut in a break back that would have penetrated a specialist's defence. Still 28 runs adrift, Doug Wright came out as Hutton's and England's last hope.

Hutton accelerated by taking a couple of boundaries from Valentine — one a square hit laced with risk, quite out of character but struck imperiously, then a single to keep the strike. Goddard was so accurate, so difficult to get away that, despite Hutton's class, he played out a maiden. Wright kept his ground during a Valentine maiden and still Hutton failed to get the single and the strike off Goddard – testimony to Goddard's best spell of the series.

Eventually Hutton squeezed Goddard away for two to bring up his double hundred and the next ball forced away to leg looked like two, but breathtaking fielding allowed only the single. Wright blocked a couple, then inside edged the sixth delivery to fine leg for two. Eighteen runs had been added and Goddard, growing concerned, replaced Valentine for Ramadhin. Again Hutton had to be content with a maiden, singles were too difficult against a ring of fielders with the sole purpose of preventing one. Goddard to Wright again and this time, fourth ball, an off cutter pinned him in front. England came off, ten short of the follow on with Hutton undefeated on 202 made from a total of 344.

> Nobody who saw his effort of concentration and perfect stroke play will forget the great attempt he made to save his country.

Hutton hoped, indeed yearned, for Freddie Brown, the skipper, to allow him a rest. Hutton needed to recharge, take a shower and rehydrate. He felt that to ask would be rude. It did not occur to Brown to rest Hutton. So after a ten-minute rest and a cup of water Hutton once again went out to bat. This time he scored just two and England fell away to 103 all out, to lose by an innings and 56 runs. Valentine took ten in the match, Ramadhin four and Goddard five including his first innings analysis of 17.4-6-25-4.

England were plagued with injuries in 1950 but there was too much of an overreliance on Hutton, Washbrook, Edrich and Compton. When one or more of these were injured, the batting was simply too vulnerable.

West Indies 503 (Worrell 138, Rae 109, Gomez 74, Goddard 58*, Wright 5–141).
England 344 (Hutton 202*, Compton 44, Goddard 4-25, Valentine 4-121) and 103 (Valentine 6–96, Ramadhin 3–38).
WEST INDIES WON BY AN INNINGS AND 56 RUNS.

Fifty Finest

Innings Ranked Number 50
Gooch's 196 at the Oval in 1985

Opponents: Australia.
At stake: Ashes.
Bowling attack: Lawson, McDermott, Gilbert, Bennett, Border, Wessels.
Pitch: Bouncy, firm and true.
Game situation: Gower won the toss for England and without hesitation elected to bat first.

Just three days before the start of the fifth and final test against Australia, Zola Budd had broken the women's 5000m world record by an astonishing 10 seconds. Set against this euphoria was the rioting in Brixton; a black woman called Cherry Groce had been shot during a police raid.

On the second day of rioting, and whilst 200 were arrested by police, Gower won his fourth successive toss on the trot and without hesitation elected to bat first. Gower was in the form of his life, fresh from 166 in the third test at Trent Bridge, followed by 215 with ridiculous ease at Edgbaston. The Australian bowling attack had been totally savaged. Botham came in with complete license to entertain the crowd with the score on 572-4; he struck his first delivery, bowled by the young fiery Craig McDermott back over his head for six, and performed the same feat two balls later. England won that Edgbaston test to take a 2-1 lead in the series. All they needed to do was draw the final test and the Ashes would be reclaimed in England for only the third time since 1926.

Graham Gooch, the Essex opener, had scored 291 runs in eight innings so far in the six test series at an average of only 36.38, similar to his overall test average at the time. He went out to bat with Tim Robinson, knowing that over the ten years battling against Australia – and across 40 innings – he had still never made an Ashes hundred.

Gooch sported the white helmet but without the grill pad. Both he and Robinson negotiated the first quarter-of-an-hour and realised the pitch had both pace and bounce, easily the fastest of the summer. Before long McDermott, the pick of the Australian attack, bowled Robinson for three, the score 20–1.

Gower the skipper came in determined to build a platform from which to make it impossible for Australia to win. Luck came Gower's way early on and he gloved a rising ball from McDermott that lobbed over the slips but not by much. Gower also appeared slightly unnerved by the pace and gave further half chances at 31 and 35 off the luckless Geoff Lawson.

All the while Gower flirted with disaster, Gooch remained completely absorbed in his task. There were enough bad balls from an errant Australian attack for Gooch to keep his score moving forwards. He clubbed the over-pitched deliveries and smacked the short stuff. Gower settled down and at lunch England had countered the new ball sufficiently well to reach 100–1.

That afternoon, as the ball softened, Border gave his second-change bowlers lengthy spells to rest his spearheads, McDermott and Lawson. Dave Gilbert looked short of pace and rather innocuous with his brand of medium-fast, right-arm over, and Murray Bennett resembled, frankly, a pub bowler. Bennett bowled his spell of slow, left arm hidden behind a pair of dark sunglasses.

Gooch had spent the hour before his innings in the nets, getting his eye in and almost successfully punching holes in the netting. Gower just stroked and blazed away with apparent contempt in a calculated way to totally take the game by the scruff of the neck. Gooch remained orthodox, content at this stage to take the back seat but putting the bad ball away with aplomb. Gower swept Border for four to bring up a cavalier hundred from facing just 123. Tea came with the score exactly 200–1.

Soon after tea, McDermott raced in and over pitched a straight thunderbolt at Gooch's pads, easy pickings for the batsman who leant into an on drive for four to bring up his century. The pace quickened further with Border ruing the fact that he had omitted Jeff Thompson on the speediest track of the year.

First the rampant Gower cut Gilbert for four then pulled a McDermott bouncer over mid-wicket with insulting ease. Border returned to Bennett and the crowd sensed a run orgy. After tea, no Australian bowler could stem the flow, and Gooch advanced out to

Bennett and whacked him over mid-off. He swept a two and then clubbed a respectable good-length ball over square leg for another four. Clutching at straws, Border chucked the ball for Lawson in the hope of meeting fire with fire, but Gooch imperiously hooked him for yet another boundary. Border looked up with the score fast approaching 300.

For Gower, this was the highlight of his test career, sitting back on his bat handle with 150-plus to his name, watching Gooch move into over drive. The 300 came up, then the 300 partnership and all too easily the 350 amid scenes of public euphoria. Then with the score on 371, the stand worth 351 and all England anticipating new records falling, Gower cut McDermott to Bennett in the gully, who accepted the chance albeit with a sting to his hands.

At 371–2, Gower (157) walked off once again to a standing ovation in a golden summer which he harvested to the tune of 732 runs, comfortably the record number of runs scored in an Ashes series at home. He had his moment of Ashes history, a series labelled after him, and on the 29 August, as riots took over Brixton for the second successive day, he and his opener, Graham Gooch, had flayed the Australian attack at 4.6 an over for almost six hours.

Gatting failed for once, but Gooch took England to the close for a majestic 179 not out. England finished day one on 376–3, all hope of Australia retaining the Ashes over barring a miracle.

Day Two saw the Australians fight back in impressive manner. Gooch got caught hooking off a no ball, but next delivery fired a McDermott full toss straight back to the bowler who grabbed an athletic catch, with his right hand, just inches from the ground. Although quite obviously disappointed at falling so short of a double century, Gooch left the arena as he had started it over seven hours of playing time earlier, with the blank expression of a man intense in thought, fully focussed in mindset, unchanging through the mood spectrum, a rock for Gower to smile over.

In a scorecard remarkable for its inconsistency, Gooch had 196, Gower 157 and the next highest – excluding a whopping total of 50 extras – was Downton's 16. England, expecting a total of 600-plus had to make do with 464, all out just after lunch. Australia rocketed to 35 before Botham once again tempted Hilditch into a bouncer and, for the third time in the series, perished at deep square leg. From then on a steady progression of wickets fell. Australia followed on, but with the Ashes gone, her spine fell apart, and she lasted all but 47 overs;

Border the only defiance caught brilliantly by Botham at second slip.

Scenes of jubilation followed as Gower addressed the crowd on the pavilion balcony as Hutton had done back in '53, colleagues spraying him with beer and champagne to the delight of the nation – happy golden days that defined an era.

England 464 (Gooch 196, Gower 157, Lawson 4–101, McDermott 4–108).
Australia 241 (Ritchie 64*, Botham 3–64) and 129 (Border 58, Ellison 5–46, Botham 3–44).
ENGLAND WON BY AN INNINGS AND 94 RUNS.

Innings Ranked Number 49
W.G. Grace's 152 at the Oval in 1880

Opponents: Australia.
At stake: Pre-ashes, but as the only two test countries at the time, the winners would become the unofficial World Champions.
Bowling attack: Boyle, Palmer, Alexander, Bannerman, MacDonnell, Moule.
Pitch: Flat, well prepared for the time.
Game situation: This was in the days of five ball overs and solo tests. England had won the toss and elected to bat first. W. G. Grace, on debut, opened with his brother E. M., whilst further brother G. F. (Fred) would bat at nine.
Weighted runs per wicket of the bowling attack: 27.47.

This chapter is set at a time when British forces were on active duty in Afghanistan, more specifically trying to establish authority in the southern section. This time the Prime Minister was William Gladstone, famous for befriending prostitutes, and the year 1880, early September.

> Where a great man has led many can go afterwards, but the honour is his who found and cut the path.
> *Prince Ranjitsinji, 1897*

This was the greatest cricket match that had ever taken place up to this point in history, the most keenly anticipated sporting contest in the world. 1880 was the time of the great Victorian Empire, stretching across a quarter of the world's land surface. Could the Australians beat England on English soil? This was the first official test match in England, although the two-innings format spread over several days had yet to be coined 'test cricket'. That it happened in early September was down to the stubborn refusal of Lord Harris to give the Australians the right to play a test match after incidents on the 1878/79 tour when England had brought along a home-grown umpire. During the New South Wales game the umpire gave a crucial run out in favour of the MCC (England). This so incensed the crowd that at one point a large number of 'larrikins' invaded the pitch. Lord Harris, playing at the time, defended his ground by clutching a stump which he pointed aggressively at the intruders. Given that Harris, the 4th Baron, formerly of Eton and Oxford University, was exactly the sort of Englishman that Australians have loved to hate down the years, it is to the huge credit of the rest of the England team and the match officials that Harris remained relatively unscathed although he was, along with several other England players, assaulted. The whole episode cast a dark shadow on Anglo-Australian relationships.

However the 1880 Australians had made many friends and provided excellent entertainment on the cricket fields that summer. They were popular and the game had grown to immense status. Also, Australia would provide stern competition. This summer had seen the touring Australians lose only two from thirty games. They had even beaten Gloucestershire and Yorkshire. Lord Harris remembered captaining the last England/Australia game, at Melbourne eighteen months earlier. The fact was that England got hammered and a 'demon' Australian bowler called Fred Spofforth took 13–110. At any rate, Lord Harris backed down and allowed the game to be given the go ahead.

Up until this point all tests had been in Australia. The grand total stood at 2–1 in favour of the antipodeans. This time England could field one W. G. Grace, a barrel-chested, bearded, quite tall, 32-year-old doctor, chest size – probably 48 ins. He was a giant among Victorian cricketers and easily the greatest batsman of his day, a true exponent in the art of batting. Unlike all others, 'W.G.' batted both on the front foot and the back, as the length dictated. Like Pietersen today pioneering the switch-hit stroke, so Grace pioneered this technique –

copied today by any batsman of just reasonable substance.

W.G. had already broken all manner of records. It is true that modern cricket, as we know it with over-arm bowling legalised, started in 1864 – with it the first publication of *Wisden*. Records only really go back to then. However before any other batsman, W. G. Grace scored centuries before lunch on seven occasions between 1869 and 1876. He was the first to score centuries in both innings, and performed this feat three times before any body else. W.G. was the first batsman to score a triple hundred. The second was also scored by W.G. just one week later in 1876. By 1880, W.G. had scored seven double hundreds in first-class cricket. Since 1864, with the heralding of over-arm bowling, no other batsman had even scored one. His first-class average, close to 40, towered above all others. W.G. was the champion and huge public interest would focus on him.

Lord Harris agreed to captain the team and then set about the selection of the strongest team available. He glanced at the season's up-to-date, first-class averages. He would have to pick W. G. Grace. Then Lord Harris sat back in his chair. He wanted a few of those Cambridge University heroes, the ones who beat the Australians by an innings in 1878. He wrote down Allan Steel (who had scored 59* in that game), A. P. Lucas and the Hon. Alfred Lyttleton (72); all steady batsmen averageing over 20 for the season. He pondered about the big hitting, all-rounder Billy Barnes, by all accounts a bit of a rough diamond, solid season though, reliable first change, right-arm brisk medium. Frank Penn, Lord Harris's team mate at Kent, would certainly not throw his wicket away and could be relied on to graft – a courageous player, so he would play.

It was a three-day game and runs would be vital. England had to bat deep.They needed a reliable wicket-keeper batsman. Lord Harris had already chosen Lyttleton for his batting, jolly good that he could keep wicket as well. This gave Harris the freedom to choose a player for the romantics, a thread to a by-gone era but who could offer experience at the top and was still good enough.

Harris thought back to his childhood. A day at Canterbury Week in 1861 would remain long in the memory of the ten-year-old and sway his judgement almost twenty years later. He had seen E. M. Grace, seven years older than brother W.G., and regarded as the best batsman in England at the time, strike 192* against Kent, then grab ten wickets in the innings with round-arm bowling, Kent fielding twelve-a-side. E. M. Grace was still only 39, not too old, but his first-class average was still over 20. He would open with W.G.

There was a third brother in Fred Grace, a hard-hitting, middle-order batsman who could bowl well enough to be considered an all-rounder. With Fred at number nine, the batting was as strong as possible, all of the top nine averaging over 20 in first class cricket – the benchmark for selection.

Lord Harris then thought long and hard about which two specialist bowlers to pick. He needed speed so he chose the Nottinghamshire left-arm quick Fred Morley, good at getting rid of tailenders. Harris digested the fact that Morley had taken 100 wickets in a tour of Canada and the USA at the ridiculous average of 3.54.

Finally Harris wanted control, tight lines to frustrate good batsmen out. In 1880, one bowler had taken 170 odd wickets at under nine, the vastly experienced Alfred Shaw, a prolific wicket taking 38-year-old, the finest slow, medium trundler of all time. Shaw bowled more overs (four or five ball) than he conceded runs throughout his entire career.

'Funny thing' thought Harris out loud, 'That's the strongest England team of all time, and apart from myself, only A. P. Lucas remains from the team that were thrashed in Melbourne.'

'Go to sleep darling,' his wife whispered.

September 6th was warm and sunny with the settled look of a contest that would run its course. 'D'you 'ere that?' some Cockney whispered in the queue for the turn styles, 'Spofforth's broken his finger!'

Lord Harris read out his team sheet one by one to W. L. Murdock, the heavily-moustachiod Australian skipper. Harris seemed to pronounce W. G. Grace with particular accent, as though he was the Titan, someone to be afraid of.

England won the toss and elected to bat first. A large round of applause from a record attendance of 20,814 spectators greeted brothers W.G. and E.M. as they entered a whole new arena, bathed in late summer sunshine. Such was the build up to the greatest sporting spectacle of all time that the ground was full to bursting with thousands having to stand all day.

Instantly recognisable, W.G., in peaked cap with the distinctive yellow and red MCC colours, looked distinguished, long dark beard, broad shouldered, beefy, hungry slit-like eyes. He wore a black belt, pads seemingly several sizes too small and spiked gloves. With his older brother E.M. for company, and an adoring mother watching from the pavilion, the stage was all set. E.M., obviously the shorter, took first ball.

The Oval was a vast amphitheatre with an old wooden pavilion looking on in regal splendour. There were no other stands, just terraces for spectators. In those days cricket was a game to be watched intently during the passage of play, with no need to speak to others. Just three policemen looked on, each standing transfixed at proceedings in a fixed spot so as not to block the view of others.

Cricket was still evolving. For example in the Victorian era five-ball overs were bowled not six. Also a batsman was awarded only a five if he hit the ball over the boundary rope, not six The pitches were poor in general terms, although the wicket for this test was as flat as nineteenth-century technology allowed. Crucially the weather was dry as there were no covers.

Palmer needed watching, his fast off cutters had wreaked havoc throughout the land that summer; to support him was the medium paced accuracy of Henry Boyle. Maidens were played out and runs came at a trickle. Both Grace brothers had learnt their defence techniques in the orchard they cleared away at the back of their house years earlier. A straight bat was fundamental. Even so, the crowd gasped as W.G. missed a yorker from Palmer that shaved the stumps.

W.G.'s first boundary brought up a welcoming cheer and soon both batsmen were into their stride. Lord Harris looked in good spirits. None of the Graces had ever played a test match before. The intrigue in the contest between one Gloucestershire family and Australia made for riveting viewing.

Scorecards provide the numerical evidence but, as this game took place in the mid-Victorian era, only so much has been recorded and much is left to the reader's imagination.

The run rate remained between two and three for most of the England innings. One imagines where the Grace brothers scored their runs. W.G. was noted as a powerful driver and cutter, but rarely played the hook shot – most of his runs would have come on the off side, between third man and long off, so too E.M.

Ninety-one runs had been added before E.M. departed, caught by Alexander off the part-timer A. C. Bannerman, a lapse of concentration. But his solid 36 gave the start England wanted and justified Harris's faith in him. In came A. P. 'Bunny' Lucas, one of the 23-year-olds fresh from Cambridge. He had been selected on the basis of his fine defence, a gritty right-hand batsman, but capable.

Together the pair mastered the Australian bowling in a grand stand of 120 during which W.G. raised his bat for the first ever England century. Without the sting of Spofforth, the Australian bowling grew weary on an unresponsive track. After an accomplished 55, Lucas fell to Bannerman and in came Billy Barnes. The momentum continued wih another decent stand to take the total beyond any previous scored by either country. Then with Barnes falling, bowled by Alexander, Grace reached his 150 to a rapturous reception. He had hit twelve boundaries, all along the ground as God intended, ran a further ten threes, fourteen twos and forty-six singles before Palmer bowled him through the gate with the score on 281.

W.G.'s 152, before being bowled by Bannerman, was achieved against an opening attack compromising Boyle and Palmer – statistically one of the finest combined test-career figures of any opening attack in history. Whether they were that fast is a moot point but nonetheless Boyle and Palmer combined to take 120 test wickets at just over 21.

England closed on 410–8 thanks to an excellent 52 by Harris. After England reached 420 on the second morning, Australia then collapsed to 149 all out, thanks to five wickets from the paceman Morley and three more to the gifted Allan Steel.

Following on, Australia countered with a century as equally grand from W. L. Murdoch (153 not out). Interestingly he and W.G. had a wager on who would score the highest innings. Having reached 327, Australia set England just 57 to win. At 31–5, W.G., coming in at number seven, saw England home with nine not out in company with Frank Penn.

Official attendance figures for the whole test were a record for any cricket match in England at the time: for the three days — 44,154. Most arrived at the ground on foot or by horse-drawn carriage, some from the shires by steam train.

W.G. went on to represent England when available until 1899 when he was a portly 50 and 320 days old – surely too old? Yet in 1895, at the age of 47, he was still good enough to score 1,000 first-class runs before the end of May. He held onto the record for the highest ever score for 24 years, became the first to reach 100 centuries and went on to score 126 in all (over twice as many as the rest of this England team put together), a record that stood for 53 years. Even today, he still shares the record for carrying his bat through an innings, no less than 17 times. This compares favourably to Hobbs and Sutcliffe with seven times each, and Hutton's four times. Clearly he was a colossus of the time, the Bradman of his age

It is said by A. A. Thomson (in 1967) that the catch Fred Grace took to dismiss Bonnor in the first innings, was the highest hit ever made at the Oval or, probably, anywhere else. Sadly, he was to die of pneumonia just a fortnight later.

Eighteen months later Australia won a four-test series down under by two tests to nil. The Ashes were born the following summer when Australia duly defeated England once again at the Oval by just seven runs. Requiring only 85 to win, England collapsed to 77 with W.G. contributing a massive 32 in defiance.

W.G.'s legacy is vast. He discovered modern batting. It is fitting that this innings makes it into the finest fifty ever played by Englishmen in test-cricket history. The day the greatest batsman of his time proved his worth on the grandest stage of them all.

England 420 (W. G. Grace 152, Lucas 55, Lord Harris 52, Bannerman 3–111).
Australia 149 (Morley 5–56, Steel 3–58) and 327 (Murdock 153*, Morley 3–90).
England 57–5 (W. G. Grace 9*, Palmer 3–35).
ENGLAND WON BY 5 WICKETS.

Innings Ranked Number 48
Hammond's 231 not out at Sydney in 1936

Opponents: Australia.
At stake: Ashes won by Australia in 1934.
Bowling attack: McCormick, Sievers, Ward, O'Reilly, Chipperfield, McCabe. Runs per wicket average: 38.75.
Pitch: Good.
Game situation: England, having won the first test by 322 runs, won the toss in this the second of five tests in the series. England elected to bat first.

The second test at Sydney started just a few days after a stunned and shocked Britain had been informed that King Edward VIII had abdicated in order to pursue his relationship with Mrs Wallis

Simpson, just divorced from her second husband. All this against the background of the bloody Spanish Civil War, which seemed and was thousands of miles away from the real action, the 1936/37 Ashes series.

Between 1930 and 1948 world cricket was enthralled by the batting feats of a genius who broke all comparable records. Sadly for England, this was not in the commanding form of Hammond who announced himself on the world stage with 905 runs in the 1928/29 Ashes series. Ever since then, Hammond's records had been eclipsed by the batting phenomenon, Don Bradman. Bradman averaged 99.94 in a twenty-year test career. No other batsman in world cricket, playing more than five innings, has averaged higher than Barry Richards of South Africa, except Bradman. Richards averaged 72.57 in seven completed innings, as opposed to 70 for Bradman.

Occasionally, however, Hammond reminded the world of his prowess. One such occasion was the 231 not out during the second test of the 1936/37 series. He had experienced a long, lean period in international cricket since returning from gorging himself on New Zealand's bowlers in 1933. There, in back-to-back tests, Hammond had scored 227, followed by 336 not out, itself a new test record which he managed to take from Bradman.

There was speculation in high places that perhaps Hammond should be rested for a year or two, and that his performances since would not have been tolerated in any other batsman's case. By now Hammond felt the pressures of an international sportsman and complained of back ache. His throat seemed sore from the effects of too many cigarettes. With his place in the England team being questioned, he at last found form in the summer of 1936 where he fed like a bear fresh from hibernation on Indian bowlers.

After missing out on the first test, Hammond recovered his health and took 167 at Old Trafford, then bullied a further 217 and five not out at the Oval. He was back after apparently batting from memory for the last few seasons.

England won the first Ashes test by 322 runs, thanks to a century from Maurice Leyland and ten wickets in the game from Bill Voce for just 57 runs, a magnificent performance.

The Australian attack was spearheaded by McCormick, a fast bowler with a distinctive windmill action. Together with McCormick was Morris Sievers, who was to play a brief but successful test career as a fast-medium pacer, able to extract extra bounce.

On at first change was the honest toiler, Francis Ward, and the far more famous Bill O'Reilly, a leg spinner with a bowling average that compares favourably with even that of Shane Warne. Batsmen McCabe and Chipperfield completed the attack. This was statistically far from the most potent bowling unit in history, but then wickets lacked both pace and bounce. In fact, in decent weather, large numbers of runs were available to the batsmen who eschewed risk and waited for the bad ball.

Hammond entered with the fall of Arthur Fagg (who was to gain a reputation in 1938 by performing the unique feat of scoring double hundreds in the same first class game, for Kent v Essex at Colchester), who had achieved no success.

Hammond began in partnership with Charlie Barnett and together the pair added 91 before Barnett was bowled by the honest Ward. Maurice Leyland, a left-handed Yorkshireman, with forearms like Yorkshire hams, came in to dismantle the attack alongside Hammond.

The pair put on 129 before the part-time bowler pinned the stout Yorkshireman in front for 42. In came Leslie Ames at 247–3. Ames remains the only wicket-keeper batsman to score 100 hundreds. His figures compare favourably, even alongside Alec Stewart's from the 1990s. The pair took England to 279–3 at the close of the first day with Hammond on 147.

Hammond continued to dominate with another century partnership on day two before a clutter of wickets encouraged Gubby Allen, the skipper, to declare at 426–6. Rain had affected the wicket and stoppages had taken time out of the game.

Hammond remained undefeated on 231, scored in 458 minutes and including 27 fours, a typically powerful Hammond knock.

England went on to romp to a 2–0 victory, thanks principally to Bill Voce, arguably the best left-arm seamer England has ever produced and veteran of the bodyline tour four years previously. Voce took seven for 76 in the game and Australia slumped to 80 all out in the first attempt, then 324 in the second innings. Bradman, with 93, gave the Australians some comfort for the three remaining test matches.

Australia were to win the final three tests with Bradman scoring 270 at Melbourne, coming in at number seven to avoid the worst of a sticky wicket, 212 in the fourth test and 169 in the decider also at Melbourne.

As for Hammond, he produced one of his finest innings under the most trying circumstances, 32 out of 76 on a Melbourne sticky in the next test but it was not enough. A fifty in the final test after the game was lost was the only other significant innings for Hammond on the tour.

Australia went on to retain the Ashes for the next 17 years, an entire generation of cricketers later. England might just have won the Ashes in 1938 had the wickets not been so slow and dead for the bowlers.

Many beleived that Hammond did not actually seek records and, according to the Australians, his 32 on a deadly sticky at Melbourne surpassed even the 231 not out. In his career he scored more than 50,000 runs, including a then world record 7,249 in test cricket – 253 more than Bradman, although Bradman batted in 60 fewer innings. Hammond scored no less than 36 double hundreds, which dwarfs the previous record holders, Hobbs and Fry with sixteen, Ranjitsinjhi fourteen, W. G. Grace thirteen. In all history only one other batsman compares. Around the same time span as Hammond too, he scored 37. Guess who? Only the most craggy, veteran cricket enthusiast will remember Hammond. Septuagenarians today can, according to A. A. Thomson, imagine Hammond if they witnessed Tom Graveney. The comparison Thomson made in 1967 was:

> ... the best of Graveney, which is very good indeed ... is like good, ordinary Hammond. But the best of Hammond is something you cannot hope to see again.

What a shame there exist no 'flickers' of Hammond in action, just photographs with some fortunate to catch the glorious Hammond cover drive.

England 426-6 declared (Hammond 231*, Barnett 57).
Australia 80 (Voce 4–10, Allen 3–19) and 324 McCabe 93, Bradman 82, Hammond 3–29, Voce 3–66).
ENGLAND WON BY AN INNINGS AND 22 RUNS.

Innings Ranked Number 47
Hobb's 126* at Melbourne in 1912

Opponents: Australia.
At stake: Ashes.
Bowling attack: Cotter, Whitty, Hordern, Kelleway, Armstrong, Minnett, Ransford: 26.19.
Pitch: Fine.
Game situation: England need 219 to win the second test in the five-match series and draw level with Australia.

There are perhaps people still alive today who remember seeing Jack Hobbs bat, though their numbers are very few and far between, relics from a golden era. Almost certainly their memories would be post-war, and by post-war, I mean the Great War and of the middle aged sage. The post-war Hobbs was prolific and statistically superior even to the younger Hobbs, but the post-war Hobbs was content to play the waiting game and eschewed the sensational shots of his youth. He stated that this was a deliberate attempt to modify his game to his advancing years, for Hobbs played test cricket until he was 47 and still scored first-class centuries when rising 52.

The pre-war Hobbs, the athletic son of a Cambridge University groundsman, stood 5ft 9ins and batted in a style that more than one contemporary journalist described as 'Trumper-like', after Australia's greatest pre-Bradman batsman. Though strong on the off side, Hobbs's leg-side play was simply awesome, peerless, and broke new ground. Perhaps his greatest shot was the nonchalant flick off his legs – not behind square, for that patent was Ranjitsinhji's – but in front.

The previous winter Hobbs had dominated a series in South Africa where he averaged, on the matting wickets against the world's best googly bowlers, 67.37. The next highest was less than 34, Hobbs stood alone.

The 1911/12 tour of Australia began disastrously for England. 'Plum' Warner, the captain, fell terribly ill and took no further action in the series aside from as an on-looker and member of the selection panel. Under J. W. H. T. Douglas's leadership England had lost the first test. S. F. Barnes, still regarded by many as the greatest bowler of all time, was furious. Douglas had chosen to open with himself and the left-arm pace of F. R. Foster. S. F. Barnes picked up 3–107 coming on first change, not bad when Australia had racked up 447, but Barnes felt he should have opened and used the new ball.

At Melbourne for the second test, S. F. Barnes opened the bowling for England after Australia had won the toss. Although the 38-year-old Barnes felt unwell, he stormed through the Australian line up with the wickets of Bardsley (first ball), Kelleway, Hill and Armstrong; all in a spell of 4–1.

A score of 184 felt below par on a reasonable wicket, but England's bowling and Barnes in particular, had been majestic. England replied and reached 38–1 at the close of the first day, Hobbs having fallen, flicking a wide one from Cotter to Carter the wicket-keeper for the second time in consecutive test innings. Next day J. W. Hearne (at 20 years and 324 days) became the youngest Englishman to score an Ashes century and England were dismissed just before the close of the second day for 265. Wilfred Rhodes, the great Yorkshire all-rounder, helped with 61.

Australia countered with 290 to set England 219 to level the series. Realistically for England to stay in the series, they had to win this test. Hordern's leg spin and googlies had wreaked devastation in the three England innings to date in the series. Hordern had 16 wickets already, but he had not dismissed Hobbs.

It was 40 minutes before lunch on the third day when Hobbs and Rhodes began England's pursuit of 219. Albert Cotter, the experienced spearhead, bowled in a slinging style similar to that of Jeff Thomson in the 1970s, right-arm fast. Cotter provided the pace and, at 29, was in his prime. Bill Whitty at the other end bowled left-arm medium fast and swung the ball prodigiously. He was younger (aged 25) and apt to be moody when umpires decisions went against him.

There followed an offensive of breath-taking magnificence. First Hobbs and Rhodes stole outrageous singles by defending the ball out square towards cover point and sprinting to the other end before Ransford, the finest cover point in the world, had time to react. Both batsmen took boundaries off the bad balls, Rhodes rock like, Hobbs in dashing manner. Though Cotter and Whitty had bowled several maidens, Hobbs and Rhodes found little difficulty.

Clem Hill needed quick wickets with the new ball but in the first half-an-hour none had been forthcoming. Hill grew anxious so for the last over before lunch Hordern came on, but Hobbs danced down the wicket and hit him back over his head for a defiant four before rocking back into his crease to pull the last ball through mid-wicket for another boundary. In 40 minutes the pair had put on 52–0.

Hobbs and Rhodes had formed a formidable opening partnership against South Africa in 1909/10 with stands of 159 in the first test, 94 in the second and 221 in the fifth, yet this was their first stand of more than 50 against Australia.

Rhodes fell, caught at the wicket, soon after with the score on 57. To maintain the momentum, Douglas elevated the big-hitting George Gunn from four to three. Gunn kicked off from the start and like Hobbs, danced down the track to hit the bowlers back over their heads. On came Cotter for a second spell and this time Hobbs cut him swiftly and with great execution both to cover point and behind square. There followed a delicate late cut to complete the mastery.

Hordern kept bowling more in hope than expectation as Clem Hill, the Australian captain ran out of options. Runs came at a steady rate. It was in this passage of play where Hobbs unleashed his full repertoire of scoring shots. At the crease he stood splendidly side on, peaked cap, black belt around his waist. Hobbs was a lean $11^{1}/_{2}$ stone, about the same dimensions as Ricky Ponting.

When facing Hordern, Hobbs played the ball from the pitch. He could not read Hordern's googly but, by playing well forward to the full pitched deliveries, he smothered the spin, and by playing right back on his stumps, could thrash the slightly short ball through mid-wicket and mid on for four.

Hobbs had just turned 29. For one of England's greatest ever batsman, widely considered the greatest and certainly the finest of his era, 30 seems quite an old age for a debut Ashes hundred, but Hobbs had only started playing cricket at twelve and did not play in first-class cricket until he was 22. He looked youthful, clean shaven.

Hobbs was self-taught. His genius was to be seen most under difficult conditions and against the finest bowlers. There his technique and mastery would become obvious, head and shoulders above his peers, a true master.

Australian crowds grew to admire Hobbs. The 126* Hobbs scored just a week after his twenty-ninth birthday from 207 deliveries proved a watershed in his career. Though he had shown glimpses of genius against Australia before, this was his first Ashes century. Steadily over the next twenty years Hobbs was to break all records. Following his 126* at Melbourne, came 187 at Adelaide in the third test and then a 178 once again at Melbourne in the fourth test.

England took the series, not just because of Hobbs, but also because England had the luxury of her greatest opening bowlers in history: Sidney Barnes and Frank Foster. Australia, despite going 1–0 up at Sydney, were hammered 1–4.

Jack Hobbs lived until he was 81, whilst Albert Cotter was shot by a sniper in 1917.

Australia 184 (S. F. Barnes 5–44).
England 265 (Hearne 114, Rhodes 61, Hordern 4–66, Cotter 4–73).
Australia 299 (Armstrong 90, F. R. Foster 6–91, Barnes 3–96).
England 219–2 (Hobbs 126*, G. Gunn 43).
ENGLAND WON BY 8 WICKETS.

Innings Ranked Number 46
Cowdrey's 102 at Melbourne in 1954

Opponents: Australia.
At stake: Ashes.
Bowling attack: Lindwall, Miller, Archer, Johnston, Benaud, Johnson.
Average runs per wicket: 25.48.
Pitch: Lively, lots of lateral movement.
Game situation: England in trouble, Cowdrey enters the Melbourne arena at 21 for 2 in front of 63,000 partisan Australian supporters.

In the year when Bill Haley's *Rock Around the Clock* was Number 1, England and Australia were engaged in a classic Ashes series. Both sides had fire power in the fast-bowling department. Australia still relied on Lindwall and Miller as they had done since the war. England possessed Brian Statham, an accurate fast medium, rather like James Anderson today, though statistically a notch above, and Frank Tyson, who passed into legend as possibly the fastest fast-bowler of all time, anywhere. The difference between the sides at the start of the series lay in the experience of the opening bowlers. England's attack was raw, potentially wayward but hostile, whilst Australia's had been around a long time.

England lost the first test by an innings and 154 runs. Hutton had won the toss and inserted the Australians, who amassed 601–8. England subsided feebly in both innings. Apart from fighting 88s apiece for Bailey in the first innings and Edrich in the second, and 40s from May and Cowdrey, England had looked out of their depth.

Runs were equally hard to come by in the second test. Only tail-ender Wardle reached 30 in England's first innings total of 154, but England through Tyson and Statham had restricted Australia to a lead of 74. May, the bright 25-year-old, replied with 104, adding 116 with Cowdrey, a portly 22-year-old amateur just down from Oxford. Because of this bright pair of colts, England reached the lofty heights of 296. Towards the end, with growing frustration, Lindwall unleashed a 90-mile-an-hour bumper that knocked Tyson out.

Australia, set 222 to win, perished at the hands of a very angry Tyson who was certainly wayward but incomparably quick. He took six in the innings. The Australians hated the pace and the series seemed to be coming down to a dual between these magnificent bowling attacks, and whichever side could streak enough runs.

At Melbourne with the series at 1–1, Bill Edrich opened with Hutton in a desperate attempt to find a reliable partner for the great Yorkshire veteran. The sky was overcast, damp even, and on a fresh wicket Lindwall began proceedings by sending down two bumpers which Hutton just managed to evade. A third, Hutton fended off from near his throat and the ball lobbed just short of two diving gullies. The gargantuan crowd of 63,000 roared out their approval. This was gladiatorial, like the Colosseum in Rome.

Though Lindwall moved the ball late, his direction wavered and runs were leaked from the edges of both batsmen; understandable as their 38-year-old eyes had to contend with 90 m.p.h. deliveries; initially runs came through the cordon of an umbrella field, set by skipper Ian Johnson.

Bill Edrich had not reached thirty in his last four innings The 38-year-old now lived on past glories. Fighting for his place, Edrich at last got a ball from Miller that strayed towards leg. It was only Miller's second over but every single previous delivery had been in that narrow corridor of uncertainty and Edrich wanted to counter-attack, somehow, but the leg glance ended in Lindwall's hands at leg slip, the perfect trap. Peter May played out the rest of the over. Hutton took a single squeezed onto the leg side off Lindwall, then May on strike gloved Lindwall's first delivery, a tremendous snorter, to Benaud in the gully. Pandemonium broke out.

The advantage of winning the toss had evaporated away under the sultry and quite windy conditions, despite the bull-ring lay out of ground. Into this hothouse amphitheatre stepped the young Oxbridge man, just turned twenty-two on Christmas Eve. Cowdrey walked almost apologetically onto the ground, sporting a blue cap and the generous waistline of an undergraduate at ease with himself in the world.

Cowdrey took guard in a gentlemanly manner and settled in to face Lindwall. Decibel levels rose as Lindwall hurled himself into that magnificent final stride, modelled on Larwood, and unleashed an away swinger of good length which Cowdrey slightly edged all along the ground through the vacant third slip area for four. Lindwall cursed his luck, and next delivery sent the ball towards Cowdrey's pads which the young man glanced to fine leg for another boundary.

Hutton came over for a mid-pitch chat between overs. Hutton had been Cowdrey's greatest inspiration and now here he was batting with the England legend.

'Just think' said Hutton, 'you aren't even getting paid for this!'

Cowdrey smiled. It was typical Hutton humour. England's first professional captain was in charge of an England team partly comprised of genuine amateurs, such as Cowdrey, cricketers who plied their trade for pleasure not money.

Watching Miller unleash everything he could at Hutton, was to see two titans in action. Hutton could just about cope until a short of a length out-swinger took his edge and Hole snaffled a quality catch low down at second slip. Cowdrey now faced the prospect of seeing Miller *v* Compton at close quarters, probably the greatest dual in the game's long history. A rising delivery thumped into Compton's body which the 36-year-old chested downwards out of harm's way with barely a grimace. The next took off as a substantial leg cutter which Compton couldn't get within inches of. Neither legend spoke, no one said a thing until Miller walked passed Cowdrey at the non-striker's end.

'I don't know, Col – I've played against Compo since 1946, and still he doesn't get any better.'

And so it played out, Compton drove Miller passed cover for three, the first runs off Miller. Cowdrey drove a two, also through the covers off Miller, but otherwise Miller reined supreme all morning. His spell reached such heights of perfection that all England's batsmen could do was batten down the hatches and wait for the storm to pass. Compton too was ageing, and Miller was simply too quick and his deliveries too unplayable for him to survive. Sure enough, Compton on four edged Miller to Harvey in the slips and England at 41–4 were deep into a crisis.

Miller at 35 was still in his prime but his dodgy knee began to creak.

Out came Trevor Bailey, and together with Cowdrey the pair saw England through to lunch. Miller had bowled throughout the morning session and his nine eight-ball overs included eight maidens and the scalps of Hutton, Edrich and Compton for just those five runs. Cowdrey ate his lunch happy with his 17 not out. He, and he alone, had looked in touch. Cowdrey seemed to have had more time than his peers. He got into line early fearlessly against the rising delivery.

Miller's storm passed away and the 35-year-old had thrown everything he could possibly muster at England. His body now ached so Johnson gave his trump card a nice long rest in the slip cordon.

After lunch the horrors from the morning vanished, the pitch dried and conditions for batting improved. Archer and Benaud replaced Lindwall and Miller. Cowdrey drove straight for four and again through cover, then played the ball skilfully off his legs. Bailey meanwhile called for a suicidal single in a moment of madness and had Archer, successfully shied at the stumps Cowdrey would have been run out by five yards. He missed and soon after the 100 came up for England. Cowdrey then played an exquisite late cut for four to bring up his 50, even the partisan crowd gasped in admiration.

Cowdrey had hit Benaud out of the attack and Johnson replaced him with the left-arm pace of Bill Johnston. Cowdrey batted now in complete comfort but just as anxious England nerves were soothing in the afternoon sun, Bailey succumbed for 30, edging to the keeper. England at 115–5 were still deep in the abyss, but better for the stand of 71. The perky figure of county team mate Godfrey Evans joined Cowdrey.

Cowdrey, however, now fell becalmed and for a period of 35 minutes became stranded on 64. Ian Johnson's well-flighted off breaks drifted from leg to off with the strong breeze. Evans offered encouragement in between overs, especially when the crowd barracked Cowdrey with slow hand claps. Cowdrey panicked, danced down the wicket and hoisted Johnson over mid on. The ball flew just over the finger tips and sped away for four. Cowdrey wiped his brow, certain in the knowledge that had he been dismissed so recklessly he would have been lambasted by Hutton as vehemently as Compton was by Hammond back in '38.

Tea came and went. Cowdrey soon started middling everything again and swept Johnston – cutting his pace down to medium – for four. Wickets fell though, Evans for 20, LBW to Archer, England 169- –6. It was Cowdrey, all alone, who had kept England in the game but only just. Archer now bowled a wide half volley which Cowdrey caressed to the ring with a glorious cover drive, left elbow up, head and poise in perfect harmony – as though Cowdrey's bat was an extension of the man himself.

Cowdrey glanced at the scoreboard, 97 not out. An excited chatter broke out amongst the crowd. Next ball Archer dropped short of a length and Cowdrey hit wide of mid on for three. The crowd, at times hostile, now clapped their appreciation as Cowdrey scampered through for his 100. Cowdrey raised his bat to acknowledge the applause and time stopped still whilst 63,000 communicated their admiration.

Wardle, the 31-year-old left-arm orthodox spinner could bat a bit but not today. Archer cleaned him up. Next over, and after Cowdrey had maintained the scoring with a couple of singles, Johnson flighted another off break which moved through the air from leg to off. Cowdrey drew his front foot forward freakishly forwards outside the off stump. The ball pitched right into the middle of the rough – created by Johnston earlier in the day – and ripped passed Cowdrey's left pad to roll comically between his legs off his right pad then tragically onto his stumps.

Cowdrey's 102 sparkled with perfection and occasional brilliance on a day Australia dominated from start to finish. It was the finest innings under the circumstances, often quoted as chanceless and almost every shot played, every question asked, was met with the most appropriate response.

With Cowdrey gone, England subsided for 191. This was the lowest team total to include an Ashes century, equal with Bradman's achieved during the bodyline series. This record still stands today.

Australia gained a first innings lead of 40 to which England replied with 279 with May scoring 91. But runs were easier to come by after illegal watering and rolling had closed some of the first day cracks –

although this claim was soundly denied by the groundstaff.

Australia, requiring 240 for victory and the chance to go 2–1 up, were blown away once again by Frank 'Typhoon' Tyson. According to Godfrey Evans the wicket-keeper, Tyson's spell of 7–27 was the fastest piece of bowling he had ever seen, a view backed up by Ritchie Benaud.

It was however Cowdrey's gem of an innings, 102 out of 160 scored in the four hours he was at the crease, which prevented England losing the game within the first two sessions of play. Cowdrey eventually went on to score a further 21 test centuries to equal the England record.

For 20 years Cowdrey answered England's call. He was the only batsman ever to face both the Lindwall/Miller and Lillee/Thompson threats.

England 191 (Cowdrey 102, Archer 4–33, Miller 3–14).
Australia 231 (Statham 5–66).
England 279 (May 91, Hutton 42, Johnston 5–85).
Australia 111 (Tyson 7–27).
ENGLAND WON BY 128 RUNS.

Innings Ranked Number 45
Gower's 173 not out at the Gaddafi Stadium 1984

Opponents: Pakistan.
At stake: First ever test series defeat to Pakistan.
Bowling attack:Mohsin Khan, Sarfraz Nawaz, Abdul Qadir, Wasim Raja: Average runs per wicket: 33.6.
Pitch: Slow and low.
Game situation: England conceded a first innings lead of 102 and are 38–2, still 64 runs behind, with over two days to go. England trail 1–0 in the series.

According to an old sage in the pavilion of the St Lawrence ground, David Gower batted just like Frank Woolley. Both were graceful left handers, blond and elegant. It was Gower's 154 not out at Sabina Park three years earlier that evoked memories of Woolley's brace of 90s in the Lord's test of 1921. Few spectators could appreciate the similarities between the two for half a century separated their contribution to cricket. Youngsters in the 1920s would be OAPs in the 1980s. Nevertheless, one can extrapolate back through the fine works of Cardus and Warner and attach that code to the DNA supplied by Martin-Jenkins and Woodcock – safe to say that on their day spectators became equally entranced at the ease in which both players leant into their shots. A century from either left a warm glow of intense satisfaction, an emotion of deep rooted contentment as though everything in life was fine.

David Gower had an enormous burden placed upon his 26-year-old shoulders. He was not supposed to be captain, Bob Willis was. However Willis had to depart the tour through hepatitis with England 1–0 down in the three test series, so Gower as vice-captain took up the reins. Also, talismanic all-rounder Ian Botham withdrew and returned to England for a knee operation. Despite these setbacks Gower played quite superbly after the brace of 50s in the first test which, whilst still under Willis's command, England lost in the end narrowly by three wickets. Gower's 50s represented the only England innings over 28 in either innings. Abdul Qadir, the maestro leg spinner, claimed 8–133 and swinger Sarfraz Nawaz 6–69 in the match.

In the next test at Faisalabad Gower took 152 from the same attack. Vic Marks, the England off-spinner, helped Gower add 167 for the seventh wicket and Gower enjoyed the luxury of a declaration following a first innings lead of 97. Nonetheless, the pitch at the Iqbal Stadium in Faisalabad was too bland for a result, so England went to the third and final test at the Gaddafi Stadium in Lahore with only the prospect of a series levelling win.

It was not a happy party of England cricketers that arrived at Lahore. By now the Pakistani Government had met to discuss the Botham comment regarding Pakistan as the perfect place to send one's mother-in-law. As a consequence, England found themselves with no caterers since the staff at the Hilton refused to serve food as a protest to Botham's deep insult. In the end, Bernard Thomas, the team's physio, had to serve up baked beans on toast (according to Gower in his autobiography).

So with only the prospect of a drawn series to whet England's appetite, Pakistan once again won the toss and elected to put England in to bat. Sarfraz and Qadir grabbed nine of the wickets to fall, all except Gower who nicked a Mohsol Khan seamer to wicket-keeper

Anil Dalpat for nine. England totalled only 241 in 78.5 overs. Again Marks came to the fore and with Graeme Fowler added 120 for the sixth wicket – Marks enjoying his promotion to number seven.

This looked reasonable with Pakistan struggling to 181–8 with Foster already celebrating a five-wicket haul but Zaheer Abbas and Sarfraz, the number ten, shared a crucial partnership of 161 for the ninth wicket. It took the part-time off spin of Chrics Smith (older brother of Robin) to separate them. Sarfraz fell for 90 to a catch by Gatting. Pakistan gained a 102-run lead on the first innings.

Gower re-jigged the batting order to allow Fowler to open with Smith. This allowed Gatting, not an opener by choice, to drop to three, Gower to four, Lamb to five with Randall at six. Smith and Fowler started well but both departed about an hour before the close of day three to leave England stuttering on 38–2. Gower and Gatting took the score tentatively to 65–2 at the close, still 37 in arrears with only eight wickets left.

The crowd for day four was as sparse as test cricket gets. *Wisden* describes the stands as showing 'acres of spare terraces' but that Gower rarely seemed in trouble against Wasim Raja and Abdul Qadir's googlies, top spinners and leg breaks. It is quite astonishing to think that so few locals attended a game that could on day four go down in Pakistan's short history as their first series win against England. In terms of crowd interest, this test is similar to the famous timeless test in South Africa just before the war. Just like then though, the cricketers on both sides fought intense attritional cricket. Gower and Gatting kept the score ticking along and posted a 100 partnership.

Gatting had reasons to be grateful for batting with the left-handed Gower. The scampering of singles mid over allowed Gatting to feed off the inevitable errors in line. Just as England looked to have reached parity, tragedy struck and one of England's finest players of spin bowling departed, run out for 53, with the score on 175–3, a lead of 72.

Again Gower had to stay there and eke out runs when naturally he would want to score freely and boldly. A batsman playing against his natural flair deserves praise. Gower as batsman had already harvested his full quota of runs to justify his place and ranking as England's best batsman, now he sought runs for his country. He cared not for entertaining the partisan crowd, these were the days before satellite television brought the game into people's lounges. Gower's job was pure and simple, to bat England into a decent lead to facilitate a sporting declaration on the last day.

Lamb, deceived by the guile of Abdul's flight, soon fell for six making this a most miserable series for the South African, just 78 runs from seven completed innings. Randall fell immediately after and England had crashed to 189–5, just a lead of 87. Gower afforded a smile as Vic Marks, the diminutive Somerset off spinner, arrived at the wicket. Gower, standing with bat held behind his back, told his Somerset colleague to relax, enjoy the challenge but above all not to get out.

Sure enough Marks once again justified his position at number seven. The 200 came up, followed by Gower's courageous hundred. The cheer from the crowd was of course muted. When the spinners pitched too full, Gower drove with panache. When just too short, Gower moved back and flicked or pulled to leg. Mostly he mixed watchful defence coming forward with soft hands to smother the ball. The 250 came up and by the close Gower and Marks had taken the score to 273–5, Gower held firm throughout the day to reach 124 with Marks closing in on a third half century, undefeated on 41.

Day five saw a spirited acceleration from England and particularly Gower. Marks duly collected his third successive 50 before chancing his arm to Qadir and getting caught. Foster came and went for one at which stage England led by 207. Cowans promoted to ten above the veteran wicket keeper Bob Taylor, swung and missed for three, whilst Gower accelerated passed the 150 and onwards with delicate leg cuts, a lofted on drive and a flick to mid wicket.

Taking his score to 173, Gower declared for the second successive test to leave Pakistan to chase down 243 in 59 overs, gettable, if Pakistan wished to win by a greater margin. In all Gower had batted for just over seven hours, faced 284 balls and hit sixteen fours in an exhibition of craftsmanship against top-quality leg spin that today leaves the mouth-watering fantasy of just how well Gower would have played Warne in the 1993 series, rather better I would wager than most other Englishmen.

It is interesting to note that whilst Gower scored 449 runs in the three test series at an average of 112.25, he clearly rates his 157 at the Oval in 1985 as the better knock. On that golden day, with Gower and Gooch taking the Ashes away from Australia, the two Englishmen played supremely well in front of a delirious nation. Television brought Gower's 1985 series into the front rooms of the entire country so there was an audience of millions rather than a few hundred at Faisalabad.

What makes the Faisalabad century worthy of a place in this book ahead of any in Gower's 1985 landmark series, was the quality of the bowling attack. In Pakistan, Gower rose head and shoulders above all other Englishmen with over twice as many runs (449) as the next man (Marks with 218). This was a depleted England team with players like Graham Gooch opting for the higher wages in the apartheid ridden South Africa. In 1985 England had their strongest possible team to select from and there was no shortage of runs, against the weakest Australian bowling attack to arrive at these shores since possibly the 1860s!

I remember this innings well, following radio bulletins every hour on the hour. By the end of March 1984 it seemed that England had one of the two greatest batsmen of the modern era, with Viv Richards from the West Indies the other. Certainly, on his day Gower made batting look so easy. He was forever criticised for giving his wicket away, handing it to the opposition, wafting outside the off stump. Much of the criticism came from journalists and commentators hooked on Gower's successes. To attend a day's test cricket graced with a Gower hundred was to thrill at a genius casually revealing his gift – rare timing, extraordinary grace, a marvel of human achievement.

I witnessed a day in the washed out Centenary Test at Lord's in 1980. Gower had been recalled after losing his place against the West Indies. In ran Dennis Lillee, nicely accelerating up to the stumps from the Pavilion End. He was fired up by the scent of startled England batsmen, Gooch and Athey back in the hutch, victims of the great man's pace. Gower, then a fresh faced 23-year-old, had just joined Boycott. One would expect nerves to betray the south paw, instead Gower cut, hooked and drove Lillee for three scintillating boundaries in one over that lit up Lord's like pulsating electricity.

Too readily criticised when he failed, Gower was guilty solely of being too good at what he did.

England 241 (Marks 74, Fowler 58, Qadir 5–67).
Pakistan 343 (Sarfraz Nawaz 90, Zaheer Abbas 82*, Qasim Omar 73, Foster 5–67).
England 344–9 declared (Gower 173*, Marks 55, Gatting 53, Qadir 5–110).
Pakistan 217–6.
MATCH DRAWN.

Innings Ranked Number 44
Gooch's 153 at Sabina Park in 1981

Opponents: West Indies.
At stake: National pride, England were already 2–0 down and this was the last test.
Bowling attack: Holding, Marshall, Garner, Croft, Richards. Average runs per wicket: 26.14.
Pitch: Bouncy but true.
Game situation: West Indies won the toss and inserted England.

The West Indies team of 1980/81 comprised a truly fearsome fast bowling quartet. Not even statistically more successful West Indian teams, such as the 1984 'blackwash' side, possessed quite such a devastating battery of fast bowlers.

The Sabina Park attack on 10 April 1981 was made up of Michael Holding, now a genial TV commentator but then known as 'whispering death', a name derived from a supreme athlete's light-footedness on approach to the wicket. A wonderful free-flowing delivery stride launched the ball at extreme pace. I once asked the Surrey stalwart at the time, Graham Clinton, who the fastest bowler he ever faced was. 'Holding,' came the reply.

At the other end, the youthful Malcolm Marshall provided skiddy pace accurately directed at the batsman for the most part and designed to cramp the batsman up or cause a retreat to the leg side. Shorter than six feet, Marshall was brought in because it was felt by the West Indian selectors as though Andy Roberts had lost his edge. The West Indies think tank wanted no such comfort zone. This was the only series where front-line England batsmen were seen to back down the leg side in fear.

First change was the imposing 6ft 4ins Colin Croft who came from round the wicket and banged the ball from a furious heavy-weight boxer's physique into the batsman's rib cage. Croft had already collected 21 scalps in the three previous tests. No one liked his angles of delivery and, of the four, Croft was the most frightening.

The fourth seamer, and obviously the most potent fourth seamer in history, was 'Big Bird' Joel Garner, a 6ft 8ins specimen who produced steepling bounce that made him almost impossible to drive. He would peg batsmen back with just short of a length rising deliveries then fire in a toe-crushing yorker.

To make the point, there are parallels here with the 1946/47 Ashes series. The opponents were different, but both series were played on lightning fast pitches against a battery of pace bowlers. On both occasions England's batting comprised four players who could cope and seven players who simply could not. Test-match cricket has a cruel habit of weeding out the mediocrity from the great and good. In 1946/47 those four capable England batsmen were Hutton, Washbrook, Edrich and Compton. In 1980/81 they were Boycott, Gooch, Gower and Willey. Throughout the 1980/81 series no other player in 44 completed innings scored more than Roland Butcher's 32, a disparity significantly greater than 1946/47 where at least Ikin, Yardley and Hardstaff scored 60s.

This was the era of no number three worthy of the name. England went through a period of 34 runs scored by number three batsmen in ten completed innings. Gooch and Boycott formed the masterful opening pair. Gower was the flourishing number four and Peter Willey a number six or seven, there to front up to pace, because he was brave and never mind the bizarre open-chested stance.

Clive Lloyd won the toss amidst the noise from the crowd and on a typically hot, dry Caribbean day. Whistles blew and the stands were packed. In the days before cheap flights and the Barmy Army, most spectators were local partisans, jigging to music, drinking rum and dancing a calypso to any drum beat going. It was party time. Sensing the crowd behind him, Lloyd chose to bowl first and put pressure on England from the off.

Boycott, the 40-year-old veteran, and Gooch, the 27-year-old were the perfect opening pair for England at the time. Boycott accumulated his runs in sensible low-risk manner. He knew the value of quiet, steady adjustment to the light, of playing passively from the start and building a long, long innings. Boycott had opened for England for sixteen years either side of a self-imposed three-year exile which some critics saw as a fear of fast bowling. Indeed at Bridgetown Barbados three weeks earlier, Boycott had faced the nastiest possible opening over from Michael Holding. You can see this on 'You Tube'.

Gooch faced the first ball. He already had a 100 to his name in the series and an 83 at Antigua. Boycott also had enjoyed some success, a

70 in the opener at Port-of-Spain and a fine 104 not out to deny the West Indies, also at Antigua.

The initial salvos from Holding and Marshall were brisk enough, yet the pitch seemed calmer and less inclined to climb. Both batsmen settled down first to the task of survival, allowing play to carry on around them. In this zone batsmen allow balls to go by outside the off stump, sway out of short pitched deliveries and wait for the drift to leg.

A punched back-foot drive through the covers off Marshall screamed to the boundary. Gooch, erect and moustachioed like a Mexican, sniffed the air and felt it could be his day. Boycott ran the singles, leant into the occasional drive and square cut purposefully during the morning session, but it was Gooch who dominated.

Marshall skidded through a short ball which Gooch imperiously hooked for six over square leg. Boycott grinning like a Cheshire cat rolled back the years and purred along to 40 before gloving a Garner lifter to Murray, England 93–1.

Croft came on in place of Holding and Garner superseded Marshall but Gooch was ready with his eye in and the pitch was sound. Croft was the bane of Englishmen on this tour, the causer of lost sleep. At once Gooch used his bat like a bludgeon and smote Croft through square on both sides of the wicket. Angry, Croft ran in seemingly possessed and fired an errant bouncer well wide of off stump, Gooch thrashed at it and sent the ball over third man for six. Runs rattled along now and England threatened to take the game away for the first time all series. The 50 partnership came up for the second wicket, the first such 50-plus partnership for the second wicket for ten months. Bill Athey, shell shocked and in no frame of mind for number three duties, watched from the non-striker's end whilst Gooch dominated Croft in a blistering assault which cost 56 runs from his first eight overs.

In amongst the carnage, Holding penetrated Athey's defences, bowled for three in a stand worth 55, England 148–2. Enter Gower, the dazzling left hander and one of the few with the necessary timing and speed of reaction. Gooch continued to blaze away, mixing watchful defence with an eye to attack. A boundary brought up his hundred, an astonishing performance, made by the fortieth over and with the score on 155–2.

Gower kept Gooch company but just as the game was stretching out into calmer waters for England, Gower fell, bowled by Croft and

England were 196–3, Gooch still there, having just overhauled his previous test best of 123.

Out strode Willey, 102 not out in the previous game. He blocked for 23 deliveries but fell for only four in a decent comeback spell from Marshall, 210–4 and the day's play swung back towards the hosts.

Roland Butcher of Middlesex now joined Gooch and proceeded to play with rare calm and fluidity. Butcher pounced on the bad balls from the now tiring attack and struck a couple of sweet boundaries. Gooch continued on and passed 150. On his 213th delivery, with 153 to his name, and with the score on 249, Gooch snicked Holding to Murray and one of the most masterful, attacking innings from an Englishman came to an end.

Gooch walked off, sweat dripping from his head, shoulders hunched over, almost disconsolate to a generous, rapturous applause from the large crowd. Skipper Botham passed him at the gates with a rare look of admiration.

The England innings stuttered to the close of play on 278–6 with the test match, thanks to Gooch, evenly poised. Even Botham was not out at the close, on 12 – a good day's cricket played around a single masterful innings.

England subsided to the pace of Holding in the first 40 minutes of play and ended 285 all out with the last four wickets falling for two runs.

West Indies cruised to 193–3 by the end of the second day in the face of tight, but largely impotent, England bowling. They finished 157 ahead and England, including Gooch slumped to 32–3 on the fourth evening. Defeat looked a surety, but Gower and Willey stayed to the close in an undefeated stand of 102.

Gower batted through the last day, helped by three hours of drizzle, and with Paul Downton guided England to a draw. Gower's valuable knock of 154 not out, with Gooch's 153 in the first innings allowed England to return home with at least some semblance of pride. They would need to bolster both batting and bowling departments before the very good Australian team arrived, but at least Willis was set to return.

Both Gooch and Gower failed to last the course of the 1981 Ashes series. Gower's 89 at Lord's was the only innings of substance from either. Both would return and reach new peaks for over a decade with Gooch batting long into his forties.

England 285 (Gooch 153, Boycott 40, Holding 5–56).
West Indies 442 (Lloyd 95, Gomes 90*, Haynes 84, Greenidge 62, Dilley 4–116).
England 302–6 declared (Gower 154*, Willey 67).
MATCH DRAWN.

Innings Ranked Number 43
Trescothick's 219 at the Oval in 2003

Opponents: South Africa.
At Stake: England needed to win in order to square the series.
Bowling Attack: Pollock, Ntini, Hall, Kallis, Adams. (Weighted runs per wicket: 32.4).
Pitch: Superb, made for strokeplay, fast outfield.
Game Situation: South Africa, dismissed soon after lunch on the second day, had scored 484.
Attendance: 88,000.

South Africa, second in the international rankings at the time, had the air of supremacy. They had dominated a rain-affected first test which ended in a draw, then crushed England by an innings and 92 runs in the second at Lord's. A sub-standard pitch at Nottingham flattered England to level the series but South Africa bounced back to win at Leeds thanks to Jacques Kallis's nine wickets in the match.

After winning the toss at the Oval, and needing only to draw to secure their first series win in England since 1965, South Africa duly elected to bat. At 290–1 on the first afternoon they appeared to have the game and series sown up. Bookmakers at tea on the first day placed odds of an England victory at 40–1. Onwards South Africa accumulated but wickets fell steadily. A score of 362–4 at the close became 484 all out in the afternoon session on the second day. England, though frustrated by a tenth wicket partnership of 52 between Pollock and Ntini, had clawed their way back into the game but only just. No England team had won a home test match after conceding so many in the first innings.

Requiring 285 to avoid the follow on, but more pertinently 600 plus to force South Africa onto the back foot, Michael Vaughan the skipper and Marcus Trescothick strode purposefully down the pavilion steps.

Vaughan began in stirring form, driving with panache whilst Trescothick fretting at the other end was badly dropped in the slips on one. Soon, as so often besets a Vaughan innings, a bright start was terminated by a millionaire's drive pouched in the slips, England 28–1, Vaughan dismissed for 23. Enter Mark Butcher, England's consistent number three, who proceeded also to pebble-dash the advertising boards with thumping drives and deft deflections. On 32 at about a run a ball, Butcher got a beauty from Hall that swung in to rap him on the pads. At 78–2, things were looking bleak but at least the Somerset opener remained.

Graham Thorpe entered to provide a balanced, experienced calm to the battle. A weak over from Andrew Hall then saw Trescothick awake from his self-imposed hibernation with fours apiece from a rasping drive and two cuts. By the end of the day these two left handers had accumulated an unbroken stand of 87 and the day, just, went to England.

On the third day, England began to claw the game back even more as Thorpe and Trescothick fed off wayward bowling, directed unwisely towards leg stump by, of all people, Pollock and Kallis. Smith rotated his bowlers but, despite using five, including Jacques Rudolf before lunch, the pair of south paws had added a further 106.

England's only chance of squaring the series rested heavily on these two seasoned pros. Thorpe, the senior partner, acted as the pace setter whilst Trescothick waited for the bad ball. The afternoon session provided a rare feast of indulgence from England's batsmen with Thorpe punching the air in delight at reaching his twelfth century. He departed shortly before tea, his defense breached by Kallis bowling round the wicket. The partnership of 268 broke the Oval third wicket record set back in 1939.

Still Trescothick batted on. Ed Smith, the scholarly Kent batsman who was enjoying a prolific run of form in the county championship, spent an uncomfortable hour for sixteen. Then, at 379–4, Alec Stewart strode out for his very last test innings, amidst a deafening roar and a South African guard of honour. He immediately pierced the field and went on for a worthy 38. Soon after, in company with Flintoff, England took the lead. By this time Trescothick had been smashing the ball to all parts.

Finally, after 374 balls sprinkled with 32 fours and 2 sixes, a tiring Trescothick top edged a hook to be caught in the deep off Ntini. It has to be said that the bowling by this stage was wilting with the worst offender, Paul Adams, delivering rank long hops. Nonetheless, Trescothick's knock put England eighteen ahead at the end of the day.

Pyrotechnics from Andrew Flintoff in his prime ensured an eventual total of 604 on the fourth day. The South African attack sore and shamed was simply lashed. Flintoff's 95 included 85 from the last 72 balls. So effective was Flintoff at farming the strike that, in a ninth wicket partnership with Harmison, the tail-ender only contributed three in a stand of 99.

South Africa, shell-shocked and drained, collapsed with four wickets apiece to Bicknell and Harmison. England, set just 110, romped home by nine wickets. To complete an excellent test match, Trescothick snicked the winning boundary over the slips to finish on 69 not out.

England: Marcus Trescothick, Michael Vaughan (captain), Mark Butcher, Graham Thorpe, Ed Smith, Alec Stewart, Andrew Flintoff, Ashley Giles, Martin Bicknell, Stephen Harmison, James Anderson.

A warm glow of weighty ambition engulfed Duncan Fletcher's England team. The momentum gained from this victory carried the England team through a golden period lasting through until that unforgettable Oval Test in 2005. England went on to beat the West Indies – post-Ambrose and Walsh – in the West Indies, for the first time in 36 years, and a decisive 3–0 at that. Only Lara's record 400* in the final test prevented a clean sweep.

2004 saw a complete whitewash of England victories, 3–0 against New Zealand, then 4–0 against the West Indies. Further to this, England dismantled a strong South African side 2–1 the following winter. There followed the greatest Ashes series, possibly ever, with England winning the series 2–1 against a mighty Australian team.

Glancing at the Oval 2003 England team, one can appreciate the strength and the symbiotic mix between 1990s stalwarts such as Thorpe, Butcher and Stewart, and the Ashes heroes of 2005: Flintoff, Trescothick, Harmison, Vaughan and Giles. This was Martin Bicknell's first test in a decade, third in all, and final act. Alec Stewart meanwhile enjoyed 133 test appearances before bowing out as the greatest wicket keeper-batsman since Les Ames back in the 1930s. Anderson, the 21-year-old seamer, still had his best years ahead.

South Africa 484
England 604–9 declared (Trescothick 219, Thorpe 137, Flintoff 95)

South Africa 229
England 110-1 (Trescothick 63*)
ENGLAND WON BY 9 WICKETS.

Innings Ranked Number 42
Hutton's 205 at Sabina Park in 1954

Opponents: West Indies.
At stake: Squaring the series.
Bowling attack: King, Gomez, Atkinson, Ramadhin, Sobers, Walcott, Worrell, Stollmeyer.
Pitch: Plumb perfect.
Game situation: West Indies had been dismissed for 139 in the final test of a five-match series. England were trailing 2-1 in the series.

The Ashes winning team of 1953 had lost the first two test matches in the series despite runs from Hutton and Compton. Both came into the final test having each registered centuries in the series. Hutton had also scored four fifties and Compton a 64 and a 93. England had been outgunned in the batting department because up against England's bowlers was a formidable West Indies top eight.

Not only did the West Indies middle order contain the 'three Ws' – Weekes, Worrell and Walcott – but also Holt who, until the fifth test, averaged 70.7 in the series. Stollmeyer skippered the team and opened the innings. He averaged 42.33 in 32 tests. So the line up was as strong a top five as any in West Indies history. Then came the all-rounders: Atkinson (career test batting average 31.8), Gomez (30.3), McWatt (28.85) and, making his debut at number 8, none other than Garfield Sobers (57.8).

The West Indies won the toss and, by an immaculate piece of medium-fast bowling, Trevor Bailey claimed 7-34. Bailey benefited from a strong cross breeze from cover that helped his inswing. Bailey bowled a full-length outside off stump. Holt snicked Bailey to slip whilst trying to execute a cover drive; Everton Weekes played on; Stollmeyer was caught behind. Later he trapped Atkinson in front, removed Gomez and McWatt, and finally bowled King the tail-end fast bowler. It was nothing less than a magnificent series swinging sixteen overs, taken in two spells, before a rain interlude close to tea, and a third one with a wet ball to wrap the innings up.

West Indies had stood like rabbits stunned by headlights and, with a run rate of two an over, crawled to 139 all out.

Hutton and Bailey, as a makeshift opener, batted out the last 35 minutes of this momentous day. England closed on 17–0, Hutton eight not out and Bailey nine.

The second day saw a very slow run rate as England sought to bat the game out of reach. At lunch England had crawled to 41, crucially with both openers still there. Frank King, the spearhead fast bowler, bowled with fury and hit Bailey a sickening blow on the jaw. Unbroken, Bailey batted on though visibly shaken.

Hutton began the day by leg glancing King for a single, but then he and Bailey played out twelve overs before the next run. King bowled a lot of chin music, once three in four balls. Neither batsman risked the hook. England reached 50 but, second over after lunch, Bailey snicked behind for 23 to give Sobers the first of 235 test wickets. In came May to imprint his genius on the game. First ball May drove handsomely through the covers. Hutton survived a torrid over from King, almost playing on.

Nonetheless the partnership was gathering pace with Hutton suddenly breaking out. He clubbed Sobers over mid-wicket, then next ball just over the head of Stollmeyer at mid off. In due course Hutton swept Ramadhin to reach a three-hour 50 and May brought up the 100 with a fine straight six off Sobers.

May refused to allow anyone to pin him down. He reached a fine 30 before driving a wide Ramadhin delivery that swirled fast and hard towards extra cover. Pairaudeau, substitute for Walcott, dived full stretch and picked himself off the grass and earth clutching, according to E. W. Swanton, a hatefully good catch. 104–2.

Compton, the cavalier genius, began with a cover drive for four, then another boundary from the thinnest of trickles to fine leg. He stabbed the ball deliberately through the slips. On one occasion Compton guided a missile that bounced painfully onto the knee cap of Everton Weekes at second slip. Things slowed down before tea, with Hutton and Compton reducing risks ready to face the second new ball. England at tea were 129–2 and looking to take a significant first innings lead.

The King–Compton duel after tea was brief but thrilling. Compton, a hooker, faced the hostile bumper King. One such scalper hit

Compton's glove, the next flew off Compton's bat with such velocity that it penetrated the wire meshing beyond the long leg boundary. Then, tragically, Compton evoked memories of his greatest test match innings by treading on his stumps, for a highly entertaining 31. England were by now in the lead, 152–3.

The West Indies clawed their way back into the game with the quick dismissals of Graveney and Watson. At the close, England had reached 194–5. In occupation all day, a rock on which England's fortunes once again rested, was Hutton on 93. It was slow, the run rate for the innings as a whole was just over two an over. Crucially though Hutton was still in occupation.

On the third day, Hutton proceeded to build on his record of achievement, widely believed to be only second to Sir Donald Bradman. In tropical heat, Hutton showed outstanding concentration and physical stamina. The West Indies wilted visibly.

The day started with King unable to bowl due to a thigh strain. Hutton accumulated sensibly the seven runs required for his century, made in 340 minutes. Then Hutton had another mad spell and lashed out. He hit Ramadhin twice over the head of mid on for four before reining himself in. By lunch time the softening-up process had gone on long enough. England had a lead of 105.

For some bizarre reason Stollmeyer did not choose to take the new ball immediately. Evans fell to Ramadhin, perhaps that's why. West Indies obviously missed King. Wardle batted with the luck of the devil, whilst Hutton took the score beyond 300 with a dazzling straight six off Atkinson. Wardle sent a Ramadhin off-break out of the ground and over a white wall, and only then was the new ball taken.

The fact that the new ball had a different bounce and quicker speed through the air made no difference to Hutton who was rapidly moving up the gears. He reached his double hundred with an exquisite cover drive for four. Hutton's second hundred had taken half the time of his first, 165 minutes.

First ball after tea having put on 105 with Wardle for the seventh wicket Hutton fell to Walcott, edging a cut. His 205 was a monumental effort. As Hutton walked to the pavilion the match was as good as won, the score was 392–7, a lead of 253.

England added a further 22 runs with Wardle smacking 66. West Indies made a better fist of it second time around under a gloriously calm sky. Walcott, hooking freely against Trueman, scored a glorious hundred. England required 72 and achieved that with the loss of only

Graveney. Watson and Graveney opened this time, with May striking 40 not out at the end.

The West Indies were a strong team who provided stern opponents for England, but this was an England evolving into a World Champion team. In the years ahead England would defeat Australia convincingly (both in Australia and at home), the West Indies, South Africa and New Zealand.

This was Hutton's last great innings for England. He finished with only 25 fewer runs in test cricket than the great Bradman, and at an average, not since exceeded by any Englishmen, of 56.67.

West Indies 139 (Walcott 50, Bailey 7–34).
England 414 (Hutton 205, Wardle 66, Sobers 4–75).
West Indies 346 (Walcott 116, Stollmeyer 64, Laker 4–71, Trueman 3–88).
England 72–1 (May 40*).
ENGLAND WON BY 9 WICKETS.

Innings Ranked Number 41
Edrich's 219 at Durban in 1939

Opponents: South Africa.
At stake: Series: England is 1–0 up after four tests. The last test at Durban has been deemed 'timeless'. This is to ensure a result so that South Africa has a chance of squareing the series.
Bowling attack:Newson, Langton, Gordon, Mitchell, Dalton.
Pitch: Featherbed, built to last.
Game situation: England require 696 runs in the last innings. Hutton and Gibb have made a solid start but Edrich arrives at the crease following Hutton's dismissal for 55. The score is 78–1.

Poor Bill Edrich had the most inauspicious starts to what eventually became a successful career. Born of a cricketing family steeped in the traditions of the summer game, Bill came from Norfolk. A strange three-year qualifying period meant that Edrich had to wait three years to qualify for Middlesex and the first class arena. He scored 2,154 runs in 1937 at 44.87 so earned a call up for Wally Hammond's England team at the start of the 1938 Ashes.

Hammond was a great fan of Edrich. He liked the youngster's fielding ability and the enthusiasm of Edrich's bustling approach to bowling.

Hammond's pet, as Edrich became unkindly named, made scores of five, nothing, ten, twelve, twenty-eight and twelve that summer – just 67 runs in six completed innings in a summer of record England scores. Keeping his place in the team for the winter's tests in South Africa, Edrich continued his abysmal run of form: four and ten in the drawn first test at Johannesburg, a duck in the second test at Newlands, he did not bat in the third test, then scored only six in his solitary innings in the fourth test. All of the cricketing pundits saw this as Edrich's last chance. At only 23 Bill Edrich would come again, now it was time for a pragmatic approach.

However, in the warm up match before the last test, Edrich secured a brilliant 150 coming in at three. Once more Hammond chose Edrich. Afterall he liked the lad's bowling and fielding skills. England had not been short of runs. Edrich in many ways helped to balance the side. His slip fielding in a side short of slip fielders swung it.

The final test at Durban was to be played as a timeless test with England 1–0 up in the series. The pitch was made from loamy clay from the bed of the nearby Umgeni River. Heavy rain the previous day had allowed the heavy roller to create a batting haven.

South Africa won the toss, elected to bat and posted 530 in 203.6 overs, each over consisting of eight deliveries. It was after lunch on day three when England began her first innings. By now only the players seemed concerned about the game. Timeless tests were one thing, but not for spectators; even the South African Cricket Board believed that such long drawn-out events would be bad for the game.

Edrich failed yet again, coming in at six. He was miserably tense at the crease with the South Africans grinning at him and moving in close. Edrich prodded forward at Langton's brisk medium pace and gave a catch to silly mid on. Off he walked horribly disconsolate for one. England's innings closed for 316, 214 behind. Everyone scored more than Edrich.

A partnership of 191 for the first wicket in South Africa's second innings took the game away from England. Eventually South Africa finished with 481 and set England the improbable target of 696. Never before had a side scored more than 400 to win a test on the last innings. Only two sides in all first-class cricket had scored more than 500, and none had ever scored 600. Here England were asked to score more than 100 more than any side in the history of the game.

Hammond had a touch of inspiration. Over he went to Edrich in the changing room to inform his young recruit that for this final innings Edrich would come in first wicket down, so emulating the position from which he scored 150 in the recent state game. The evening of day five Hutton successfully appealed for bad light after just one ball and Edrich took his pads off and trooped off to a party, England 0–0 requiring the small matter of 696 to win.

Bill Edrich apparently was a real party animal. He enjoyed drinking, smoking and laughing at amusing anecdotes. This side of Edrich was hidden as the youngster wrongly sought to cut down on the partying in an attempt to improve his performances on the field. Cutting down on partying had made Edrich uncharacteristically tense, perhaps the real reason for his failures. This night he partied hard on champagne, content in the knowledge he could do no worse. Next morning Edrich grinned at the slight headache brought on by excessive alcohol the night before and his mouth tasted like an ash tray. Nonetheless he was content and more relaxed, philosophical even, about his fate.

Edrich had to wait to get in. Hutton and Gibb started well but with the score on 78 Mitchell bowled Hutton for 55. Edrich had ten minutes to negotiate before lunch. As he picked up his bat, Hammond went over and adopting an encouraging note told Edrich,'You can make runs Bill, if you try. Don't be afraid to go for the ball if you can see it. If you can get a double hundred, we might stand a chance!'

Once in the middle, Edrich noticed the smug grin on Mitchell's face and told himself to hit the first ball to the fence. Edrich stood short and slight but compact and wiry. First ball from Mitchell pitched fractionally short. Edrich stepped back and across his stumps and pulled the ball to the mid-wicket fence. An exhilaration fell upon him. Now he watched Gibb from the other end play out a maiden in dour mood. Facing Mitchell again, Edrich on drove him for another boundary, then stole a single. In Langton's last over before lunch Edrich took a single off a solid hit partially blocked by the fielder. At lunch the score was 88–1 with Edrich already in double figures.

Edrich had a tetchy lunch, anxious to get back out. He replayed that pull shot first ball in his mind. The sweet sound like a rifle shot, still this was only the beginning. 'Just express yourself Bill' Hammond said, handing the young man a smoke from his silver cigarette case. Ten minutes later Edrich and Gibb squinted their eyes into the sun and walked purposefully back to the middle where they were met by glorious sunshine. Bruce Mitchell and Norman Gordon, fast medium shared the attack but bowled, if anything too short. Edrich cracked these splendidly to the boundary and looking for runs all the time, raced along at a run a minute.

Gibbs proceeded cautiously, picking off the ones and twos, and let Edrich take the risks. Edrich, displaying a bold drive to a ball that wasn't there, thin edged a boundary down to fine leg. Luck was clearly on his side and now Edrich had moved passed his previous test best of 28.

Langton took over from a tiring Gordon, but Edrich at once straight drove him for four to overtake Gibb who had a 96-minute start. A hook in Langton's next over sped to the boundary – this was the Edrich all Middlesex knew. Hammond was no mug, he knew the sort of cricketer Bill Edrich was, flamboyant, skilful yet honest. He would win tests for England one day. Waiting to bat behind Bill Edrich in a test match before the war was traumatic for the next fellow. The poor blighter sat on the edge of his seat expecting to start his innings at any moment. Not so with Hammond who simply lit another cigarette. Another four whistled along the ground to mid-wicket to take the score passed the 150 mark. Edrich now had scant respect for Mitchell's leg breaks and googlies. 'Sod it,' he thought, the next one's going. Up to the wicket Mitchell came, more an opening batsman than a front line bowler, so Edrich hunted down the wicket and slammed the ball on the half-volley gun-barrel straight back along the ground to the wickets. Mitchell returned to his mark with a dot ball but felt rather intimidated. Next ball Edrich thumped back passed the bowler for four to take him to his maiden test 50.

He soaked up the applause and the crowd, bored stiff and, having hating the timed-test concept an hour earlier, now greeted the young Englishman with respect. Edrich had lit up a dull game. He took a single then cross batted Langton straight back in a manner similar to Pietersen in 2005 off Brett Lee at the Oval on the last afternoon. All the while Edrich mauled Langton and Mitchell, Gibb at the other end remained static on 41.

Edrich continued scoring mainly boundaries and singles whilst cloud cover grew. Soon Gibb had problems with his glasses misting over in the drizzle but play continued. Gibb reached his 50 and at tea England were handily placed at 197–1, Gibb on 53 not out, Edrich on a scintillating 77.

Edrich changed tack after the interval. He had up until now been fighting for his reputation and place in the side. Now he was batting for England. Hammond must have spoken of the need to dig in and master the bowling, so much so that Edrich played the percentages game and only accrued five in 45 minutes. In the first hour after tea only 32 runs had been added but Edrich had advanced into the 90s with a well timed on drive for four.

The crowd cheered every Edrich run. A two off Langton through cover took Edrich to 99. Next ball, Langton overpitched and Edrich punched the ball back hard and it was only partially fielded by the bowler. Gibb and Edrich ran through for a quick single and he lofted his bat with tremendous relief. Even the South African team applauded to a man. Sympathy for the underdog who had fought through the hard times was never expressed more warmly by an appreciative but modest crowd of 4,000.

Reg Parks, England's tall, broad-shouldered, opening bowler waved a white elephant from the balcony – the lucky mascot he had given Edrich before his knock. At close of play on the seventh day, England had advanced to 253–1 with Edrich on 107 and Gibb 78. Clouds continued to build and a weather system moved through to prevent play on the Saturday. Sunday was a rest day, so the players all had in effect a full weekend off.

More parties and champagne flowed. Edrich packed his bags in readiness for the train journey on the Tuesday night. Only two more days were possible. England simply had to catch that train to connect with the boat from Capetown.

By the Monday, the crowd had thinned to a few hundred. Unfortunately few, except the players, were bothered about the outcome. The match had gone on and on seemingly forever and the start of the match felt impossibly remote. Events in the middle remained at fever pitch, a test match had to be won and players fought tooth and nail to preserve their records and reputations, runs and wickets, simple as.

Edrich continued in positive vein, running quick singles with Gibb which helped accrue overthrows. He lofted Mitchell over square leg and treated all bowlers bar Langton with ease. Gibb reached his hundred after six hours and Edrich took his passed the 150. Soon after he broke through the shackles imposed by Langton and swept him repeatedly down on one knee to the boundary. At lunch England were 333–1. A small matter of 362 remained to be scored to achieve the impossible.

The crowd swelled to 3,000 in the afternoon sun. On, Gibb and Edrich batted, breaking the Hobbs–Sutcliffe record stand for any wicket against South Africa – 268 at Leeds in 1924. Finally, Dalton bowled a leg break through Gibb's defences for 120. The partnership realised 280. Gibb only scored two boundaries and on the leg side but his value to England's needs was incalculable.

Out strode Hammond with England having only an outside chance of achieving the seemingly impossible. He cut a daunting figure at the crease, still in his prime at 36 and what he lacked in terms of a 20-year-old's reaction times, he made up for in wisdom. Face creased more than his years suggested, Hammond nevertheless started awkwardly and his timing was out. This contrasted markedly with the gaiety of Edrich's sword as the latter hunted down the wicket again to the spinners, then stepped back and pulled them through mid-wicket. Edrich's aggression enthralled the crowd who cheered every shot. A four off Melville and a quick single took Edrich to 200. At tea, England were in the box seat, especially now Hammond had established himself with 34. England were 442–2, now a gettable 254 short of a mountainous record that, like Bradman's 1930 records, would surely stand the test of time.

Eating sandwiches at 215 not out is a feeling few have ever experienced, but one can imagine the deep-rooted satisfaction, a smugness. Tour manager Flight-Lieutenant A. J. Holmes poured Edrich a glass of champagne which, of course, he accepted gratefully.

Six runs into the afternoon session, Edrich glanced a leg-side ball from Langton straight and firm to short leg who took a decent catch. In $7^1/2$ hours Edrich had hit a career saving 219.

That evening, the eleventh in fact since the start of the match, England were just 200 short with seven wickets intact. They did not quite make them. The rain came to wash out play after tea on day twelve, the last day. England had advanced the score to 654 for five, just 41 runs short with five wickets remaining. So close, yet in the end it was time in a timeless test that thwarted England. Had they won, this would have been a record even today.

As for Edrich, war intervened for six long years. When he returned to England action on the Ashes tour in 1946/47, he scored the most runs by an Englishman in the series. He will always be linked with Denis Compton for their immortal run accumulation during the 1947 summer. Compton hit 3,816 in the season, Edrich 3,539.

Bill Edrich continued playing for England on and off for the next eight years. His last fighting knock was a defiant 88 in a losing cause against Lindwall and Miller at Brisbane in 1954.

South Africa 530 (van der Bijl 125, Noure 103, Melville 78, Grieveson 75, Dalton 57, Perks 5–100).
England 316 (Ames 84, Paynter 62, Dalton 4–59, Langton 3–71).
South Africa 481 (Melville 103, van der Bijl 97, Mitchell 89, Viljoen 74, Farnes 4–74, Wright 3–146).
England 654–5 (Edrich 219, Hammond 140, Gibb 120, Paynter 75, Hutton 55).
MATCH DRAWN.

Innings Ranked Number 40
Randall's 150 at Sydney in 1979

Opponents: Australia.
At stake: Ashes.
Bowling attack: Hogg, Dymock, Hurst, Higgs, Border: runs per wicket 31.02.
Pitch: Fair.
Game situation: England, 142 runs behind on first innings are 0–1 off 0.1 overs with Boycott back in the hutch.

It had not seemed to matter too much that Lillee and Thomson were both omitted from the Australian side. They, along with Greg Chappell, Rodney Marsh, Doug Walters and other regulars, had been banned from representing Australia due to their involvement in Kerry Packer's World Series Cricket. In their place, Australia still had a formidable attack. Spearheading it was the burly, blond six foot Rodney Hogg who was to claim 42 wickets in the six-test series at 12.85. Very fast, Hogg proved too quick on more than one occasion even for Geoff Boycott who was to have his worst series against the old enemy.

Supporting Hogg was Alan Hurst, a mainstay reserve for much of the mid-1970s. He was taller and almost as quick as Dennis Lillee. The best Australian leg spinner between the Benaud and Warne eras, James Higgs added variety, so did Geoffrey Dymock's left-arm seamers and Alan Border's orthodox slow left arm. This was quite an attack and certainly one good enough to regain the Ashes, won by England in 1977.

In the series to date, England had won the first two tests comfortably with a balanced attack and vital innings by both Randall and Gower. The third test was lost with no England batsman even scoring a 50. In the fourth test, England won the toss and elected to bat. Again they struggled, all out for 152 at a rate equivalent to just over two an over. Only Botham offered resistance with a steady 59.

Hurst grabbed five for 28 including Randall's for nothing. Australia then appeared to bat England out of the game with 91 from Darling and a not-out 60 in his second test from A. R. Border.

Veteran openers Boycott and Brearley went out in the second innings under considerable pressure. First ball and no more than a gentle loosener at about thee-quarters pace, Rodney Hogg defeated Boycott with a breakback for nothing. Boycott had shuffled across his stumps and, sure enough, to the astonishment of all, recorded his first duck in 67 test innings. It seemed, after England had won the first two tests, as though momentum had swung around. Australia won by 103 runs at Melbourne thanks to ten wickets from Hogg, and looked to be squaring the series at Sydney.

At any rate England, on 8 January, were in a mess. Their last three innings had not reached 180. As Randall jogged onto the arena he became completely overawed by the sound of a partisan crowd and the extreme heat. Also under pressure with only 61 runs in the previous five innings, Randall prepared to face Hogg. England were 142 in arrears and their best batsman, Boycott, was out for a golden. Touching his peaked cap nervously, an already sweating Randall was a hyperactive, nervous wreck.

Slowly, cautiously, he and Brearley withstood the rest of the early barrage. Both survived close LBW shouts. It was not pleasant viewing for anyone, but then Randall executed an off drive of class and timing off Dymock to release the tension. England fans listened and frowned on the radio sets in the chill of a British winter night. Australian fans sweltered in the heat as not much happened and no wickets fell. Lunch came and went with the batsmen thankful for the replenishment of liquids.

These were the days of eight-ball overs in Australian cricket, about which more later. The 50 partnership came after 86 minutes in the early afternoon without too much of an applause, as the Australian crowd grew impatient. Randall played a couple of straight drives and an excellent hook to keep the scoreboard ticking along at a rate that barely seized the initiative.

Giving the seamers a rest, Yallop handed the ball first to Higgs then Border. At least the run rate would rise and with it, the best chance of a batsman being lulled into a false sense of comfort. Brearley and Randall talked in-between overs conscious of the mind game. They kept their heads and wickets intact just content to go along at a little over two an over.

Tea came with England on 74–1. Mike Brearley, taking advantage of loose deliveries down the leg side from Hurst, was on 33 with Randall on 37.

Significantly Randall who had fretted against the leg spin of Higgs, on-drove him impeccably for four. Brearley did well to survive a three-over burst from a fired up Hogg. When the 100 came up, both batsmen were 47 not out. The drinks break saw players and officials resting in the shadows of one of the big chimneys, so hot was the occasion.

Eventually at 111–1, Brearley was bowled by Border. England were still 31 behind and now both openers had gone. For company, Randall had the 24-year-old Gooch, who was still to record his first test century. Together they took England into a slender lead, Gooch contributing 22 in a stand of 58. Randall had by now become horribly tetchy. Far from being the lordly batsman who had played a long innings and had mastered the attack, he fretted and missed several full tosses that he would normally have dispatched to the boundary in a flurry. After each delivery, he would mutter himself, walk away from the wicket, twitch, touch his cap, all the time burning off valuable energy just through nerves. Both men batted through to the close of play, Randall's 65 not out had helped England gain a lead of nine.

On the fourth day, again in sweltering heat, crowd numbers were down to disappointing levels. Part of the blame lay with the weather as it was simply too hot to enjoy watching cricket without air conditioning or shade. The temperature rose to 100° Fahrenheit. Hurst began to run in to bowl to Randall when suddenly the batsman pulled away. Close to the sight screen behind a man was being carried away on a stretcher, a cameraman had fainted, fallen twenty feet onto concrete and fractured his skull. He survived.

Soon Gooch was caught at short-leg off his pad, England were ahead but equivalent to 27–3. Already England had surpassed her first innings total. The delay with the second new ball spoke volumes for the trouble Higgs had inflicted on Randall.

Enter Gower, enjoying a decent first Ashes series but feeling sick. The right hand/left hand combination worked well for a while with Gower's youthful exuberance immediately blossoming, the perfect foil for the dour Randall. At once Gower showed his fresh genius driving his first ball from Higgs through mid-off for three, then in the same over another off drive for four. In the next over from Higgs, Gower swept for four then on drove for two.

After the lunch interval, Gower again pierced the off side with a drive for four and after 84 overs Yallop took the new ball. Immediately a fresh lease of life flooded into Randall who obviously preferred the new ball which was coming on to him at pace. With a confident swivel he firmly hooked Hogg's second ball to square leg for four to move to 99. Hogg bounced Randall again and this time the swivel-pull powered the ball in front of square for four. Randall's hundred had come off 355 balls in 431 minutes. Again in the same over Randall hooked Hogg for a third boundary.

Then Gower on 34 flashed a square cut to a wide Hogg delivery and edged to Maclean the keeper, to the relief of every Australian. The partnership had made 50 in an hour.

On Randall batted, losing about a pound in weight per session. Indeed for 92 minutes, together with Botham either side of tea, the batsmen defended resolutely and in a grim manner. The score crept along. Botham fell for just six, unable to ignite in a partnership of 30.

Randall and Miller combined to add a further 30 priceless runs and the lead grew to 125, enough to make things uncomfortable. Bob Taylor, a true wicket-keeping genius but modest batsman, joined with Randall to further wear down the Australian bowlers.

Randall benefited from three lives. On 113 he was dropped in the slips off Higgs, then again by keeper Maclean off Hurst when on 117. Finally, after tea, Randall was dropped again, and again off Higgs by which time he was on 124. Weary but willing he proceeded with utmost caution, pushing singles to mid-wicket and extra-cover with the occasional firm pull.

Finally, with the England total 165 ahead, Randall at last perished through fatigue to an inswinger from Hogg that rapped him fatally on the pads for a monumental innings of 150. Totally different in character to Randall's immortal Centenary Test epic, this innings spanned a massive 571 minutes and was the slowest 150 in terms of balls faced in the history of Ashes cricket by either side.

The tail wagged sufficiently for a total of 204 to be set and for Randall to replenish his fluid levels back in the pavilion shade. In all Australia bowled 146.6 overs of eight-ball length. This is equivalent to over 205 normal overs, a very long time.

The Australians never threatened the target, crumbling to off spinners Miller (3–38) and Emburey (4–46) and lost by 93 runs. The last two tests both went England's way with the Australians never once reaching 200.

Randall drifted out of test cricket a year later after a lean run once again in Australia. He returned triumphantly in 1982 with hundreds against New Zealand and Pakistan. The following winter, he topped the England batting averages in the 1982-3 Ashes with 365 runs at 45.62. He ended his test career with failures of zero and one against the West Indies in 1984. After that no amount of runs could earn him a recall – harsh.

England 152 (Botham 59, Higgs 5–28, Higgs 3–42).
Australia 294 (Darling 91, Border 60*).
England 346 (Randall 150, Brearley 53, Higgs 5–148, Hogg 4–67).
Australia 111 (Embury 4–46, Miller 3–38).
ENGLAND WON BY 93 RUNS.

Innings Ranked Number 39
Vaughan's 183 at Sydney in 2003

Opponents: Australia.
At stake: National Pride, Ashes already lost.
Bowling attack: Gillespie, Lee, Bichel, MacGill, Waugh: 30.81.
Pitch: Fine to satisfactory.
Game situation: England, one run behind on the first innings, start their second innings. England are already 4–0 down after four tests and staring at a whitewash.

When England lost the Ashes in 1989 I almost cried. I remember walking down the New Dover Road in Canterbury, can't remember why but on my Sony Walkman was a hit from the Kinks: *Thankyou for the days*. I thought of the Ashes battles of my childhood, spoilt really by the exploits of Boycott, Gower and the giant, strapping, Somerset all-rounder Ian Botham. The 1989 Ashes sealed off an era and the remnants of my childhood were gone for good. Through the 1990s the misery persisted, brightened only for a few wonderful weeks in '97 when Ben Hollioake lit up the one-dayer at Lord's and England swept to victory 3–0 in the shorter game, then the Edgbaston test to boot. The nation re-awoke briefly only to slumber back.

In the 2002–03 series Nasser Hussain won the toss at Brisbane in the first test and seeing the fright on his batsmens' faces elected to field. Australia raced to 600 and retained the Ashes in the shortest possible time: by an innings at the WACA, having lost only 34 wickets in the first three tests. The fourth test gave Australia a 4–0 lead in the series but at least this time England put up a fight after conceding 281 on the first innings. That England managed to set Australia the small matter of 107 to win after following on owed much to a splendid 145 from Michael Vaughan. Australia lost five wickets getting there, two to Harmisan and three to Caddick.

So to Sydney and with the Ashes gone, could England avoid the first Ashes white wash for 82 years? England packed their team with six specialist batsmen and perhaps the greatest England wicket-keeper/batsman of all. The line up read: Trescothick, Vaughan, Butcher, Hussain, Key, Crawley and Alec Stewart. Three seamers in Hoggard, Harmison and the leader of the pack, Andy Caddick, made up the rest of the team with Dawson the off-spinner woefully out of his depth.

England won the toss and faced an attack without Glen McGrath or Shane Warne. Thanks to Mark Butcher's 124 and 70s from Hussain and Stewart, England reached a respectable 362. Australia just topped that with 363, all wickets going to the seamers.

Although perishing for a duck first time around, Vaughan was in the form of his life. His year had started slowly in New Zealand but he had taken 115 off Sri Lanka, then 100 against India (both at Lord's), followed by 197 at Nottingham and 195 at the Oval. Not content with this he plundered 177 against the Australians at Adelaide in the second test and 145 at Melbourne. 2002 had been a glorious year, but what was 2003 going to offer?

Trescothick and Vaughan began England's second innings at roughly mid way through the test, in the middle of the afternoon on the third day. As they made their way to the centre Vaughan said,

'Here we go, I'm on a pair again' to which Terscothick replied, 'Don't worry. I'm at the other end backing up. You hit it and I'll run.'

Third ball and inside edge slammed against Vaughan's pads and Trescothick scampered through. Next over Vaughan eyed up Gillespie who had long served under the twin umbrellas of McGrath and Warne. Genuinely quick, Gillespie had enjoyed his fair share of Ashes successes, but this time he spearheaded the attack. Vaughan sought to dominate. Sure enough to a leg-side bouncer from Gillespie, Vaughan dispatched a pivot pull which flat batted the ball over the square leg boundary for six. Later in the over he leant into a quite splendid cover drive which raced over the unprotected turf for four

Steve Waugh, the veteran skipper, sensed trouble. Without Warne as an option, he turned early to Stuart MacGill – good enough as a leg spinner to be in most test sides at the time. Trescothick slammed three fours in the spinner's first over to raise some serious issues before, unluckily, he played on to the brute pace of Brett Lee. England 37–1.

Mark Butcher held on to the number three slot under pressure but came good with a beautiful 124 in the first innings. Vaughan sensed a relaxed look on the left-hander's face. At once Butcher looked comfortable and the pair took the score passed 50.

Vaughan then cut MacGill for an exquisite boundary through extra cover. Waugh chewed heavily on his gum then chucked the ball to Gillespie. Again Gillespie bowled short, but this time not too short and quite close to Vaughan's off stump. Instead of leaving this or making room to cut, Vaughan pulled outrageously through mid on for four. Overcompensating, Gillespie hurled another with greater width outside the off stump which Vaughan thrashed through the covers for another glorious boundary. Gillespie, rarely so contemptuously treated, walked back to his mark and now he showed signs of fatigue. Last ball of the over, Vaughan pulled majestically to mid wicket to race the score onto 70–1.

Gillespie stood down again, reeling from the punishment. Lee now worked up a head of steam; a magnificent young athlete and probably the fastest bowler on the planet, youthful, lean, blonde, clean shaven, but he bowled wide outside the off stump and Vaughan cut deliberately upwards and over gully for four more.

The scoring slowed for a while with Butcher and Vaughan playing the percentages as Lee and MacGill calmed the rate down, all the same though Vaughan looked in complete control. A cut for four through gully off MacGill took Vaughan to his 50, and 500 for the series.

Waugh brought on Bichel who bowled wide outside the off stump to a packed off side. Vaughan once again brought out the pull shot which thrashed the ball along the ground passed mid on for four. Under the hot sun, England had reached 100–1.

Butcher edged MacGill to slip with the score on 124 and out came the England skipper Nasser Hussain. Hussain, an intense batsman with a fierce desire to succeed, had brought a tough discipline to the England team. Mostly he craved beating Australia. No way did he wish to have, on his CV, the first England captain to endure an Ashes whitewash since Johnny Douglas's 1920/21 team.

At this stage Hussain's job was simple: push the score along and give the strike to Vaughan. Vaughan unleased a pull when MacGill dropped short to reach the 70s. A little later, Vaughan pulled another MacGill long hop for four to enter the eighties. By this stage Hussain was 'in' and he too came to the party and, before people had fully realised, had sensibly nudged, nurdled and hit his way into the 20s.

There he stayed on 21 whilst Vaughan cut Lee uppishly over the slips for a full-blooded boundary. Lee, knocked off his stride, chose variation next ball and hurled in a thunderbolt at Vaughan's pads, striving for a yorker. Lee over-pitched the ball and Vaughan square drove him for another boundary; this brought up the 50 partnership to a rapturous reception from the 'Barmy Army'.

Desperate for a breakthrough, Waugh brought on Damien Martyn, a specialist middle-order batsman to bowl steady medium to a tight line. After a maiden played by Hussain Waugh gave Martyn another over; this one was okay but not really threatening. Waugh gave Martyn a third over but by now Vaughan was facing and he square cut a timely boundary just behind square to reach 97. Then a leg stump half volley Vaughan flicked nonchanently down to the square leg boundary to bring up his third century of the series – the first time an England player had done so in an Ashes series in Australia since Chris Broad in 1986/87. Only a very few select Englishmen have ever achieved this; Jack Hobbs in 1911/12, Herbert Sutcliffe in 1924/25, Walter Hammond in 1928/29, Chris Broad in 1986/87 and now Michael Vaughan. All of the time Hussain, mainly watching from the non-striker's end, remained on 21.

On 102, Vaughan gave a relatively straight forward chance to Justin Langer at mid-wicket and much to Langer's embarrassement, he spilt the offering. Vaughan grinned at his opposite number.

A sumptuous cover drive from Vaughan brought up the England

200 and by the end of the day England had reached 218–2. Vaughan had displayed a quality of strokeplay rarely seen since the days of Dexter. He walked off to a standing ovation from the Barmy Army, undefeated on 113.

I remember the Vaughan/Hussain stand well. Flying back from New Zealand to start a new job, I had to kill a couple of hours in the departure lounge somewhere in Malaysia. On the screen was the Ashes, England were approaching 300–2. Vaughan and Hussain seemed to bat together so comfortably. Similar to the last test in the '74/'75 series with both Lillee and Thomson injured, so this time England had no worry from McGrath and Warne

Another scorching Vaughan boundary through the covers off Bichel and a contented grin smothered my face. Close of play and still 45 minutes to go before the flight. I wandered around the shops to kill time. There in the queue of some sunglasses shop was a brash Australian male about 40, grotesquely overweight and smelling of beer. Tattoos adorned his shoulders and arms.

'Excuse me', I enquired, 'you don't happen to know the Ashes score do you?'

'Er yes', he began, ' the Poms are in front … something like 2 for 300.'

'I know', I replied, '… just wanted to hear an Australian tell me.'

'Ar yer bastard.'

On day four Vaughan initially showed a degree of circumspection but still put away the bad balls for four and occasionally even perfectly acceptable deliveries. One cover drive had such precise timing that the crowd gasped at its execution. He remained cool, calm and collected throughout the morning session and by now the wicket started to show signs of wear and tear.

Hussain reached his 50, and soon after Vaughan pulled MacGill once more for four. A little later, Vaughan dabbed a two behind square on the off side to being up his 150. All the way to the last over before lunch Hussain and Vaughan accumulated runs until, with just two balls to go before lunch, Hussain snicked Lee to Gilchrist and was gone for a crucial 72 – to complete a brace of 70s in the game. The partnership between the pair of right handers was worth 189.

Robert Key hung around for a while but this was not the greatest of series for the Kent right hander and he fell, as the pitch cracked further, for fourteen. John Crawley at six and Stewart at seven meant Vaughan could still carry on and make a play for R. E. Fosters 287.

Vaughan remained positive by the prospect but, on 183 and with the score on 345, Vaughan received what is still considered to be a shocking decision from umpire Tiffin: LBW to a delivery that would have obviously bounced over the top of the stumps.

England totalled 452 with Stewart stranded on 38. Nonetheless, although the pitch now showed disturbing signs of deterioration, Australia limped to 91–3 by the close.

Next morning Andy Caddick continued to exploit the variable bounce to claim 7–94. Australia, requiring 451 to win, fell 225 runs short. So England won yet another consolation victory after the Ashes battle had already been decided, much like in the last test of the 1993 series, then again in 1994/95, then again in 1997, then again in 1998/99, then again in 2001.

The next Ashes series in 2005 provided the greatest test series for England certainly since 1981. In fact the turning point for English cricket came with Vaughan 183s. England drew with South Africa in a pulsating series later on during the English summer and within two years had regained the Ashes and climbed to second place in the world. Vaughan's mauling of Gillespie scarred the bowler and he was never the same force in an Ashes contest again.

England 362 (Butcher 124, Hussain 75, Stewart 71, Bichel 3–86).
Australia 363 (Gilchrist 133, S. R. Waugh 102, Hoggard 4–92, Harmisaon 3–70, Caddick 3–121).
England 452 (Vaughan 183, Hussain 72, MacGill 3–120, Lee 3–132)
Australia 226 (Caddick 7–94).
ENGLAND WON BY 225 RUNS.

Innings Ranked Number 38
Randall's 174 at Melbourne in 1977

Opponents: Australia.
At stake: One-off test match to celebrate 100 years of test cricket between England and Australia.
Bowling attack: Lillee, Walker, O'Keeffe, Gilmour, G. S. Chappell, Walters: 31.30.
Pitch: Standard.

Game situation: England had been set 462 runs to win in the fourth innings in front of close to 100,000 baying Australian supporters.

The Australians would probably reckon they were the unofficial world champions at the time. They had pummelled the West Indians in an enthralling series 5–1 just a year earlier. Their bowling attack for this test included one of the greatest fast bowlers of all time in Dennis Lillee, right in his prime aged 28. Opening with him was the unorthodox right-arm fast medium pace from Max Walker, less celebrated than the injured Jeff Thomson (torn shoulder injury from a collision with Alan Turner in the outfield in the previous series against Pakistan), yet his wickets were purchased slightly cheaper (27.47 v 28.00) in tests. Gary Gilmour, a talented left armer, with a still better average of 26.03 completed the seam bowling line up.

The pitch was fast and bouncy and in the first innings neither side could muster the wicket. England won the toss and inserted Australia, who collapsed to 138 all out, wickets shared between John Lever, Bob Willis, Chris Old and 'deadly' Derek Underwood. England fared even worse – shot out for just 95. Lillee 6–26.

With a lead of 43, Australia then amassed 419 with a century from wicket-keeper Rod Marsh. In reply, Randall started his account with the score on 28–1. Woolmer LBW Walker for 12, a disappointing test for him.

Randall faced 353 deliveries, wearing only a peaked cap for head protection, and hit 21 fours. His most breathtaking shots were the repeated hooks for four along the ground and just in front of square, off of all people a wound up destroyer in Lillee. This was as courageous as any innings since Compton's just after the war against the 1948 Australians.

Nervous at the crease, Randall forever fidgeted whilst the bowler ran in. Off Lillee would come, tearing in with visual acceleration, then the most sublime action released the ball at 90 mph. The bouncers were head high yet somehow Randall swivelled around and hooked downwards and imperiously along the ground. He would glance at Lillee and doff his cap like a jester whilst the crowd threw the ball back for more.

On one occasion in the first innings Lillee felled Randall as a ball whistled passed his head. 'No use hitting me there mate, nothing to damage' quipped Randall.

There were moments too where the unbelievable assault on such a daunting target seemed possible but just when England winched themselves back into the game, Randall would lose a partner. His whole innings fought to gain equity. Yet at 113–1, Brearley fell LBW to Lillee. Dennis Amiss then provided solid support in the quest for 462. They put on 166 to take the total to 279–2. Amiss, in what turned out to be his last 50 for England, got bowled by of all people Greg Chappell a part-timer. Fletcher fell soon afterwards for one, snicking Lillee to Marsh.

Still the fight was on. On one famous Lillee bouncer at the height of their duel, Randall swayed back to avoid collision only to turn the event into a backwards summersault, pure entertainment.

Randall found support from the giant all-rounder Tony Greig. Randall moved past 150 and then at 161 he was given out caught behind, yet Rod Marsh in a rare gesture of good faith and sportsmanship admitted the ball had not quite carried. This was a hard-fought celebration test, a one off. The Ashes were not being contested but still the game carried enormous interest. Such was Randall's entertainment value that Rod Marsh sensed such an innings of rare quality deserved a proper send off. If Australia were going to win they were going to do it fairly. At 346–4 and with only 116 more runs to win and Randall on 174, he played forwards to a length ball from leg break bowler Kerry O'Keeffe and Gary Cosier, diving from short leg, held on at full stretch.

The end of a truly great innings was applauded by the sell out Antipodean crowd. The clowning Randall won the plaudits and took the man of the match award ahead of even Dennis Lillee. 'If Lillee was going to take wickets he was bloody well going to have to earn them!' was Randall's comment to the papers on the next day.

Upon dismissal, Randall walked in the wrong direction confused by the shadows of the pavilion. He ended up close to the Queen and the Duke of Edinburgh's enclosure before security guards ushered him in the appropriate direction. On his return to Nottingham, Randall was granted the freedom of his home town.

In all Randall batted for 446 minutes and although the Ashes were not at stake for this one-off contest, the cricket was played in a highly competitive manner throughout. In the end England fell just 45 runs short, by a strange quirk of fate the same margin as the very first test between the two countries back in 1877 and on the same ground too.

Kerry Packer then came along with his alternative coloured-clothing brand of World Series Cricket. More Australians were drawn in than English cricketers and so, during the Silver Jubilee tests of 1977, the Australian camp became obviously split. England won 3–0.

Randall continued to represent England in test cricket until blitzed by the 1984 West Indians. No one has batted quite like Derek Randall either before or since. His test hundreds, and there were seven, were always worth watching for sometimes, like in Melbourne in 1977, he would throw caution to the wind. He tended to bat either in an entertaining manner with millionaire shots pinging from his bat, or when the situation dictated, he'd slug it out, overcome exhaustion and dig in for victory. Inconsistency prevented Randall being classed as a great, but he certainly played a couple of great innings!

Australia 138 (Underwood 3–16, Old 3–39).
England 95 (Lillee 6–26, Walker 4–54).
Australia 419–9 declared Marsh 110*, Davis 68, Walters 66, Hookes 56, Old 4–104).
England 417 (Randall 174, Amiss 64, Lillee 5–139, O'Keeffe 3–108)
AUSTRALIA WON BY 45 RUNS.

Innings Ranked Number 37
Stewart's 164 at Old Trafford in 1998

Opponents: South Africa.
At stake: Possibility of going 2–0 down in a five-test series after the third test. England had not won a five-test series at home since 1985.
Bowling attack: Donald, Kallis, Ntini, Adams, Klusener, Cronje, Cullinan: 26.74.
Pitch: Devoid of both pace and bounce.
Game situation: Following on 369 runs behind, England were 11–2 when Stewart, England's wicket-keeper batsman and captain arrived at the crease.

England had been out played in the series to date. Much of this was as a result of South Africa's potent pace attack. In fact it is a tribute to the 1998 South African bowling attack that three of England's finest 60 innings stretching back to 1877 actually came from batsmen who each played out of their skins in this series. The one narrowly missing the final 50 was Atherton's infamous 98 not out, involving the hand from God which cancelled out Maradona's in the football World Cup of '86.

The first test at Edgbaston was rain affected but England gave a decent account of themselves, Atherton 103, Cork 5–93 were the highlights, but the game petered out tamely as a draw. Lord's, and the second test saw Southern Hemisphere dominance emerge. Though Cork again cut a furrow through South Africa's early batsmen to leave them vulnerable at 46–4, they recovered through a stand of 184 between Hansie Cronje (81) and the ever popular Jonty Rhodes (117) and reached a respectable 360. England capitulated to Donald (5–32) and Pollack (3–42) and were dismissed for a paltry 103. Some resistance from Atherton (44), Hussain (105) and Stewart (56) saved the innings defeat but only just, South Africa winning by ten wickets. Though this depressed England supporters there was no doubt South Africa possessed an awesome opening pair. Elsewhere in this book, Donald and Pollack have been described as being like lions tearing into England batsman as though they were a fresh kill. The amount Pollack swung the ball at nearly 90 mph seemed to compliment the hurricane-force thunderbolts from the long-legged and angry Donald.

Old Trafford saw more of the same with South Africa winning the toss and batting for no less than 199 overs. During this time on a bland surface, England could only extract five batsmen for 552 runs before Cronje mercilessly elected to declare. By now an hour had been eaten up of the third day. It seemed that South Africa merely wanted to grind England in to the dust, to make impossible the chance of a South African defeat and to ensure that they did not have to bat much in the second innings.

South Africa batted staunchly, with few easy pickings by a balanced England attack. Kirsten took 572 deliveries and over ten hours in compiling a daunting, monolithic 210 – the third longest South African innings in history. Kallis, normally more flamboyant, took just under six hours to rack up 132 and Cullinan five hours for his 75.

The placid pitch however came alive when the South Africans tore in and on the back of a couple of wickets to Donald and the youthful Ntini, spinner Paul Adams cashed in with 4–63. With 162–8 at the end of day 3, England eventually reached 183. No wonder crowds started to stay away. After the crushing disappointment of Lord's, even on the first day, the ground was barely half full with just 11,200 spectators.

More of the same followed on that fateful fourth day and England soon lost Knight and Hussain in the second innings. Out strode the multi-purpose captain, specialist batsman and wicket-keeper, Alec Stewart.

Had Stewart not carried the burdens of wicket-keeping he might have reached greatness with the bat over a fifteen-year career. Statistics may lie occasionally and some batsmen may gain a selfish reputation by playing for their average. Others may just bat in a showmanlike manner and throw their wickets away foolishly. Then there is your Alec Stewart-type batsman, a team player, always positive and never afraid of his responsibilities.

It was once said that an England batsman gets the first 60 runs for himself. Its usually enough not to get dropped for the next test. After the first 60, batsmen then have to concentrate and garner extra runs for the team cause.

Stewart always commanded respect. First picked for England when his dad was in charge, eyebrows were initially raised yet he soon proved his worth in extracting hard runs in high pressure situations. His twin tons in Barbados back in 1994 would each have warranted a place in England's top 100 innings, so too the 69 not out carrying his bat against Wasim and Waqar. Yes, Stewart was a classy cricketer.

Gradually Atherton and Stewart settled down and the 50 came up, then the 100. Pollack was injured for this test but Kallis and Ntini rose to the occasion and backed up the spearhead Donald with minimum fuss and tight lines.

Nonetheless, between lunch and tea Atherton and Stewart stole 121 runs, batting as fluently as at any time in the series. Well though South Africa bowled, their lines and length were spot on, the pace attack tired in the evening session and both batsmen were there at the close with England now 211–2. Atherton, as was typical, staunchly kept his wicket intact and waited for the rare bad ball. He slept on 81 not out, whilst the more flamboyant Stewart had stroked a masterful undefeated 114.

On the last day with six hours to bat out, Atherton clawed his way onwards in first gear whilst Stewart kept the scoreboard ticking along. Stewart's role was to keep playing positively to reduce the deficit, Atherton's to use up time. After an hour, Atherton had a rush of blood and hooked a Kallis bouncer down to fine leg. The 228 partnership ending with a soft dismissal. England trailed by 141 runs.

Undeterred, Stewart kept blasting the bad ball. He increased the tempo in a desperate attempt to clear the arrears. Eventually, playing by the sword and entertaining the last-day crowd, Stewart hooked fatally at Donald and fell for a magnificent 164 spread over seven hours. *Wisden* describes the innings as 'an astonishing performance from someone carrying so much responsibility.'

It must have narked Stewart as he trudged off. England had to bat for twelve hours to save the game and there were still four hours to go. Now, sensing blood once more, Donald went in for the kill. Thorpe, suffering back pain and now a passenger, immediately got cleaned up for no runs. Cork, now batting in the all-rounder's number seven slot fell to Adams and 40 minutes later Donald pinned Ramprakash, the last specialist batsman for 34.

Ashley Giles playing in his first test had a torrid time. His 36 overs had cost 106 runs for Cullinan's wicket. Though undefeated on sixteen in the first innings, he fell once again to Donald and England had slumped to 329–8, still 40 runs in arrears.

England's hopes now rested with Darren Gough, the talisman, and the Welsh off-spinner, Robert Croft. There were 90 minutes left and only Angus Fraser still to come in. Both tailenders ate up time and the South African's became irate. For 78 long minutes Gough held back from his natural exuberance and dug in. Eventually he fended Donald off to short leg to give the great 'white death' six wickets in the innings.

Fraser and Croft survived the last 43 deliveries. The crowd cheered as Croft knocked a single to draw the scores level and make South Africa bat again. Then one final Donald over to Fraser, loud LBW shout off the last ball, but Fraser, England and the series was kept alive. Croft played out a maiden from Adams despite the fact it was too late for South Africa to bat.

The sense of relief for England cricket fans, starved of success for so long, was palpable and similar – so I am told – to the Lord's 1953 Ashes escape by Watson and Bailey (too young to remember) and the Cardiff escape of 2009 (on holiday in Brittany at the time and without radio contact).

England managed to win the last two tests to earn a 2–1 series win. The South Africans were so distraught at the result and what they believed to be a catalogue of umpiring errors that on return the team were still paid their win bonuses by the board.

According to witnesses in the England team at the time, animosity festered between the two sides for the rest of the series – a shame because some cricket of breath-taking theatre came to pass!

Stewart cut an athletic figure, 6ft tall and super fit. Though quite tall for a wicket-keeper, he kept playing for England bowing out on his own terms five years later, when into his forties – the last Englishman to do so. A pang of regret filtered through this *author* as Stewart was the last England cricketer to be older than *him*, a dream over.

South Africa 552 (Kirsten 210, Kallis 132, Cullinan 75, Cronjé 69*, Gough 3–116).
England 183 (Atherton 41, Stewart 40, Adams 4–63) and 369–9 (Stewart 164, Atherton 89).
MATCH DRAWN.

Innings Ranked Number 36
Gower's 154 not out at Sabina Park in 1981

Opponents: West Indies.
At stake: National pride, England were already 2–0 down in a five test series and this was the fifth and final test.
Bowling attack: Holding, Marshall, Croft, Garner, Richards, Gomes, Mattis and Haynes. 36.60.
Pitch: Fine.
Game situation: England were 157 runs behind in the first innings. Gower arrived at the crease with England on 10–2 and there were still $7^1/2$ hrs of the game to go.

Margaret Thatcher's early years in government coincided with troubles times. The populace of Britain weren't happy. In London, a black youth was arrested in Wiltshire Road. Nothing unusual in that except a crowd tried to intervene and free him. The infamous Brixton riots saw hundreds of black and white youths rioting against the police, hundreds were injured on both sides. Bobby Sands, an IRA politician, had just won a by-election yet was in the process of starving himself to death. Across the Atlantic, President Reagan recuperated after receiving a bullet to the chest. An Oxford lady, Susan Brown, became the first woman cox in the history of the University Boat Race, steering the Oxford team to victory.

Meanwhile, in the Caribbean the England cricket team struggled against the fastest bowling attack in history. This was the tour where England's batting averages were bipolarised. Four batsmen averaged over 40 throughout the series, yet no one else averaged over 20. Quite staggeringly for a cricketer with the batting skills of Botham, this tour represented a nightmare with the bat: 73 runs at 10.43.

The four batsmen capable of standing up to 90 mph missiles, on fast bouncy wickets included 39-year-old Geoffrey Boycott, Peter Willey, Graham Gooch and the left-handed, 24-year-old David Gower.

Boycott was the great barnacle of the batting line up, the man England supporters would chose to bat for their lives. He played a percentages game and sold his wicket dearly. Famed for being a coward, Boycott declined to play test cricket during the three years when Lillee and Thompson were at their peak, but proved those critics wrong, turning out five years later against an even more formidable unit.

Opening with Boycott was the harder hitting 27-year-old Graham Gooch, capable of playing supremely well but inconsistent at this time in his career. Nonetheless Gooch and Boycott provided a sound opening pair.

Peter Willey was reputedly the strongest cricketer in England, apparently defeating Ian Botham in an arm wrestle. Around the era from 1976 to 1986, he was the one selectors chose to stand up specifically to fast bowling. Willey showed no fear, and at the first sign of gun smoke the selectors always gave Willey a call.

Coming in at four was a very special player in David Ivon Gower, a boy from King's School Canterbury, who played in a manner that had the purists cooing. On this day, 14 April 1981, Gower arrived at the crease with England staring down the barrel of possibly another innings defeat in the series. 10–2, including the prized wicket of Gooch after his magnificent 153 in the first innings, Gower walked out to join the veteran Boycott.

Marshall was in the processes of breaking down, but there was still Michael Holding, the quickest on the planet. His first over at Boycott in the third test has gone down as one of the most frightening ever delivered – trembling from shell-shock, Boycott's stumps were shattered on the last ball of Holding's infamous over. He was the spearhead.

Colin Croft, bowler of the meanest throat balls on the planet with his powerful 6 ft 4 ins body frame, came from over the wicket in a chest-on action. Croft snarled like a maniac killer, a colossal man, and simply not a person to mess with.

Gower also had to face Joel Garner, a strongly-built giant of 6 ft 8 ins. Certainly the tallest express-paced bowler of all time, quicker than Bruce Reid for instance, Garner delivered steepling bounce, allied with swing and seam. Think of Ambrose, add a further inch, and you have Garner. Ambrose's career lasted longer and was even more impressive than Garner's, but Garner caused freakish problems. The game was not invented for fast bowlers to deliver a cricket ball from over nine feet high. There were sight screen issues as well as the safety of such bounce.

Some batsmen irk bowlers, Pietersen for example must be hated. How many bowlers has he humiliated? Boycott was another, so too Atherton, but for different reasons. They were stubborn buggers and hard to remove and needed prising out. Gower however played beautiful shots, rarely out of anger, just clipped or touched to the boundary. The ball rarely clanged off the blade, just pinged off, an exquisite noise rather than a violent one. Gower could pacify fast bowlers with his charm and grace.

Famously Gower played and missed several times at the start of his career to Dennis Lillee. Lillee became ever more exasperated. In the heat of the battle Gower apologised to Lillee, 'I'm sorry sir, you're just too good!' Cowdrey had it, so did Gower: a gentlemanly calmness that dissipated a fast bowler's anger.

Eventually of course the bowlers would tire of Gower endlessly nudging and nurdling runs, clips of leg that rocketed to the boundary, cuts, drives, hooks, pulls, all accomplished with such ease and without appearing to break sweat. Gower was a poodle in terms of technique. His technique did not include the mongrel of a Botham, it was pure like freshly driven snow.

So it was that Gower bedded in for the last four sessions of the test. With the score at 32, Boycott fell to Croft. England were 125 behind, Gooch, Boycott and Athey in the hutch with Peter Willey the last specialist batsman as company.

Willey had a stance as front on and offensive as Chanderpaul's. He had a strong cut and, like Brian Close before him, never flinched. Marshall strained a rib muscle, so Clive Lloyd rotated his fast bowlers, careful not to overload the remaining three. He added Viv Richard's containing off-breaks at the end, just in case either batsmen's concentration waned before the close.

With the occasional alarm Gower and Willey added 102 defiant runs but still England closed 26 runs behind. Gower, the dominant partner, dined on 70 not out with Willey still there on 44.

Gower's career to date had been lit up with sparkling cameos. Unlike other great England batsmen like Hutton and Gooch who failed to trouble the scorers in their first innings, Gower's first ball in test cricket, a bouncer, was despatched to the square leg boundary for four. His hundred on Ashes debut the following winter was an exquisite innings, and he took a double hundred off the Indian attack a year later. As the final day unfolded Gower had to bat all day to ward off defeat. This tremendous burden provided Gower with the task of staying there and gutsing it out with his Leicestershire colleague and strong man Peter Willey.

Lloyd started with pace as expected and the score crept along for the first hour of the final day, during which England took a slender lead. Lloyd, crafty as a cat, threw the ball to Richards. Willey, perhaps in a state of calm relaxation tamely offered a catch to Greenidge. Immediately Croft returned and claimed his twenty-fourth wicket in the series by pinning the unfortunate Roland Butcher right in front. 168–3 became 168–5, eleven in front when Botham came out to bat. Botham was in a disastrous run as captain. It was not that he lacked tactical nous; basically the pressures of the job were affecting his batting. Botham's greatest knocks have always come from allowing the genius a free spirit to play how he likes. Captaincy drew uncertainty into his batting. Should he slog or get his head down? Gone for his entire spell as captain was the flair, hidden, dormant until some time in the future...

In his most miserable series, Botham stayed to add an intense 47 with Gower, now becalmed in a bubble and batting as though his life depended on it. Paul Downton, his partner, has not gone down as one of England's finest wicket-keeper batsmen. His scoring shots were limited, but there was a defiance against pace which propelled Downton into the England team. No England Packer player had made it back into the England team yet, so no call up for Alan Knott. Bob Taylor was a gritty wicket-keeper too, but lacked the youth and vital nerve of Downton.

So it was that Lloyd took the second new ball, his last throw of the dice. For England two cricketers brought up on Kent's public school pitches, one from King's, the other from Sevenoaks, gritted their teeth and dug in. Expecting quick wickets, Holding, Croft and Garner gave it everything but tired more easily as the length of Gower's innings drained their pace. Neither batsman erred when Lloyd flicked the challenges around and offered Gomes's medium pace, five overs of Mattis and even an over from Desmond Haynes.

England forged a lead of 145, with Gower batting in total for 465 minutes. In all he hit a six and sixteen fours and remained undefeated when the captains shook hands. By his side for the last four hours Paul Downton returned to the pavilion with the job completed successfully. He made 26 in the partnership of 87.

The West Indies took the series 2–0, this after securing a 1–0 win in England the previous summer. Lloyd's West Indians had lost a narrow test to New Zealand a year earlier but that is sport, sometimes minnows emerge on top. Isn't that the ingredient so alluring in the third round of the FA Cup? Other than that defeat in a one-off test, the West Indies were indisputably the best team on the planet. They would continue to evolve reaching their greatest heights in the summer of 1984 when they white-washed an England team 5–0.

England were to lose the next series 5–0 in the West Indies in 1985/86. Interestingly, and highlighting the daylight between the West Indies and the next best, sandwiched in-between these series, England had won not only in India, but also regained the Ashes. The truth is that the West Indies at this time beat pretty useful England teams!

England 285 (Gooch 153, Holding 5–56).
West Indies 442 (Lloyd 95, Gomes 90*, Haynes 84, Greenidge 62, Dilley 4–116).
England 302–6 declared (Gower 154*, Willey 67).
MATCH DRAWN.

Innings Ranked Number 35
Washbrook's 98 at Headingley 1956

Opponents: Australia.
At stake: Ashes.
Bowling attack: Lindwall, Archer, Mackay, Benaud, Johnson: 27.27.
Pitch: Some lateral movement early on.
Game situation: Washbrook enters the Leeds arena with England 17–3 on the first morning having won the toss and elected to bat.

Cyril Washbrook, England's reliable opener in the immediate years after the Second World War, had last played for England on a disastrous tour of Australia back in 1950/51. The right hander was 35 then and initially declined to tour for business reasons. Later, his business associates agreed that he could go. Washbrook averaged 17 and England lost 1–4. The wickets had changed since 1946/47 so Washbrook had less purchase from his square cuts and pulls. By the summer of 1951 the England selectors went for J. T. Ikin, then F. A. Lawson, R. T. Spooner, R. T. Simpson, anyone it seemed but Washbrook.

Nonetheless Washbrook kept his hand in the game and still represented Lancashire. As the years passed, he dropped down the order. His 40th birthday came and went and, no longer harbouring thoughts of national recognition, he agreed to accept the invitation to become an England selector. It seemed a sensible choice. Washbrook still had a hand in the game and could valuably use his time spotting talent around the counties.

From 1953 onwards England ruled the world, more out of the considerable strength of the bowling with all sides covered than the quality and depth of the batting. May, Graveney and Cowdrey had come through from the young brigade, but although Cowdrey had days when his genius surfaced, May was the only consistent performer. Gradually the pre-war veterans departed the test scene; W. J. Edrich in January 1955, L. Hutton in March 1955 and D. C. S. Compton still played for Middlesex, albeit without a knee cap.

In the '56 series, the first test was rain affected and drawn, a relatively low-scoring affair. The second test at Lord's was another such game, but England lost by 185 runs. The batting looked ragged; despite a brace of 50s from Peter May, no one else scored higher than Bailey's 32 in the first innings. Team scores of 171 and 186 were below par, so the selectors convened at a private club in the West End with the notion of change.

Sat around the table were Leslie Ames, Wilfred Wooller, Gubby Allen (the chairman), Peter May (the England captain) and Cyril Washbrook. All agreed that the batting department had to change. Only Peter May himself was a shoe-in with three fifties in three knocks. Cowdrey and Richardson had scored 81 each at Trent Bridge and so hung on to their places.

They needed a batsman who could bowl a bit, so chose Alan Oakman, the tall 26-year-old Sussex right-hander to make his debut. They wanted some grit, a fighter who would not give his wicket away;

they chose the 30-year-old Doug Insole of Essex, a steady accumulator.

Gubby Allen then demanded that Washbrook fetch the beers whilst they considered his name. Rather perplexed, Washbrook did as asked. Allen Ames and Wooller were in no doubt that Washbrook could provide the experience and pugilistic qualities required to bolster the middle order – to be the perfect number five to fight a rearguard action. May wasn't so sure, but the others pointed to his fielding, still as good as ever despite his 41 years. May pointed out the lack of hundreds Washbrook had made that season, to which the others stated the several staunch knocks when Lancashire were in trouble. May felt five years out in the wilderness was too long. A 41-year-old who finished his test career with a bad series when still in his prime, being picked to solve a batting crisis? The fact was, Compton, another veteran, was still working his way back from injury and David Sheppard was also unavailable. On Washbrook's return from the bar, Gubby Allen said: 'Washy, we want you to play at Leeds, will you play?'

'Has it really come to that? ... in that case I'll be only too pleased to try to fill the gap' replied Washbrook.

As the news broke, the press and the public raised no objections to the removal of Graveney and Watson for Oakman and Ikin. However the Washbrook selection caused a sensation with some journalists stating it to be the worst selection blunder in the history of the game. That evening hoards of reporters with cameras waited outside Washbrook's home. He made a statement for the public, something along the lines that 'One doesn't refuse to play for England.'

So to Leeds and on the day Washbrook came in as the extra batsman for Brian Statham, Trueman's opening partner. By anybody's reckoning this selection was seen at the time as a colossal gamble, with the selectors leaving themselves open to vitriolic abuse from the press should this bizarre decision backfire.

England won the toss and elected to bat. Washbrook put his feet up and relaxed, gone were his days of opening. Cowdrey and Richardson, the Kent pair, walked out in the knowledge that Lindwall had recovered from injury and was back in the side, but although Miller was also picked, it was just in his role as a batsman as his knee needed rest.

The wicket had that tinge of green and England had still never won an Ashes test at Headingley in fixtures going all the way back to 1899. It is with some trepidation that both openers started out. Richardson edged a two through-gully off Lindwall from the first ball of the match, Cowdrey played out a maiden from Archer without appearing to time the ball.

Archer, bowling right-arm medium fast, pitched the ball in the right areas. Cowdrey played a back defense at a spiteful delivery which pitched just short of a length, then flew off to take the edge. England 2–1. Oakman played out the maiden. Both bowlers hit the perfect length and swung the ball through the air. Under typically humid and overcast Headingley conditions both bowlers made the ball move appreciably through the air. Add in the green pitch and only four runs were scored in the next half-an-hour.

In Lindwall's fifth over, Richardson took a single and Oakman drove a three through the covers. He seemed to have settled down and got to grips with his debut innings but, next over, Archer sent down a terrific 'breakback' which shattered Oakman's off stump, England 8–2. Washbrook completed his body armour and sat down on the player's balcony to get acquainted with the light.

Washbrook inhaled sharply as May's first shot took the edge through gully for two. Archer's seamers, bowled to a full length, were perhaps the finest he delivered in his entire career. What was plain to the Yorkshire crowd that day was the score was down to great bowling rather than bad batting. After the first hour, Lindwall was replaced by Ken Mackay, another right armer, but more in the team for his batting. After a couple of overs Mackay gave way to Ritchie Benaud the young leg-spinner.

Archer, now in his ninth over, tempted Richardson into a drive and Maddocks gratefully accepted the edge. England, now 17–3 in a critical Ashes test match, already 0–1 down in the series, had to dig themselves out of yet another batting collapse.

Down the steps came a stocky middle-aged man, fit-looking in a chunky way, but greying at the sides. A cap jauntily placed at a slant, shirt sleeves rolled up, Washbrook entered the game to a tumultuous applause from the crowd. Despite the extensive criticism from the press, the Yorkshire crowd cheered their approval at the veteran.

Washbrook took guard in the old-fashioned way, just a couple of pats on the turf and no long stud-scratched line running down the pitch. He glanced around, this tough throwback from pre-war years. Some old boy in the crowd claimed to have seen Washbrook face up to Fleetwood–Smith back in '34. 'Did he score a century?' the grandson asked. 'LBW for nought boy ... but he got 143 against a better attack in 1948.'

Washbrook blocked the last two from Archer and felt the ball come nicely onto the bat. The pitch seemed fine. Benaud concerned him. He had faced Benaud six years earlier but simply could not remember what he was like. Next over, May took a single and exposed the old against the new. Down Benaud sent a well-flighted, good length ball but Washbrook used his feet well and stepped back into his crease then nudged the ball to square leg for a single – another boost from the crowd with support equivalent to a 50.

Between the overs Wasbrook asked May to take Benaud until lunch, just so that he could take a good look from the bowler's end. May welcomed the long distance approach that Washbrook adopted.

A huge appeal followed from a thud into Washbrook's pads in Archer's tenth over, but umpire Buller disagreed – going over the top. Washbrook winked at Johnson, the Australian skipper, and exuded calm but inwardly shook from the shock. Between deliveries Washbrook spent nervous energy prodding at fictitious blotches on the wicket.

The crowd sat looking on intensely with barely a murmur, furrowed brows and real concern. Archer, closing in on lunch, pitched a trifle too shot with slightly too-much width outside the off stump. Instinctively, Washbrook leaned back and thumped it through the covers with his trademark square cut. A massive long cheer, not heard since the relief of Mafeking, had not quite died down before Washbrook took a single from the next ball. Before Archer's over was complete, May flicked him beautifully through mid-wicket. Johnson asked Miller whether he would reconsider but Miller had stated his case earlier. He would save his last great bursts for the final two tests, no sense in aggravating an injury by returning too soon. Johnson understood. Someone needed to relieve Archer. His great spell had yielded thirteen overs, eight maidens, 3–13, quite remarkable. Johnson tossed the ball to Miller's great partner, Lindwall, himself working his way back to full fitness. England had clawed their way to 30-3.

Lindwall overpitched and Washbrook launched into a massive off drive which rocketed to the boundary. Now Washbrook felt alive. No one had hit the ball that hard all series. May meanwhile hit Benaud for a couple more fours and the crowd basked in the sunshine willing the partnership to continue, willing above all else, the veteran. Lunch came with England on 54–3. May had 30 to Washbrook's 14 but the two had inspired hopes of a genuine recovery.

The afternoon session began with Johnson bowling his off breaks and Archer continuing from the Kirkstall Lane End. Washbrook watched as Johnson pitched a touch short and twice cut him for four. Both May and Washbrook drove Archer to the boundary, then Washbrook survived another appeal for LBW but umpire Dai Davies ruled not out.

Following that, May drove Benaud twice for four in one over, a commanding cover drive followed by an on drive squeezed between the bowler and mid on. Johnson switched Benaud to the Grand Stand End and brought back Lindwall. Washbrook pulled his first ball to mid wicket and reached both England's 100 and his own 50 at a stroke. Next over Washbrook square cut Johnson straight at catchable height to Miller, standing at cover. Miller lost sight of the ball through the crowd and grassed the chance. The batsmen scampered through.

Back came Archer and the progress slowed once more to a trickle. Tea loomed and both batsmen wanted to be undefeated by the time the new ball came around. Switching to survival mode, both walked off with 65 not out and England a respectable 140–3.

Straight after Johnson took the new ball and a concerted effort was seen from both Archer and Lindwall, now at his quickest in the day. Washbrook and May defied the attack and managed to push the scoring along. Both reached their seventies when Washbrook unfurled another pull at Lindwall's rib ticklers that flew to the mid-wicket boundary, a resounding shot that bounced like a bomb to the ring fence. England's 150 arrived in the process.

Soon after Washbrook glanced a leg-side delivery only for the diving Maddocks to grasp then drop the harshest of chances. Was it a life? Unperturbed, Washbrook carried on playing his shots, making the most of the situation as though racing against May for the first to a 100. A full-length delivery angling into Washbrook's stumps from the durable Archer was then dispatched imperiously back passed mid on.

May survived a half-chance hit with force just inches from the ground back to the bowler where it richocheted off bowler Mackay's shins. Both advanced into the 80s. Then with May on 92, to Washbrook's 88, the captain stroked a brace of boundaries off a Mackay over to reach the landmark first. Then with tragic luck Johnson bowled May a full toss which May hit handsomely but fatally straight to Lindwall at backward square – gone for 102, after a partnership with Washbrook lasting $4^1/_2$ hours and harvesting 187.

Astonishingly, this was England's highest partnership against Australia since the Oval test match eighteen years earlier. Tony Lock came in as nighwatchman and Washbrook held firm to the close, undefeated on 90.

Washbrook tossed and turned all night, reliving the glories of the previous day. He just could not get to sleep and ordered a cup of tea from the overnight porter at 5.30 am.

At the start of day two Washbrook played out three consecutive maidens from Archer and in the first half-an-hour added just a couple of singles to take his score to 92. Then facing Benaud, he swept a four and cut a two to go to 98. Benaud, wily beyond his years, conferred with Johnson and fielders were brought into a ring. Washbrook would have to hit out for his hundred.

Lock played out an Archer over, then Washbrook faced Benaud again. This time Benaud bowled a quicker slider straight onto Washbrook's stumps. Washbrook sensing it was short enough to pull, leant back, unleashed a pull/hook, but the ball thudded onto his pads. This time the umpire had no hesitation and much to the disappointment from the crowd, their hero, a Lancastrian at that, walked off initially to a stunned, desperately disappointed silence. The score stood at 226–5, some recovery from 17–3.

It was only when Washbrook was half-way back to the pavilion that the clapping started and all able-bodied persons rose as one to acclaim the most fairytale of comebacks since Wilfred Rhodes 30 years earlier.

Ian Johnson, interviewed later on in the year and asked his reflections of the series, had this to say about Washbrook's batting '... my hunch is that cricket history will rate Cyril's performance as the one which swung the destiny of the rubber.'

England had Bailey and Evans to thank for taking the total up to 325. From there the Australians disintegrated for 143 and 140, an astonishing turn around. Laker and Lock the spinners shared eighteen wickets.

England made more successful comebacks, one each in the next two tests. During the fourth test at Old Trafford, Jim Laker's match figures of 19–90 decided the Ashes after a fluent 113 from the Rev D. S. Sheppard. Finally Compton returned with only one knee cap and creamed 94 and 35 not out in the drawn fifth test.

Washbrook played through the series but in three innings this was his only proper contribution. Job done at test level Washbrook kept playing until 1964, in his 50th year.

You may well ask why Washbrook's innings is rated as higher than May's, for May's 101 does not quite make the top 50, yet Washbrook's does. The reason is Washbrook had far more to lose if he failed on that day than May. He had his dignity to preserve, his role as a selector questioned and entered the fray under the greatest pressure. He knew he really had to succeed.

England 325 (May 101, Washbrook 98, Lindwall 3–67, Archer 3–68).
Australia 143 (Laker 5–58, Lock 4–41) and 140 (Laker 6–55, Lock 3–40).
ENGLAND WON BY AN INNINGS AND 42 RUNS.

Innings Ranked Number 34
Atherton's 98 not out at Trent Bridge 1998

Opponents: South Africa.
At stake: South Africa are 1–0 up in a 5 test series. This was the fourth test.
Bowling attack: Donald, Pollock, Elsworthy, Kallis, Adams.
Pitch: Fair.
Game situation: Fourth innings requiring 247 to win.
Weighted runs per wicket of the bowling attack: 26.06.
Attendance: 49,820.

This was the fourth test of a series and England were one down, a typical thrashing at Lord's. In the previous test England had held out for a draw by the thinnest of threads, thanks mainly to a stand of 226 between Stewart and Atherton. In the end, England hung on grimly with one wicket intact and a close appeal for LBW turned down on the last ball. There is no doubt that the South African bowling attack was their best since reintroduction into test cricket in the early 90s. One can see from the bowling runs per wicket combination of 26.06 that some had to have been great.

That summer Alan Donald, comfortably the fastest 'white' bowler on the planet, was in his pomp. In partnership was a right-arm fast medium bowler, seen for the first time on these shores in the form of Shaun Pollock, an outstanding swing bowler with potent accuracy.

This was a time of outstanding bowling attacks around the world filled with some of the finest exponents of their art ever to grace a cricket pitch. This to some extent explains why batsmen as good as Atherton, Hussain, Hick and Stewart all averaged less than 40 in their careers – the standard benchmark of a good test batsman – and Ramprakash under 30.

Sadly attendance figures had been low so far that summer. Old Trafford had been a half-empty stadium and England had not won a five-test series at home since 1985, a whole generation of cricketers ago.

In the fourth test South Africa led by 38 on the first innings. Fraser then pulled England back into the game with ten wickets in the test and South Africa failed to ignite once more, this time for only 208. This left England a target of 247. No England team had scored that to win a home test since the Oval Test in 1902, that long ago.

Atherton and the young Mark Butcher walked out to bat midway through the afternoon session with a day and a half to get 247. If England could just withstand Donald and Pollock, keep their heads and wait for the bad ball they stood a chance. One batsman had the technique and the reputation to wear down Donald and that was Michael Atherton. His reputation for long innings against quality attacks was made in the West Indies in 1994, then South Africa in 1995. This was a time when Atherton's wicket was the most prized English wicket, such was his unwavering powers of concentration.

An uneventful start saw runs coming slowly before Butcher departed in the eighteenth over. Mid-way through the evening session Hansie Cronje the skipper called on Alan Donald to start a new spell. The tall, blond South African speed star marked out his long run. Atherton entered his bubble, taking the team's responsibility entirely on his shoulders. Both combatants recognised this as the crucial phase in the test match. This was Donald's second spell, South Africa's best bet for a quick wicket or two.

According to Michael Atherton himself, the passage of play for the next 40 minutes was the most intense of his test career. The dual demanded depth. Let me take you there.

The first over is an introduction, a warm up at between 85 and 88 mph. One delivery, short and wide outside the off stump, was cut for four just behind point.

After one delivery of the next over, Donald switches to around the wicket. Atherton takes this as a statement of intent, a sign that Donald is ready to crank it up a gear. Atherton clips a short one off his hip to fine leg, nice to rotate the strike.

The storm arrives in the next over. England are 82–1, with Atherton on 27. Donald steams in and fires a short missile that rears up at Atherton's throat. Instinctively Atherton's lifts his bat to defend himself and the ball brushes a glove on the way to Boucher behind the stumps. Donald, arms outstretched in jubilation, passes Atherton on his way to congratulate the keeper. Atherton remains unmoved, poker faced, impassive and waits for umpire Dunne's finger to go up ...

Donald looks back at Dunne following the look of bewilderment on Boucher's face. The finger stays down, Dunne did not see it. Atherton remains calm. Donald, livid, flushes red with growing anger. Unable to control himself South Africa's spearhead screams out, 'You f****** cheat!'

The crowd of home support, beered up under the sun, had now come to life, so too had the summer. Here in the midst of everything were two gladiators in their prime, a head-on battle with everything at stake. Donald was not about to give up easily. He glowered at Atherton, who stared back calmly, unresponsive. He knew Donald had to overt his eyes and walk back to his mark.

Next ball is fast, furious and pitched up at the stumps. It takes a thick inside edge, whistles passed leg stump and shoots away for four down to fine leg. Donald is now on full, raw throttle. Next delivery rises swiftly and Atherton just manages to duck and jump out of the way. A rising missile later in the over strikes Atherton on the chest. Abuse follows as fielders change round at the end of the over.

Nothing of note happens at the other end. It is all about Donald and Atherton. He brings in a leg gully and short leg to signal more short stuff. Atherton hooks over the infield for two, not well controlled and a fielder moves back immediately. A single off his hip next ball takes Atherton off strike and allows Hussain to take some of the heat. Atherton remembers Boycott's advice against the quicks: rotate the strike and watch from the other end.

Hussain, on 23, drives and snicks at a full ball that flies as a regulation chance to Boucher who drops it. Donald screams out 'No!' at the top of his voice and looks disgusted. Boucher and the infield stay more silent now as the storm begins to lose that rare intensity. Donald bowls just one more over before Adams the spinner replaces him. That night Donald took a cortisone injection on his ankle and had less to give on the final day.

This was not a fluent innings by any stretch of the imagination. Hussain batted all the way through to lunch on the final day and when he was dismissed for a valuable 58, Stewart entered to smash a cameo 45 off 34 balls. He did relent to give Atherton the pleasure of hitting the winning runs, a straight drive back passed the bowler. Atherton walked in 98 not out more concerned with victory than any personal landmark. England had squared the series 1–1 with one final test to play, at Headingley.

England went on to win narrowly at Headingley, with some contentious decisions once again going England's way. It was England's first five-test series win at home since 1985. The pace bowling trio of Gough, Fraser and Cork did just enough. Atherton, Stewart and Hussein all made heroic contributions during the course of the series.

However the shining light was all too brief. The winter of 1998/99 saw another Ashes defeat, this time 3–1, with Atherton averaging a miserly 13.75 in four tests.

England went on to lose 2–1 the following summer to New Zealand after having hosted the World Cup and been ignominiously eliminated before the quarter finals. It was a low ebb. At one point England were ranked the lowest test playing nation, bottom of the pile including Zimbabwe.

Radical changes were brought in for the new millennium with the County Championship split into two divisions, and England cricketers becoming centrally contracted to the E.C.B. Duncan Fletcher became England manager after the debacle of the 1999 New Zealand defeat and with it, a bright new dawn.

South Africa 374 (Cronje 126, S. M. Pollock 50, Fraser 5 – 60, Gough 4 – 116).
England 336 (Butcher 75, Ramprakash 67*, Atherton 58, Donald 5 – 109).
South Africa 208 (Cronje 67, Cullinan 56, Fraser 5 – 62, Cork 4 – 60).
England 247 – 2 (Atherton 98*, Hussain 58, Stewart 45*).
ENGLAND WON BY 8 WICKETS

Innings Ranked Number 33
Hobbs' 100 at the Oval in 1926

Opponents: Australia.
At stake: Ashes.
Bowling attack: Gregory, Grimmett, Mailey, Macartney, Richardson: average runs per wicket 31.98.
Pitch: Ruined by a thunderstorm with England 49–0 overnight, a lead of 27.

Perhaps this was the greatest of all innings ever played by an Englishman. Ralph Barker, in his book *Ten Great Innings*, included Jack Hobb's 100, instead of the numerically superior Sutcliffe's 161. The two batted together at the same time and faced the same bowling on the same treacherous morning, following a tremendous overnight thunderstorm.

Rarely has the Oval experienced the same tropical feel as the start of day four. The next day the drenched ground, coupled with a warm continental breeze gave a humid feel rarely experienced in these parts – closer to Brisbane in character rather than London.

At any rate, England for so long deprived of Ashes success had lost eight test matches to none against Australia in the combined series of 1920/21 and 1921. Then England lost the first three tests on the return to Australia in 1924/25 and with it the Ashes, before at last securing a win in the fourth test, nevertheless the fifth test at Sydney was again won handsomely by Australia to the tune of 307 runs.

1926 saw the return of a veteran Australian team. Of the eleven selected for the Oval, Warren Bardsley (44) and Charlie MaCartney (40) were veterans from as far back as the 1909 series, whilst Mailey was also 40 and the average age of the team was 36, older than any of Ricky Ponting's 2009 Australians.

The England team also had an air of the Edwardian era about it (Hobbs 44, Woolley 39, Strudwick (the wicket keeper), 46) as well as Wilfred Rhodes, 49, a vintage slow left-armer who had first played for England right back in the Victorian age alongside W.G. Crucially, England's median age was lower at 33 and the team included a tearaway fast bowler, the 22-year-old Harold Larwood.

All four test matches that summer had been drawn. The first at Trent Bridge was abandoned after 50 minutes due to heavy rain. England held the bragging rights at Lord's with 100s from Hobbs and Hendren and 80s from Sutcliffe and Woolley. Australia fought back at Headingley and held a 200-run first innings lead but England, following on, batted out time with Hobbs 88 and Sutcliffe 94 sharing in a 156 partnership, their second century stand of the series. Weather again ruined the fourth test, nicely poised with England 30 runs behind Australia on the first innings with five wickets in hand. Once again Hobbs indulged, this time with 74, supported by G. E. Tyldesley 81 and Woolley 58.

Three-day test matches were a waste of time. 1926 had shown that they were either drowned out as draws like Lord's and Old Trafford or drenched in runs. The fifth test was to be played to a finish and was the most eagerly anticipated on these shores since the very first in 1880. A timeless test could last between a week or a fortnight. What a mouth-watering prospect for the nation.

Percy Chapman, only 26, was invited to captain the England team in place of A. W. Carr, ill during the last test, and thence discarded. He won the toss and elected on a flat track to bat first.

That Saturday, 14 August, England batted grandly yet threw their wickets away with too cavalier an approach. Hobbs was first to go, bowled by a full toss from Mailey for 37. Thereafter a procession of batsmen came and went, Woolley 18, Hendren 8, followed by a rasping partnership between Sutcliffe and the amateur Chapman. Promising great things in a partnership of 81, both fell by the close as indeed did the rest. Stranded at number eleven was Strudwick, who had only been included when Brown failed a fitness test just before the start. To sum up, it was an inglorious display of carefree batting that provided wonderful entertainment.

Australia in reply batted with far greater resolve. Whilst England achieved 280 in 95.5 overs, Australia scored 302 either side of the rest day in 56.2 more overs. At the close of day two Hobbs and Sutcliffe launched England's second innings reply with a carefully constructed, mature stand of 49, undefeated. They slept soundly that night, Sutcliffe oblivious to the storm.

'Pity it rained in the night' said Hobbs as the two went out on day three.

There followed one of the most famous battles for survival in

England's long cricket history. How Hobbs and Sutcliffe coped with unimaginable odds in the face of accurate, experienced bowlers, delivering an immaculate line – mainly on leg stump to a ring of short legs is the stuff of legend. The ball popped here, the ball spat there and, as the pitch dried, the surface crumbled. Maiden upon maiden from Richardson pinned the two greats at the crease. A gargantuan duel of stamina and mental strength unfolded. Slowly but surely, the odds crept upwards in favour of the mother country.

Both batsmen made sure to score at anything loose, with Jack Hobbs emerging as the dominant partner. The morning session would be remembered by all fortunate enough to be in attendance. For a full $2^1/2$ hours the most celebrated of all opening partnerships added a priceless 112 to take the score to 161 for no wicket, a lead of 139. The Australians followed the umpires towards the pavilion whilst Hobbs and Sutcliffe prodded the wicket, on a length, for a full five minutes before walking off to universal acclaim. How the crowd hoped and prayed for a Hobbs hundred in the afternoon.

Hobbs duly reached his first ever test 100 against Australia on his home ground. He had beaten almost every batting record so charismatically set by W.G. in the previous century. This was Hobbs at 44-years-of-age defying some of the world's best bowlers. There are times in an English cricket fan's life when thinking of an innings puts a tear to one's eye. There were many shedding a tear in gratitude that Tuesday so long ago, only an ever-dwindling few still breathing remember it. The most eagerly anticipated cricket match in a generation had the most sublime scorecard.

England 172 for 1
Hobbs 100

Sutcliffe continued, taking his call from Hobbs and was defeated only on the last ball of the day, for 161 – another truly outstanding batsman. These two, together with Hammond, Hutton and Compton, are the only England cricketers to complete their careers with over 50 averages in both first class and test cricket.

England won and a 48-year-old spun England to victory on the Wednesday. I sometimes wonder, on the eve of a similarly important test, in the 2009 series, with similar stakes, why Ramprakash was not picked. Like Hobbs, he played his first-class cricket at the Oval, home of Surrey. He has scored in excess of 100 hundreds and, just like

Hobbs, has matured as a batsman and now makes far fewer mistakes. We shall never know.
The game has evolved but it does remain 99% the same!

England 280 (Sutcliffe 76, Mailey 6–138).
Australia 302 (Gregory 73, Collins 61, Tate 3–40, Larwood 3–82).
England 436 (Sutcliffe 161, Hobbs 100, Grimmett 3–108, Mailey 3–128).
Australia 125 (Rhodes 4–44, Larwood 3–34).
ENGLAND WON BY 289 RUNS

Innings Ranked Number 32
Botham's 118 at Old Trafford in 1981

Opponents: Australia.
At stake: Ashes.
Bowling attack: Lillee, Alderman, Whitney, Bright: 29.87.
Pitch: Fair.
Game situation: England had taken a lead of 101 on the first innings but had slumped to 104–5 when Botham arrived at the crease about twenty minutes before lunch on the third day. With the weather set fair for the remainder of the test, this was a battle that would go to the death. England were 2–1 up in the six-test series. This was the fifth test, all results were possible.

England's summer of 1981 will remain shrouded in folklore for as long as the game is played, a pivotal moment in cricket history. The Royal Wedding between Prince Charles and 19-year-old Lady Diana Spencer had taken place just a couple of weeks earlier. It had not been a year for peace and tranquillity, Britain was in a mess – riots at Brixton in London earlier in the year had spread to the provinces with unrest in Liverpool, Wolverhampton, Birmingham, Reading, Luton, Chester, Hull and Preston. Causes included unemployment, poor housing, police harassment of the Black Community and racism. Politicians called for a curb on immigration.
Tempered with these topsy-turvy events was a phenomenal series unfolding before the nations' eyes. It had been a generation since the British public had followed a series so avidly. Classic vintage Ashes

matches, the real blockbusters that grip the nation so enthrallingly, happen about four times a century. In this regard, 1981 compares favourably with 1953, 1926 and 1902. In terms of the percentage of the population glued to the sets, 1981 compares with the post-war Bradman series. It was a year that hauled in the crowds and converted a million new enthusiasts to the game.

One man in particular gripped the nation's attention every time he went out to bat. Ian Botham had resigned the captaincy a month earlier. In the following match at Headingley his heroics helped set up a sensational victory and his spell of five wickets for one run to steal victory from the Australians in the fourth test sparked a second surging wave of euphoria around the country. Despite heroics from Bob Willis with 8–43 to clinch the Headingley victory, it was Botham who received the Man of the Match award. During the fourth test he came from nowhere to rightly get the Man of the Match once again.

In the fifth test England won the toss and had subsided to Lillee and Alderman on the first day. Tavare held the innings together in his barnacled manner and scored a slow but priceless 69. Paul Allott playing in his first test thrashed a defiant and totally unexpected 52 not out, but England had been skittled for 231.

Astonishingly, Australia capitulated in just over 30 overs, their shortest Ashes innings since 1902. Chief architects in the destruction were the all-firing seam attack of Willis, Botham and Allott. Australia bowled out for 130, were going for their shots and playing with reckless abandon.

The see-saw series then saw sustained excellence from Australia's opening bowlers and between them a turgid England slumped to 104–5. In the morning session, England lost three wickets and crawled through a full session for just 39 runs. It was painstaking and Australia had fought their way back into contention. Both Gooch and Boycott had been removed by the end of day two. Then Gower, Gatting and Brearley fumbled through the morning, scratching a pitiful existence with runs hard to come by. The nature of the series meant anything was possible and now the pendumum swung ominously in Australia's favour.

With the fall of Brearley's wicket Botham walked out to a big cheer. He was quiet before lunch, just three singles. Botham appreciated the need to get to lunch and review the situation. Unlike at Headingley, Botham chose the orthodox Hammond manner.

This was a very good Australian side spearheaded by Dennis Lillee, arguably the greatest fast bowler of all time. Lillee had slowed down his standard pace to nagging accuracy and dangerous lateral movement. This was to be his most successful Ashes series. He was partnered by Terry Alderman who was to take 41 wickets with high quality swing bowling in the six-test series. So useful were these two throughout the series that under normal circumstances they would have won the ten-week cricketing extravaganza on their own. Boycott, Gower, Gooch and Gatting all endured a poor series with the bat. Gower, normally productive against the old enemy, lost his place after Edgbaston.

In the team for this test was Mike Whitney, a curly-haired athlete drawn from the Lancashire league, who bowled left-arm seamers at fast-medium. Finally Ray Bright provided left-arm spin.

It soon became clear after lunch that something quite extraordinary was unfolding before the capacity Old Trafford crowd. Within a few overs Botham grew in confidence and soon cut, pulled and drove his way into the 30s. Targeting Alderman, Botham drove massively at a short of a length delivery. The ball rose to tremendous heights, recalling the famous Bonnor strike at the Oval in 1880. This time Whitney ran back under the swirling ball from mid-off, desperately trying to catch the horrible half chance that could decide the test. He dived and his fingertips touched the ball yet it fell to the ground a fraction before the despairing fielder. The entire crowd erupted in joy save for the pockets of Australians. Photojournalists caught the mood with the now famous image of a despairing Whitney, the ball on the ground, the BT advert 'Make Someone Happy' and a euphoric crowd in the background.

Hughes took the new ball and handed it to the veteran spearhead. Lillee had no time for Botham's rapidly growing ego. Purposefully he marked out his run. Lillee knew instinctively the critical moments that decide a series. This was the pivotal moment. Australia had batted so poorly that another 30 minutes of Botham and the Ashes would be gone. The final chance, the defining moments and his team needing a devastating spell.

During the next 30 minutes Botham produced a display of batting to rank with any batting genius at any time in history. John Woodcock of the *Times* reported the immortal words 'I refuse to believe that a cricket ball has been hit with greater power or rarer splendour.' The most breathtaking dual in my 35-year allegiance with England test cricket unfolded before millions tuned in to the BBC. Lillee ran in with all of the old hostility, one legend of cricket to another.

Picture the scene, Manchester man sups on his warm beer as Lillee roars in and propels a vicious, lifting delivery at Botham's throat, Botham shapes to pull, takes his eyes of the ball, swings his mighty bat and top edges into the stands for six The time lag between connection, roar of the crowd and the ball landing in the stands is less than three seconds and pandemonium breaks out, hardly anyone remains in their seats as the Botham missile hurtles towards them before landing four rows back. This is not a typical day's cricket and the spectators grow delirious.

Lillee, clearly fuming, walks scowlingly back to his mark, drowned out by the excited buzz. He runs in faster and unleashes another bumper, this time Botham is ready and swivels round once more and makes greater connection. The ball travels higher and further and Old Trafford has erupted. South Manchester comes to a standstill, easily the loudest noise the roar from the stadium.

Another square cut for four off Lillee and Botham reaches a barn storming 50. Just as the cries die down, Lillee storms in and bowls an attempted yorker. In the melee of the occasion Lillee does not quite land it close enough to Botham's toes, the Somerset giant rocks forward and smashes the ball off the front foot with the full swing of the bat. That Botham was not quite over the ball adds further drama and the ball races towards Lillee at just above head height. Lillee, on impulse makes an initial foray at the ball but somehow realises this would hurt and pulls away. Like a bouncing bomb the ball thunders into the advertising hoardings at long off. Ordinary folk are frightened. No one looks away just in case. From the other end Alderman is dispatched unceremoniously into the crowd at long on.

Again Lillee digs in short. Again Botham hooks. Again he takes his eye off the ball and again the ball lands in the crowd after scaling a breath-takingly magnificent parabola.

Sometimes a scorecard can be deceptive and hide the truth, yet Lillee is being thrashed by Botham for 45 runs off 18 deliveries with the second new ball. A total of 90 runs are blasted from Botham's bat on that unforgettable afternoon, from just 49 balls. A very good Australian team, one which three weeks earlier had anticipated regaining the Ashes, now stands punch drunk on the Old Trafford turf amidst the throng of ecstatic England supporters – a traumatic experience.

In amongst this carnage Tavare blocks, holding up an end and takes singles to give Botham the strike. Occasionally he strikes the ball sweetly, one through mid-wicket represents a text book flick and is appreciated by the crowd in a more soporific manner.

Botham strikes a further two sixes in the final half-an-hour. Both

Lillee and Alderman, hitherto Australia's most potent bowling combination in the series, are removed from the attack, egos battered and lines mangled. Bright comes on to bowl in order to take the pace off the ball. Botham sizes him up then launches a slog sweep over the square-leg boundary and reaches his century. This time Botham reaches the landmark in just 86 balls. A sixth six over long on follows again off Bright before Whitney, bowling left-arm seam finds the edge of Botham's bat, 118 off 102 balls in just a little over two hours.

As Botham walked off towards the pavilion he had just put both the test match and the series out of Australia's reach. The hush at the end was palpable, it was all far too good to last. Soon the applause echoed around the stand and the capacity crowd rose to its feet.

In a stand of 149 with Tavare, Botham scored a shade under 80 per cent of the runs. England are now 354 runs to the good and the Australians were once again shell shocked, shattered and traumatised. As Botham walked passed the gates and into the pavilion, perhaps at no other time either before or since has an England cricketer reached such heights of public adoration.

Quote from Sir Len Hutton (1984): 'There cannot have been many more astonishing innings in the annals of the game at any class, and I would cross mountains and swim rivers to see its like again.'

'I will always remember that as being the most exciting and emotional bit of cricket I have ever been involved in.' Chris Tavare (1993).

Tavare batted in all for 423 minutes for 78 and there were 50s apiece for Alan Knott and John Emburey, but everything was an anticlimax after Botham. England set Australia 505 to win and level the series. Yallop and Border (the latter batting with a broken finger), both scored centuries in acts of defiance, but the test match and the summer belonged to Botham and England. The sixth test was a drawn affair in a dead game with Botham still managing to achieve a ten-wicket haul. From here Botham was to plateau for a few more years without ever quite scaling the same heights again.

England 231 (Tavare 69, Lillee 4–55, Alderman 4–88).
Australia 130 (Kent 52, Willis 4–63, Botham 3–28).
England 404 (Botham 118, Tavare 78, Knott 59, Emburey 57, Alderman 5–109).
Australia 402 (Border 123*, Yallop 114, Willis 3–96).
ENGLAND WON BY 103 RUNS.

Innings Ranked Number 31
Smith's 148 at Lord's in 1991

Opponents: West Indies..
At stake: England had won the first test thanks to Gooch's 154 not out, but had not won a series against the West Indies since 1969, moreover had lost every single one since 1973/74.
Bowling attack: Ambrose, Marshall, Walsh, Allen, Hooper: 25.85.
Pitch: Good.
Game situation: England 60 for 4 in response to the West Indies 419.

Planet Earth yet again was put under pressure. The world's population had swollen to 5.4 billion which had represented a doubling time of just 28 years. Indeed, at this precise moment one daily newspaper reported that there were more people alive in 1991 than had ever lived before, a quite astonishing fact given that homo sapiens had existed for somewhere between 125,000 and 250,000 years. Such a boom came with problems. Across in the Gulf, US and British forces had just forced Saddam Hussain's Iraqi army out from Kuwait and trouble was beginning to brew in Yugoslavia with Serbia controlling the Federal Army with atrocities and mass transmigration starting to emerge.

In England, after several fraught years in test cricket, something of a stir had taken place when Gooch won the first test against the West Indies at Headingley, indeed the first test victory at home against the West Indies since 1969. The West Indies, captained by the legendary Vivian Richards, were far from pleased. They turned up at Lord's hurt, angry and looking for revenge.

There is no greater sight in cricket than seeing batsmen, dressed like gladiators, face up to the onslaught from a battery of fast bowlers. The West Indies had a four-pronged pace attack, a strategy that had proved a successful, fertile ground that conquered the world for a decade and a half. Marshall, Ambrose and Walsh were as penetrating as any other West Indian pace attack in history, as 1,300 test scalps proved. Ian Allen completed the pace attack with Carl Hooper adding a touch of off spin to complete the line up.

England's batting had just crumbled against Australia the previous winter and despite David Gower scoring over 400 runs, including two centuries and top scoring for England no less than four times in the series, Gooch, the fitness freak, had conspired to drop the golden boy of English cricket.

Nonetheless England's batting line up looked pretty impressive: Gooch, Atherton, Hick, Lamb, Ramprakash and the South African born 27-year-old Robin Smith. In fact not since early 1975 had England fielded a batting line up that was to contain three batsmen who went on to achieve 100 hundreds in a first-class career. In Australia in 1975 England fielded Cowdrey, Amiss and Edrich whilst the side in the summer of 1991 fielded Gooch, Hick and Ramprakash. The difference was that whilst Cowdrey, Amiss and Edrich all had significant success for England by averaging in the 40s at test level, only Gooch was to achieve this from the hundred club in 1991.

Test cricket was no place for flat-track bullies in 1991. Possibly at no other time was test bowling so potent as in the early 1990s. Runs were hard to come by.

The West Indies won the toss at Lord's and batted through 120 overs for 419. Carl Hooper scored his first test century and there were 50s for Haynes, Richardson and Richards. Derek Pringle, now the cricket correspondent for the *Daily Telegraph*, took his third and last five-wicket haul for England.

In response, Ambrose, Walsh and Marshall tore in with rampant West Indian support from the stands. Atherton had his stumps shattered by Ambrose the 6ft 7ins giant, then Hick, trembling in fear, edged a rising delivery to Richardson in the gully. The score of 6–2 became 16–3 as Lamb, so often the stalwart against West Indian pace, snicked Marshall to slip. Ramprakash, just 21, and Gooch the veteran hero from the first test, held the tide at bay and slowly but surely England crawled their way out of trouble. Looking confident Gooch played over a Walsh Yorker and out into the Lord's arena strode the closest resemblance to a cricketing gladiator in England. Possessed with rippling forearms, a moustache and broad shoulders, a young man at the peak of his physical powers took guard. Quite a contrast in support was Ramprakash who throughout the series consumed so much West Indian energy yet never reached 30. This time, after 90 minutes and with the mood relaxed, as Allen, on his debut, bowled his first tentative overs at test level, Ramprakash edged to slip where Richards gleefully accepted the gift. At 84–5 England were teetering on the edge of an abyss.

Smith's finest hour arrived. In partnership with the obdurate, eccentric Jack Russell the left hand/right hand combination gradually drew the sting from the assault and runs were harvested with caution from both batsman. Get that ball older.

The hard graft bore fruit though with Richards finally giving way to spin, Russell edged behind to Dujon with England still 239 runs in first innings arrears. Only Pringle and the tail remained to keep Smith company.

Pringle, never an exciting player, was the first to be touted as the new Botham when first picked for Engand as early as 1982. Then he shocked the establishment by being the first England cricketer to have his ear pierced. Scholarly, of Felsted and Cambridge, the 32-year-old Pringle now settled in to play his role in the rearguard. The 200 passed with Smith patiently waiting for the bad ball, then punishing it when it came along. Soon after the 250 arrived Smith reached an impressive century. England rose to acknowledge the feat.

Pringle fell at 269-7. Could England reach 300? Phil 'Daffy' Defreitas played many a cameo for England and chose to take the attack to the now tiring pace quartet. In a stand of 47, Defreitas actually out scored Smith but fell to the second new ball for a fighting 29.

Smith decided to move up a gear with just Watkin and Malcolm left and dominated a helter-skelter ninth wicket stand of 37 priceless runs. The only shame was that when Malcolm was last out for no runs, bowled Ambrose, Smith was left high and dry on 148 not out, an imperious knock against the best attack on the planet in a desperate rearguard action.

This most absorbing of contests played out to full houses on the first three days only to be ruined by the weather. England grabbed a couple of early wickets to leave the West Indies on 12-2 but rain prevented a result. Only 25 minutes of the last two days saw any play. England 1-0 up after two tests and on to Trent Bridge.

Robin Smith rose to second in the world rankings after this resilient knock and Gooch, for a while, sat at the top. Smith had the most ferocious cut the game had ever seen. He batted in a brave, warrior-like manner and frequently became the target of bouncers from the opposition. He took blows to the body but rarely grimaced, just took it in his stride. Though Smith averaged over 50 for his first 52 innings, a feat that only Pietersen has accomplished for England since, Robin Smith never quite reached the same peak again.

West Indies 419 (Hooper 111, Pringle 5–100).
England 354 (Smith 148*, Ambrose 4–87).
West Indies 12–2.
MATCH DRAWN.

Innings Ranked Number 30
Shrewsbury's 164 at Lord's in 1886

Opponents: Australia.
At stake: Ashes held by England.
Bowling attack: Garrett, Evans, Palmer, Spofforth, Trumble, Giffen, Jones. Runs per wicket average: 24.05.
Pitch: Rain affected.
Game situation: England won the toss for this the second test in a three-test series and elected to bat. Shrewsbury entered with the score on 27 for 1.

In the year that Coca-Cola was invented and Gladstone's Irish Home Rule proposals led to his downfall, England and Australia were once again locked in battle, this time at the centre of cricket, Lord's.

Lord's still looked more rural than urban at the time. The ground was not ringed by stands as it is today, and the 'Grand Stand' as it was then known had a tiered corrugated iron roof more akin to an orderly shanty town. The view for the spectator beyond the cricket pitch was of mature trees and the occasional building in the distance a quite extraordinary difference considering the ground's relatively central location within London today. Close your eyes and the dominant noise during play, above the whispered chatter, was still horse and carts passing by beyond the ground. A different time which no one alive today is able to recall, when cricket was watched for the most part in fascinated silence, a stark contrast to the Mexican Waves that go on today.

Arthur Shrewsbury was in his prime, a 30-year-old who, if under pressure, the English fans would probably choose to bat for their lives rather than the great W. G. Grace.

England won the toss and A. G. Steel chose to bat. Within fifteen minutes of the start of play a heavy shower changed the character of the pitch and play was suspended for 90 minutes. W.G. fell just before lunch, caught by Jarvis the keeper, off the medium-paced off spin of Palmer. Grace had eighteen in a stand of twenty-seven with the stubborn, and actually quite painfully slow, Scotton for company.

With Grace, a veteran 38-year-old now back in the hutch, the man replacing him wore a cap to hide an obvious bald patch and walked out onto the Lord's turf purposefully. Shrewsbury, smaller and leaner in stature than W.G., rarely smiled. He bore the intense look of a bank clerk, or a young school master still learning his game. Sporting a modest moustache and wearing a dark belt around his trousers he epitomised the cricket fashion of the time. His gloves were the prickly sort and the pads looked frail. With sleeves rolled up to mean business Shrewsbury took guard and glanced around the field.

The pitch, spiteful from the rain, required the utmost concentration in order to survive. There followed an uneventful half-an-hour by modern standards but compulsive viewing to the Victorian crowd, like today a blend of society from all quarters, though more attuned to the game, quieter, more reflective, ultra focussed on the battle in the middle.

Shrewsbury prepared to face Spofforth who had surpised him with his variations of pace in the previous test. The 6ft 3ins 'Demon' (a name given after he had repeatedly humbled W.G. eight years previously) had slowed from out and out pace to a rich mixture without any apparent change in action. He came off a relatively short run and began once again to test Shrewsbury's defence. The ball spat off a length from his brisk medium, swerved through the air into the right hander and the odd one held up on the pitch.

Spofforth (his 94 test wickets came at a cost of only 18.41 and a first-class career stretching over 23 years for 893 victims at only 14.95) again varied his pace intelligently and with notable subtlety, but Shrewsbury was not to be out-thought a second time. He played everything straight with a broad bat, either going totally forward to the length balls or totally back to play the ball late. Occasionally his forward defence punctured the field and the batsmen scampered through for runs. With Scotton dormant at the other end, the crowd applauded every hard-fought run.

Spofforth glared down the wicket at Shrewsbury to unsettle him. To the bowler, raising the game's intensity through intimidation was an essential part of the theatre. Subsequently the Spofforth glare would become rooted in the game to be copied a million times by any paceman of fiery heart at any level.

Australia's bowling attack was more penetrative than any other bowling unit considered in this book, bar the one that Jessop tore apart in 1902, and the Australian attack of 1950/51. Penetration or potency of attack is calculated by this author as the average runs per wicket of the bowlers based on their final test-career average, weighted by their contribution to the innings.

So, in statistical terms, Shrewsbury faced a battery of devilish bowlers more penetrative than the 1980 West Indians, on a rain-affected strip prepared without proper technology. Of course the Australians in 1886 did not have an express-pace bowler, but then what is worse: being hit on the helmet by a 90 mph bowler once during an innings, or being peppered several times by 75 mph deliveries without a helmet on a pitch of irregular bounce?

These were the days of poorly-prepared wickets, where no player was to finish with a career-batting average of over 40, the crucial benchmark for all specialist batsmen today.

In George Palmer (78 test wickets at 21.51), Australia had one of the best medium-quick off spinners in the world. They also had Hugh Trumble perhaps the very finest off-break bowler in history (141 at 21.78), who delivered the ball from a high arm to generate extra bounce.

Despite the Australian attack fielding such an awesome trio, it was the understated and durable Tom Garrett (36 wickets at 26.94) who broke through with a fast medium right-arm delivery to bowl Scotton for 19 with the score on 77.

Out strode the 31-year-old former school teacher Walter Read, rather a feisty character, unafraid to challenge authority. Dismissive of Scotton's limpet innings, Read immediately lashed out at the bowling to draw a brief period of frenzied excitement from the patient crowd. Read, eyeing up George Giffen's friendly-looking slow medium, tossed his wicket away for 22, and when A. G. Steel, the skipper, walked in front of a Spofforth break-back England teetered on 119–4.

Billy Barnes partnered the now settled Shrewsbury. If Shrewsbury was the Boycott of his day, then Billy Barnes was Botham, a strapping 35-year-old who gave the ball a good biff, particularly on the off side, and bowled intelligent medium pace. Barnes, a strong, robust man stood over 6ft and liked a drink. On this day he was to curb his natural aggression and prove what a fine all-round cricketer he had become.

The Nottinghamshire pair fought tooth and nail for survival, yet both put away the bad ball as the pitch mellowed in the late afternoon sunshine. Four-ball overs meant a lot of time wasted but by the close and despite the 90 minutes lost before lunch Shrewsbury and Barnes had taken England to 202-4.

Shrewsbury sank into a chair in the dressing room and ordered a large cup of tea. He loved his tea supping it whilst 91 not out, and within range of a second test century, on a rain-affected pitch at that, brought a warm satisfied smile. Not even the great W.G. had scored a second test century. Tomorrow, 20 July 1886, could become the defining moment in his career.

Next morning Shrewsbury squinted as the sun beamed into his bedroom. He would start cautiously, survive on the most impermeable defence in world cricket, and slowly but surely creep towards the landmark second century. From there he would open his shoulders and stake a claim on the Doctor's record Ashes score for an Englishman of 152.

As it happened both Shrewsbury and Barnes played positive cricket from the off and soon Shrewsbury raised his bat for the coveted 100. Then the crowd drew applause for the 250 total. There was applause too for the fighting half-century from Barnes and all before lunch.

At 280 Barnes fell, but there followed useful stands of 23 with the obdurate Richard Barlow and 30 with the big hitting George Ulyett, veteran of the very first test match back in 1877. It was during this entertaining stand with Ulyett that Shrewsbury broke the record England score to a rapturous reception from the knowledgeable Lord's crowd. The tail started tumbling away though and at 340-9 square-shouldered George Lohmann arrived at the wicket.

From here on both batsmen chanced their arm, struck a couple of blows before Shrewsbury fell caught in the outfield for 164. England totalled 353 with a wicket that for the most part was 'impossible' to bat on.

There are a few quotes about Shrewsbury's innings, a master piece of concentration over 411 minutes. He gave perhaps three difficult chances in an innings which rightfully remains as one of the great sticky-wicket innings ever played by an Englishman, an inspiration to future generations most notably Jack Hobbs.

According to *Wisden*, 'Too much praise cannot be afforded him for his extraordinary performance.' Plum Warner, a 13-year-old at the time, claimed Shrewsbury's knock was 'one of the masterpieces of the art of batting under conditions favourable to the bowlers.'

In all Shrewsbury hit sixteen fours, eight threes, sixteen twos and forty-four singles.

The Australians then batted in a feeble manner, causing something of an anti-climax. England's fielding was excellent, but the main hero here was Johnny Briggs a 24-year-old Lancastrian who delivered puzzling slow left-arm in the mould of Rhodes, Underwood and Panesar.

The Australians batted with extreme caution under bright sunshine and gathered their runs at an equivalent rate of just 1.36 per six-ball over. England went on to win by an innings and 106 runs to retain the Ashes.

In the final test at the Oval, England won by an even larger margin of an innings and 217 runs. The dominant feature of England's innings here was W.G. Grace. As a flat-track bully, Grace smashed 24 boundaries to eclipse Shrewsbury's record score. In all Grace scored 170 made out of 216 whilst at the wicket, an extraordinary performance, compiled on a perfect pitch for the time and against a now disgruntled Australian team.

Word has it that the 1886 Australians were a far from happy bunch, with some stories indicating violent rows emerging on train journeys between fixtures.

For several years afterwards, Shrewsbury wilted as a star but W.G. Grace, appointed captain for the 1893 home series remembered Arthur's innings at Lord's in 1886. He declared 'Give me Arthur' when asked to pick the team, despite Shrewsbury scarcely scoring a run in the 1890 series. Shrewsbury did not disappoint and with scores of 106, 81 and 66 did much to retain the Ashes. He became the first to score three test centuries for England and in 1902, at the age of 46, he finished top of the Nottinghamshire batting averages.

In the last game of that wonderful season Shrewsbury complained of kidney pains. No one thought any more of it at the time and during the winter Shrewsbury moved into a house with his girlfriend Gertrude Scott. He purchased a revolver at a local gunsmith and returned a week later to the same place concerned that the gun was faulty. The attendant duly explained that he had miss-fitting bullets and supplied Shrewsbury with the right ones.

That evening the legendary batsman walked up the stairs and asked Gertrude for a cup of cocoa. Then a loud noise came from upstairs and Gertrude shouted out. Another louder bang resonated around the house. When she burst open the bedroom door

Shrewsbury lay mortally wounded from a bullet to the head. He had tried to shoot himself through the body – the first bang – but that failed so he summoned the last vestiges of strength to fire a bullet through his head. He died, but not immediately, a truly shocking end. No note was written, but there was the typical meticulous planning evident with the recent drawing up of a new will and the statement he'd idly said to Gertrude earlier in the day, 'I'll be in the graveyard before long!'

England 353 (Shrewsbury 164, W. Barnes 58, Spofforth 4–73).
Australia 121 (Briggs 5–29, W. Barnes 3–25) and 126 (Briggs 6–45).
ENGLAND WON BY AN INNINGS AND 106 RUNS.

Innings Ranked Number 29
Hutton's 364 at the Oval in 1938

Opponents: Australia.
At stake: Squaring the series, Australia already had the Ashes as they were leading the series 1–0 (having retained the Ashes in the last series in 1936/37) with just one to play.
Bowling attack: Waite, McCabe, Fleetwood–Smith, O'Reilly, Barnes, Hassett, Bradman: Runs per wickets 71+ due to Waite bowling 72 overs and having a test bowling average of 190. This provided too much of a distortion so a new average was calculated with Waite's overs at a new lower value of 50. This has been adjusted to allow Hutton's mammoth innings an entry into the top 50.
Pitch: Featherbed.
Game situation: England won the toss and elected to bat first.

By a peculiar coincidence, on the day Sydney Wooderson ran a mile-and-a-half in the shortest-ever time, so Len Hutton, a 22-year-old Yorkshireman, began the longest and highest individual test-match innings ever played by an Englishman.

In England our cities expanded and housewives suffered from a peculiar condition known as 'suburban neurosis'. Experts claimed that this was due to wives being left at home all day with not enough housework to keep them occupied. They obviously spent too much time thinking and not enough time worrying.

For English gentlemen, the 1938 Ashes had once again disappointed, with Australia winning the fourth test so retaining the urn. Both attacks lacked real fire-power but the Headingley test at least provided a sporting, damp wicket. Up until then England could claim to have had the better of the first two drawn tests with the third at Old Trafford abandoned due to rain without a single ball being bowled.

However at Headingley, Hammond's 76 was eclipsed by Bradman's 102 in a low-scoring encounter that saw Australia home by five wickets with O'Reilly capturing ten wickets in the game for the third time in this series. Hutton was not playing, having broken his finger in a county game. He had picked up a hundred at Trent Bridge but failed twice at Lord's.

This was the summer of three England wicket-keepers: Ames, Price and Wood. Wood came in for Price for the fifth test at the Oval and Hutton returned in place of Barnett, whilst Maurice Leyland took Doug Wright's place, as England strengthened her batting in the wake of the Headingley disaster. Many felt Barnett had been harshly treated. Wa it not just three tests earlier that Barnett had started proceedings with a fine 126? In fact 98 came from Barnett's blade before lunch on the first day of the 1938 Ashes battle. Still Bill Edrich held on to his place despite just 55 runs in five innings. Edrich could bowl much like Collingwood today – that was his advantage.

The pitch looked devoid of any demons, just a flat, easy-paced surface that had been rolled and rolled again. 'Bosser' Martin, the heavily-moustachioed chief groundsman had seen to that. His was the best wicket in the country and not Trent Bridge, as was rumoured after the run glut in the first test. Whoever won the toss was bound to bat. This was to be a timeless test and 'Bosser' announced that the pitch would last until Christmas. News spread that McCormick, the Australian spearhead was suffering from a neurosis so wouldn't play. Only O'Reilly and Fleetwood–Smith remained as a threat but on such a docile track, even they would suffer if asked to bowl first. Bradman called incorrectly yet again and Hammond elected to bat first.

Len Hutton remains the last great England opening batsman to average over 50 in tests. At the Oval in 1938 Hutton broke all records in arguably the most famous England innings of all time.

'Ready' asked Bill Edrich. Hutton had to buckle his pads taking care not to use the broken middle finger. 'Ready' replied Hutton. So it was that at 11.25 a.m. on the sunny morning of 20 August 1938, that Edrich and Hutton walked out to bat for England, to start the most famous test innings played by any Englishman up to that time. As they entered the arena, the pitch glinted in the sun, an immaculate cut strip of velvet. No fast bowler, just an all-rounder in Waite partnered with Stan McCabe, a specialist batsman, called upon to bowl a few overs to see whether there was any swing. The first over from Waite was a maiden to Hutton. McCabe duly bowled the second and Edrich nudged the last delivery wide of mid-on for a single. Noting that the ball came through at a comfortable height, McCabe told Frank Chester the umpire that England would get a thousand.

There was no electric atmosphere that normally accompanies the start of a test match, no spearhead to set the spectators on the edge of their seats and the ground was only half full. Thousands of other potential spectators turned their backs on the ground assuming the place would be full.

The opening bowling was accurate and made both batsmen play at a majority of the deliveries. After a quarter-of-an-hour only seven runs had been added, then in McCabe's fourth over, Hutton leg glanced for a single, Edrich repeated the shot next ball and the misfield resulted in three. Next ball, Hutton perfectly late cut wide of second slip for the day's first boundary.

With twenty on the board Bradman brought on his main weapon, O'Reilly, a tall, balding man with the fire-and-brimstone mentality of a strict school master. Bill O'Reilly, known as 'Tiger' because of his fiery exterior, was the number-one bowler on the planet with 130 test wickets at the time for just twenty-two apiece. He bowled quick leg breaks, googlies and almost every delivery extracted more bounce than expected. Take runs off O'Reilly and batsmen could grin at the exasperated bowler seemingly tearing his hair out in annoyance, and so the key battle commenced.

The crowd could barely believe it as Hutton slogged the first ball just over wide mid-on, an extraordinary shot and the batsmen ran two Understanding came with the umpire signalling a no ball. Hutton sensed O'Reilly furious at himself. Next ball would be quicker, Hutton knew this and glanced the next delivery sweetly for four. Test series allow time for opponents to size each other up and untangle one another's mysteries. Hutton had O'Reilly from the start. Despite two short legs in place, Hutton defended with his left hand clenched deliberately harder on the bat than the right hand.

Edrich was enduring a wretched run and on this most perfect of pitches, against an attack no greater than medium pace, in a timeless atmosphere, he failed yet again. He had been dismissed by O'Reilly six times that summer. O'Reilly's rabbit prepared to face his nemesis. The bowler moved in with his long, lumbering run-up, a whirl of arms and then a straight, rhythmical release. Edrich saw it, went back when he realised he should have gone forward, and the ball spat off a length and rapped Edrich on the pads. England 29–1 off twelve overs. Not the start Hammond necessarily wanted.

Hutton assumed Hardstaff would come in next, however down the pavilion steps sauntered the familiar figure of Maurice Leyland, cap slanted, square body-shape and massive Yorkshire forearms. Hutton's favourite partner, the two often batted together for Yorkshire.

Amusingly O'Reilly's first ball to Leyland was once again a no ball and Leyland flung his bat wildly to send the ball up, up in the air and over the fuming bowler's head. The batsmen ran two. Next ball again as predicted O'Reilly bowled as quick as possible a short of a length delivery that bounced up alarmingly. Leyland swayed out of the way but the ball touched the peak of the cap only to send it agonisingly close to the stumps. It wasn't O'Reilly's day.

Bradman shuffled his bowlers around constantly. Waite, the medium-pacer, bowled around the wicket to offer variation but to no avail, Hutton and Leyland settled in and began to play wholly within the comfort zone. Lunch came with the score on 80–1, with Hutton on 39 not out.

At lunch time Hutton distanced himself from the team in order to collect his thoughts. He had no time for friendships with the Australians, not because of any obvious flaws in Australian personalities. Hutton did not believe that fraternising with the opponents was the done thing. It would not improve his game.

The afternoon session saw the introduction of Sydney Barnes's leg spin. Barnes was a net bowler who happened to drop the ball on a length from time to time. He had not bowled a single delivery on the tour to date.

Both batsmen could have been stumped off O'Reilly. Hutton was on 40 just after lunch and Leyland an hour later on 60. In fact twice Leyland heaved across the line and was bowled by O'Reilly, on each occasion the crowd gasped before realising the no-ball call. It is testimony to O'Reilly (though no-balling was his Achilles heel on the day) that neither batsman was able to score a boundary off them. Bradman set defensive fields and waited for the batsmen to lose concentration. His fielders were the best unit around.

In the last hour before tea, both batsmen neared their hundreds. Leyland, bold and provocative, danced down the wicket and drove with magnificent authority against both O'Reilly and Fleetwood–Smith. Hutton, apart from the one blemish, preferred to stay in his crease. By now Hutton's stroke-play could not be curbed. An off drive and a hit to leg took Hutton to his second hundred against Australia, and with it, England's 200. His century took $3^1/2$ hours. Bradman immediately took the new ball but even though cloud had moved in, the ball steadfastly refused to swing. Leyland clattered a half volley through mid-off in imperious fashion to reach his seventh test century against the old enemy, equal with Sutcliffe.

Bradman soon reverted back to O'Reilly and Fleetwood–Smith then, mercifully for Bradman, tea was taken. A short, sharp shower added sparkle to the wicket but only briefly. Hutton got hit on the knuckles from O'Reilly's faster ball and Leyland had to sway from a Waite bouncer.

Hutton continued to garner the bulk of his runs through the off-side. Repeatedly he off-drove the full length balls then cut the shorter ones, then as the bowlers veered to leg, Hutton glanced to fine leg. Occasionally Hutton lofted over mid on – on one occasion Hutton saw Hammond waving him down from the pavilion balcony. Hammond had a point, having sat all day in his pads the last thing Hammond wanted was to bat in murky light at the end of the day.

The mistake Bradman had hoped for came just before stumps. Leyland played a ball from Waite firmly into the covers and ran. Hutton made his ground but Badcock had predicted this, ran in and threw the ball to the bowler's end. Waite, with time to spare, stumbled onto the stumps before dislodging the bails, not out.

Reilly and Fleetwood–Smith, tired but still accurate, bowled through until close with England reaching 347–1. Hutton was not out 160 and Leyland, close to catching up on 156.

Next day unusually was a rest day. Hutton, Verity and other Yorkshire friends took a day to Bognor where they played beach cricket unnoticed in front of a large crowd of holidaymakers.

Monday morning, Hutton netted early to set himself up for another day. A heavy shower held back play for 35 minutes and the temperature was cooler, fresher but by 12.05 the sun shone brilliantly again. Leyland cut Fleetwood–Smith for two and a one, then in O'Reilly's first over Leyland stroked a two off his legs to equal the highest-wicket partnership for England in tests. A full toss from Fleetwood–Smith's first ball of his second over was stroked to the mid-off boundary by Hutton, a huge roar from the knowledgeable crowd echoed around the ground.

Once again the bowling was spot on, but the pitch was so flat the score cruised along at a run a minute. Leyland overtook Hutton. A thumping drive took the total beyond 400. On they went, then the first misfield since the eighth over of the first day saw Hassett fumble a rocket, driven this time by Hutton. Leyland called a second but Hassett chased the ball down, turned and threw at the non-striker's end. Bradman, in brilliant anticipation, took the ball and whipped the bails off with Leyland still out of his ground. Remember the saying about never running on a miss-field. So, Leyland trudged back to his team mates clapping from the pavilion with the score on 411–2. Together these Yorkshiremen, one youthful the other a veteran, had accumulated 382.

Hammond still wanted a team total of at least 600, especially considering the state of the pitch and the Bradman factor. Bradman delayed the new ball until after lunch and fed Hammond a diet of Fleetwood–Smith's spin, not a great option. Hammond had attacked Fleetwood–Smith out of test cricket in the bodyline series of 1932/33. This time he took twelve from Fleetwood–Smith's first over and lunched on twenty not out, with England 434–2 and Hutton not out 191.

Hammond and Hutton struggled to get going after lunch and the crowd sat back in soporific mood. Gradually the score ticked over, despite Fleetwood–Smith pegging both batsmen back with sharper spin. Against this Hammond thrashed a beautiful cover drive that left Bradman standing to reach his last 50 against Australia. With the score on 546 Fleetwood–Smith deceived Hammond with a leg break that kicked back into his pads, adjudged LBW for 59, the stand worth 135. By now Hutton had broken Hammond's record, set eight weeks earlier, of the highest England innings against Australia at home, 240.

Payntor walked out under a cloudy, grey sky. The murky light proved too much as Payntor soon stabbed down too late on an O'Reilly googly, misreading it for a leg break, Payntor LBW for no runs. Compton survived until tea when a sudden downpour hit the ground. It was over quickly, but after tea the black skies and Waite running in out from the pavilion gloom sent down an invisible ball that Compton played over the top of. In England's highest ever innings, there was a collapse of three wickets for nine runs. England teetered on 555–5. Enter Hardstaff.

Hardstaff was no slouch with the bat and, like Hutton, his best years were to be terminated by Hitler. Today he batted with real class. As the last specialist England batsman it was vital that he reinvigorate an exhausted Hutton and push the score along briskly so that Hutton didn't feel the need to play recklessly. On Hutton batted and at 280 a snick off O'Reilly fell perilously close to Bradman at slip. Hutton hung his head in shame. Hardstaff roused him between overs and a huge cheer from the knowledgeable crowd kept him going as he passed R.E. Foster's 34-year-old record England Ashes score of 287. Just before close, Hutton nudged a single and brought up his 300. England closed on 634–5, Hardstaff 40 not out, Hutton not out 300.

Two days of batting, interrupted only by a short shower and the loss of 50 minutes, had taken its toll on Hutton. He sank into a chair and, although unaccustomed to drinking alcohol, sank a port and Guinness at the bequest of his friend Hedley Verity. Hutton relaxed yet through the night could not sleep. In his mind he played back O'Reilly and Fleetwood–Smith.

A huge cheer on the third day greeted the two not-out batsmen from a capacity 30,000 Oval crowd. Hutton's first run of the day was greeted with cheers normally reserved for hundreds. Hardstaff set the pace, playing his part to perfection. Soon the hundred partnership came up as the crowd sensed that Bradman's record was within reach. Eight years earlier Bradman had scored 334 at Headingley, the highest Ashes score ever.

Bradman typically started the day with both spinners and Hutton especially faced difficulties against Fleetwood–Smith, being rapped on the pad a couple of times as well as playing and missing outside the off stump. The crowd thanked God when some of the overs were finished. By now Hutton had lost half a stone in weight since the start of his innings. He crept up towards Bradman's score with a couple of fine late cuts that whistled to the boundary.

Bradman tried everything, the new ball with Waite and McCabe but this only served to increase the run rate. For his spinners Bradman brought in three fielders in a leg trap, himself at forward short-leg. Hutton looked puny amongst the larger Australians, Bradman excluded. A full-toss hit through mid off just crossed over the ropes and completed the 100 partnership. Soon after Hutton edged O'Reilly to slip, perfectly pouchable to first slip except there was no slip. Every run Hutton scored was now greeted in silence as though any loud noise might disturb his concentration. After the first hour, England had taken their total to 694–5; 60 had been added with Hardstaff's share 37 compared to Hutton's 21.

Then, with Hutton on 326, Bradman recalled O'Reilly one final time. All fielders except a deep cover were brought in to save the single. Hutton would have to force his way to the record. Now there was an electric buzz in the atmosphere, the 700 went almost unnoticed as the crowd shared Hutton's concentration.

A loud appeal from Fleetwood–Smith as Hutton failed to detect the flight of the ball saw the ball bounce abruptly into Hutton's pads, not out, too high. Two further dots then the fourth ball pitched on leg, turned into the stumps and rapped Hutton on the pad right in front. A huge appeal and 30,000 eyes converged on Frank Chester the umpire. Chester had detected a faint edge and Hutton was saved.

In each of the next three overs Hutton scraped a single to take his score to 331. As O'Reilly came up, all of Hutton's home town of Pudsey was glued to the radio. The Australian delivered a ball Hutton read as a googly, it was short of a length but straight. Hutton moved back to square leg, gave himself room and cut the ball with the most juicy sound possible. As the ball sped through point for four the crowd erupted, throwing hats, papers, scorecards and cushions in the air as though a tornado had struck. Bradman walked over and shook Hutton's hand.

With the pressure eased, everything from this point on became an anticlimax. Hutton took his total to 364 and the score to 770 before hoisting O'Reilly to Hassett. He had batted in all for thirteen hours and twenty minutes.

Hardstaff went on to 169 not out before Hammond declared on 903–7. Bradman had put himself on with the score on 798 to give his bowlers a rest. Unfortunately he tripped in the scuff marks of the bowlers' boots, broke an ankle bone and had to be carried off.

Exhausted from $3^1/2$ days in the field, the Australians followed on 702 runs behind and folded meekly in the second innings, all out for just 123. The margin of victory, by an innings and 579 runs remains the single, largest test-victory by any country, ever.

England 903–7 declared (Hutton 364, Leyland 187, Hardstaff jr 169*, Hammond 59, Wood 53, O'Reilly 3–178).
Australia 201 (Brown 69, Bowes 5–49) and 123 (Farnes 4–63).
ENGLAND WON BY AN INNINGS AND 579 RUNS.

Innings Ranked Number 28
Compton's 145 not out at Old Trafford in 1948

Opponents: Australia.
At stake: Ashes.
Bowling attack: Lindwall, Johnston, Loxton, Toshack, Johnson.
Average runs per wicket: 24.99.
Pitch: Fair.
Game situation: England, 2–0 down against the strongest team of all time, won the toss and elected to bat first.

Bradman's 1948 Australians are commonly regarded as the greatest team of all time. It is possible that the 1984 West Indians and 2007 Australians were just as good. Without a shadow of doubt the 1948 team had everything a properly-balanced team should have, including a couple of express bowlers in Miller and Lindwall and the great Don Bradman.

England had lost the first two test matches having been outplayed in all departments. Compton had scored a truly memorable 184 that almost allowed England to escape in the first test but, other than that, England had been humiliated. For this test, owing to growing problems against extreme pace, the selectors dropped Len Hutton for the only time in his career. Blame his astonishingly bad knock at Lord's. He kept slashing at bumpers until dismissed, as if desperately trying to get out. Nevertheless, dropping Hutton caused a national sensation, an outrage, and in came George Emmett, a small, slight 36-year-old, to play in what turned out to be his only test.

Let us pause for reflection on Denis Compton. At the time E. W. Swanton had this to say: 'Since Hobbs, and with all possible respect of the greatness of Hammond, we have never seen an England batsman so thoroughly equipped for every sort of situation on every sort of pitch.' In the immediate post-war years Compton reached heights that no Englishman had ever reached before. In 1947 he scored 22 centuries, four in succession in Australia (including two in the fourth test at Adelaide) followed by eighteen in the English summer of 1947. Though starting to become plagued by a knee injury, Compton carried England's hopes and aspirations. It was the way Compton could cope, more conspicuously than any other Englishman, with the frightening pace of Lindwall and Miller that places his name so high up in the pantheon of great English batsmen.

England won the toss and Norman Yardley elected to bat first. 35,000 crowded into Old Trafford and, although the sun was out, the wicket was tinged with green. Twenty-two runs were added in the first half-an-hour as Lindwall and Johnston opened up and found their rhythm. Then Washbrook, having reached double figures, drove and missed at a full toss, swinging in late from leg to off. Six runs later, Emmett fended of a bouncing bomb from Lindwall with his hand in front of his face. He had not adjusted to extreme pace that well all morning, and Barnes caught it standing just three yards from the batsman.

Compton arrived at 28–2. With him was his Middlesex colleague Bill Edrich struggling for form with just 38 runs from four innings in the series to date. Compton immediately looked comfortable although inwardly cursed the fact that Barnes standing so close could be seen in his line of vision whilst the bowler came in to bowl and Edrich settled in stubbornly, protecting his wicket at all costs.

Then Lindwall sent down a bouncer at lightening speed, the umpire called a no ball and Compton shaped to hook down to long leg. Too slow on the shot the ball hit Compton firmly on the forehead and rebounded half way to the boundary rope before landing. Compton staggered away from the wicket towards point, clutching his forehead with both hands. Blood flowed onto his gloves as he was led away. The crowd grew hostile, even Bill O'Reilly the former Australian cricketer turned journalist, had this to write: '… the only difference I could see between our bowling and that of Jardine's team [England captain during the infamous bodyline series of 1932/33] was the disposition of the field.'

The sun that had shone brightly for the first hour now hid behind a blanket of cloud and a chill wind blew across the ground. Jack Crapp, fresh from a century for Gloucestershire against the Australians earlier that week, now came out for his debut innings. Both Crapp and Edrich struggled until lunch to take the score to 57–2.

Edrich had fourteen from an hour-and-a-half, Crapp eleven from an hour.

The pressure eased a fraction in the afternoon and Crapp played some decent shots, including a straight six off Johnson. Edrich hung in grimly accumulating runs at a trickle. Pre-war tests had a rule that a new ball was taken after 200 runs, post-war it was after 55 overs. Lindwall started marking his run up with the score on 87–2, a run rate of not quite 1.6 an over.

Nine runs later, Crapp, the left-handed Cornishman, had 37 before shouldering arms to a ball that swung in and panged against his pads. At this point Compton wanted to return to the fray, but Yardley the captain would not have it. Under instructions Compton netted against Pollard and Young, whilst Dollery entered and soon played over a Johnston Yorker.

After half-an-hour, Compton's turn came. Edrich made a laboured, almost tortuous 32 before edging Lindwall to Tallon behind. Crucially, by lasting 190 minutes, Edrich bought sufficient time for Compton to receive a couple of stitches to the forehead and a net.

Out strode Compton with a white plaster over his left eye in front of 35,000 applauding fans. The emotional applause lasted all the way to the wicket. Compton immediately felt confident and his partner Yardley looked more at ease than any of the others. There followed a rational period of play lasting until tea.

Soon after, Yardley played an ill-executed stroke that lobbed to mid-wicket. England were 141–6 and being outgunned badly, only Compton stood in the way. Evans, the plucky Kent wicket-keeper, capered out to the middle and played as he tended to, in a jolly, entertaining manner. He threw the bat at the ball in a manner no self-respecting batsman would dare. Some shots came off in a resounding manner, whilst others flew over the slips or were edged down to long leg. Meanwhile Compton, taking advantage of this relaxed period, reached his 50 as the scoreboard clicked along at a run a minute. He had started his innings at 12.15 that morning and it was now 5.40, a lot had happened to him in the intervening time.

Evans fell for 34 with the score on 216; thankfully England had saved face. At the close Bedser, four not out, and Compton, 64 not out, had taken the score to 231–7. With luck England might reach 300 on the second day and save the series. Tallon, the keeper, put down a couple of very hard chances and at the end of the day his palms were tender owing to the Lindwall barrage of bumpers earlier in the day. As for Compton, he retired with a splitting headache.

Next day under a cool, overcast sky and in front of a 30,000 crowd, Compton and Bedser went out to resume their innings. As predicted, Lindwall and Johnston opened. The first eight overs yielded only ten runs but the pace of the wicket had died somewhat and in any case Lindwall had lost some of his searing pace from the first day.

When Toshack replaced Lindwall Compton sniffed a weakness, an opening and at once drove him for two splendid fours through extra cover and a two to take his score to 84. Bradman at once replaced Toshack with Lindwall but only for an over. Twice Bedser snicked Lindwall over the slips for four and the crowd inhaled as one then Toshack was brought back.

The field now was set deep for Compton to encourage a single and a go at Bedser. Bedser played his part well and although troubled by Johnson's off breaks, carted him for four to leg then an edged boundary off Toshack took Bedser into the thirties. For a while Compton had to make do with singles and his score edged up to 97. Bradman brought back Johnston and set an attacking field. 'Pitch it up, bowl it straight and allow the swing to do the rest,' instructed Bradman.

Johnson knew his role and ran in to bowl left-arm medium quick, akin to Ryan Sidebottom. A nice full-length delivery swerved into Compton's pads. The crowd frenzy reached a peak as the dazzling genius Compton responded by driving passed mid-on for four His century neatly coincided with England's 300 to tumultuous acclaim. How the crowd roared their approval for the bandaged hero as Compton raised his bat to soak up the applause. Considering England were 119–5 twenty minutes before tea on the first day, this represented a superb rearguard.

Lindwall's over just before lunch was as hostile as could be and three times Compton was beaten and morally bowled. First ball after lunch, Compton drove Lindwall sweetly through mid-on, then he cut him to the third man boundary. Next over, Compton late cut Johnston for another four.

All was going well then Compton, as he was apt to do, called Bedser for a single from a tap into the covers. There was a mix up between Loxton and Bradman, both fielders collided. Bedser, back to Compton at the non-striker's end, had not heard the call or seen Compton charging to the bowler's end. Bedser grimly set off only to be run out by yards for 37. The stand of 121 thus was denied the distinction of being the highest eighth wicket stand for England against Australia.

Pollard received a thunderous applause from his home crowd. Again the field was set to give Compton the single. Pollard, off Johnson, connected with a typical tail-ender's pulled drive. The ball smacked meatily into short leg's midriff and poor Barnes slumped to the ground in agony. After several minutes three policemen came on and carried him off.

Pollard fell for eleven with the score at 352 and England were finally dismissed for 363. Most of the last 25 runs came from Compton's bat. At the end he was undefeated on 145 not out, compiled in 320 minutes. Compton carried the side's responsibilities and earned huge admiration for the way he tackled the pace bowling. Like a gladiator, Compton showed no fear as he alone mastered the bowlers.

Australia failed to ignite with the bat for the only time in the series and were dismissed for 221, Bedser taking 4–81. England responded well with Washbrook 85 not out and Bill Edrich a fighting 53. England declared at 174–3 but the rain came on Monday to deprive England of a victory.

Australia went on to win at both Headingley, set 404 to win, and the Oval, where England were dismissed for just 52 and 188. Compton scored a then Ashes home record of 562 runs in the series.

Compton continued to thrill crowds for the best part of a decade, but his genius waned as the knee cap had to be removed. Nonetheless it did not stop the selectors bringing Compton back, minus knee cap, at the age of 38 for the 1956 Oval Test where he scored 94 and 35 not out.

Denis Compton remains the last great England player to average over 50 for both test and all first-class cricket matches. The others were Hobbs, Hammond, Sutcliffe, and Hutton. No one though made their runs in a more entertaining manner. His 145 not out would have been ranked even higher had Compton not given three chances, albeit difficult, to Don Tallon behind the stumps. Nevertheless, and with the greatest respect to Eddie Paynter and Colin Cowdrey, this was the most courageous innings ever played by an Englishman.

England 363 (Compton 145*, Lindwall 4–99, Johnston 3–67).
Australia 221 (Morris 51, Bedser 4–81, Pollard 3–53).
England 174–3 declared (Washbrook 85*, W. J. Edrich 53).
Australia 92–1 (Morris 54*).
MATCH DRAWN.

Innings Ranked Number 27
Ranjitsinjhi's 154 not out at Old Trafford in 1896

Opponents:Australia.
At stake: Ashes.
Bowling attack:Jones, Trott, Giffen, Trumble, McKibbin: Bowling runs per wicket 26.85.
Pitch: Fine.
Game situation: England followed on 181 runs behind. When Ranjitsinjhi came out to bat in the seond innings England were 33–1 with the fall of W. G. Grace, still 148 runs behind.

This test took place just a month before the first 'flicker' was produced for a mass audience, the first moving cinematic picture. In Britain, the first such place that produced 'flickers' was, by coincidence the same town as Kumar Ranjitsinhi's home cricket ground, Hove. Whether Ranji had gas electricity supplied to his home is a matter for conjecture. At any rate some 300,000 households in Britain did, but few away from the main urban areas.

F. S. Jackson is accredited with being the first person of influence to spot Ranji's extraordinary emerging talent. He stumbled across a game at Parker's Pitch in Cambridge *circa* 1893. There he noticed an Indian batsman that executed cover drives and cuts with text book precision. Jackson noticed too a rare trait among batsmen. Ranjitsinjhi produced a new stroke, using the pace of the ball and with fine wrist action, straight, good-length deliveries were flicked down to long leg off middle stump. No one prior to Ranjitsinjhi ever had the facility to perform this shot with such precision and skill, time and time again.

Ranji had begun to cause a stir. He played for Cambridge alongside F. S.Jackson for the remainder of the season. It was not long before Ranji made his debut for Sussex against the MCC. Here Ranji announced his true class with 77 and 150. Then, in July 1896, he made his debut for England alongside a vintage line up that included W. G. Grace in the autumn of his cricketing years, A. E. Stoddart, R. Abel, F. S. Jackson, J. T. Brown and Archie MacLaren.

Australia won the toss and elected to bat. At one point Australia had reached 294–3 but fell away at close on the first day to be 366–8. On the second day, Australia amassed an impressive 412 with only Tom Richardson, the spearhead of England's attack, performing to his best. Richardson claimed 7–168 in the equivalent of 54.4 six-ball overs, a remarkable feat from the black-haired, black-moustached gypsy look-alike.

The bowling attack that Ranji faced on his test debut was of a commendably high standard, sandwiched between that which Watson and Bailey batted through at Lord's in 1953, and the slightly better South African attack which Alec Stewart batted through to help earn a draw in 1998.

England fell away in reply, but fifties from Kumar Ranjitsinjhi on his debut and Arthur Lilley in only his second test, saved England from total humiliation. Nonetheless, 231 ensured England had to follow on 181 runs behind (rules at the time allowed a follow on if the side batting second were 150 or more runs behind, rather than the 200 today).

England soon lost the 48-year old W.G. for his third failure in four innings. At this point Ranjitsinjhi entered the arena. He was fortunate to be ably partnered by Stoddart initially before the latter fell, bowled McKibben for 41, with the score at 76. George Giffen then claimed Robert Abel to leave England shaking at 97–3. When Jackson fell, again off Giffen, for just one run, England were haemorrhaging towards an innings defeat at 109–4. Ranjitsijhi and J. T. Brown held firm until the close on day two, Ranji not out 41.

The morning of 18 July witnessed one of the most thrilling innings of all time. In a sinking ship, Ranji opened up with some spectacular shots, most notable were the hooks off Jones's thunderbolts, the classic square cuts and gentle leg glances off the stumps that hinted at wizardry. Brown was soon dismissed at 132–5 with England still 49 in deficit. Ranji chose to die by the sword flashing in a blaze of glory. He outscored MacLaren and all subsequent partners and for a while had the Australian bowlers quite at his mercy. Though attendance was low due to the hopelessness of England's situation, at the end of day two England were still 72 behind with only six wickets left. Those present behaved in high-pitched excitement at the marvellous display of shot execution.

In the period before lunch, Ranji swished his bat like a cane to advance his score from 41 to 154 not out. *Wisden* states that 'it is fair to say that a finer or more finished display has never been seen on a great occasion.' Ranji played a chanceless innings and one where a couple of snicks represented the only minor errors.

After a promising 36-run partnership for the eighth wicket, Briggs, rather foolishly under the circumstances, advanced out of his crease to the off-spin 'Chucker' Thomas McKibbin. Briggs missed and got stumped. Hearne put on another 36 for the ninth wicket of which his contribution was nine Richardson fell for one, so England lunched at the point where Ranji ran out of partners.

He had ensured that Australia would have to bat again. In the end a target of 124 proved very challenging, with Australia at times 28–3 and 100–7. Richardson again was superb with 6–76 to make 13 in the match for 244.

It was not to be. Australia crawled home by three wickets to level the series one all with one test to play. England won the decider in a very low-scoring game by 66 runs to retain the Ashes.

Ranjitsinjhi went on to top the domestic batting averages in 1896 then went on to score fourteen double hundreds in his career, jostling for the title of most double centuries ever in first-class cricket with his Sussex team mate C. B. Fry. Ranji never again played for England after four disappointing failures in a row during the classic 1902 Ashes series. This is surprising on many counts: he had topped the English domestic batting averages in 1896 (the year of his 154 not out), then again in 1900 where Ranji topped 3,000 runs (3,065) at a princely average of 87.57. For good measure he performed the feat again in 1904. It seems strange then that he was never selected for England after 1902.

It is also a shame that no test matches took place between 1899 and 1901/02. During this time Ranji amassed eight double hundreds, all for Sussex. He did not tour Australia for the 1901/02 series but played for England in the classic 1902 series where he and his Sussex team mate, C. B. Fry could only muster 24 runs between them in eight completed innings in the series. Ranji continued in first-class cricket until the age of 48, when one eye and a weight-gain issue caused his runs to dry up. Perhaps Ranji went on too long. His first-class career average over a 27-year period was a remarkable 56.37.

At the turn of the last century, Ranjitsinjhi was the jewel of English cricket, a batting genius. It was once said that he never played a Christian shot in his life. No Englishman batted Ranji's way. He took a large slice of Indian flair and imposed this genius onto the fields of England. Cardus concluded: 'When Ranji passed out of cricket a

wonder and a glory departed the game for ever. It is not in nature that there should be another Ranji. We who have had the good luck to see Ranji, let us be grateful. Did he really happen? or was he perhaps a dream, all dreamed on some midsummer's night long ago?
    Ranji died in 1933 at the age of 61.

Australia 412 (Iredale 108, Giffen 80, G. H. S. Trott 53, Richardson 7–168).
England 231 (Lilley 65*, Ranjitsinhji 62, McKibbin 3–45) and 305 (Ranjitsinhji 154*, McKibbin 3–61, Giffen 3–65).
Australia 125–7 (Richardson 6–76).
AUSTRALIA WON BY 3 WICKETS.

Innings Ranked Number 26
Hammond's 200 at Melbourne in 1929

Opponents: Australia.
At stake: Ashes won by England in 1926.
Bowling attack: A'Beckett, Hendry, Grimmett, Oxenham, Blackie, Ryder: 39.52 runs per wicket.
Pitch: Fair.
Game situation: England 28 for 1 in reply to Australia's 397.

To get a perspective of time, figures released during this seven-day test match showed that in Britain there were no fewer than 1.6 million telephones. This represented about 3.6 telephones per 100 people. Road traffic had boomed and with the general public now free to use these vehicular 'weapons' an average of fourteen people perished on the roads each day. Smoking was absolutely fashionable and few objected to the smell; moreover it was seen as sexy. These days of optimism and jollity grew from a decade of peace and had yet to be culled by the great depression.
    Defining this chapter in history, England assembled her most powerful batting line-up of all time. The number of first class centuries scored in the careers of England's top seven for the first test has never been approached. Consider the list below:

Hobbs – 197 centuries.
Sutcliffe – 149
Mead – 153
Hammond – 167
Jardine – 35
Hendren – 170
Chapman – 27
Tate – 23
Larwood – 3
White – 6
Duckworth – 0

This represents 930 first-class hundreds. No batting line up in history can boost that number.

Hammond had just gathered the attention of cricket enthusiasts around the world as a new batting sensation who had blazed away a magnificent 251 in the previous test, the second-highest test score in test history to date.

Percy Chapman, the young skipper, led a remarkably jolly side, not just through the various state and test matches but also the grand official occasions. Chapman encouraged his team to party and celebrate – an easy matter when one is winning.

In the first test of the 1928/29 Ashes, Jack Gregory broke down after bowling 41 eight-ball overs and Australia lost by a record 675 runs. With their spearhead assigned to history by the ravages of time, Australia succumbed almost as meekly again, by eight wickets.

So, on to the third test, if England could win this they retained the Ashes. Australia, in need of fortune, now won the toss on a wondrous wicket. Centuries from Kippax and Ryder and 79 from the colt Bradman were the main contributions. However, the Australian public endured their team sliding from an entertaining 276–4 at the end of the first day, to 397 all out. Australia's caution after the early fall of overnight centurion, Jack Ryder, was both dull and disappointing. These timeless tests were becoming painful to endure.

Hammond entered after the fall of Hobbs, caught behind off A'Beckett, with the score on 28. Out he strode, a broad shouldered 25-year-old, too young to have served in the Great War, a resplendent and mighty swash-buckling symbol of British hope. Hammond, perhaps a shade under six feet, sported a brown cap, regulation pads, gloves, box, thigh pad – standard fair for thousands of village cricketers today. The bat was plain, no stickers to celebrate the maker's name. He looked around at the field, shirt rolled up to the elbow. Beyond were the tin shacks that counted as Melbourne's inter-war stands. The public ringed the boundary ropes, beyond the imposing manual scoreboard with specific name plates carefully painted onto giant wooden planks. In the distance, tall trees towered beyond the stands.

Poor Monty Noble, the legendary pre-war Australian cricketer, lamented the lack of attack from batsmen. The problem in 1928/29 was the Australian Cricket Board insistance that tests should be played to a finish. The Australian bowling attack also lacked awe, and on flat wickets, with no need to push the scoring along, batsmen tended to go for survival, grinding down the bowlers into exhausted impotence before cashing in.

Wally Hammond cut an imposing figure. He had absolutely no intention of taking risks. If a bad ball came along, he would dispatch it from his presence through the covers for four. The Australians were not learning, no one sweeping on the cover boundary again. I see.

By stumps, Hammond and Sutcliffe (the latter still waiting for a score in the series) had grazed contentedly and without alarm whilst the score ticked along at an irritating pace to 47. With only 167 runs in the day, and the match heading for another long haul, the crowd trudged disconsolately home. Not surprisingly, therefore, with the prospect of watching Hammond and England bat all day, the crowd numbers on the third day showed a big drop.

Australia fielded lethargically, as though preparing for a long spell under the sun. Their attack showed a worrying lack of talent. Blackie had no pace from the wicket which was not surprising, he was 46 poor fellow. Grimmett looked innocuous. Oxenham tried to vary his deliveries – without success – and poor A'Beckett ran in and gave it everything, about fast-medium, without the experience of offering subtle variations in pace. They wilted.

Hammond and Sutcliffe added 137 for the second wicket, feasting on the lack of a deep square-leg, of which Sutcliffe's contribution was 58. Blackie, starting his run from mid-off, curled in and at last caused one of his off-breaks to lift abruptly from just outside off stump. Sutcliffe, not enjoying the greatest run of luck, played on.

Clouds now gathered, imperceptively at first, and when the shadows vanished, imminent rain reared its ugly head. Rain was the scurge on uncovered wickets, a real devil in those days. It could change a match, a destiny vanquished by an act of God. Chapman, the skipper, sent himself in above Hendren, to up the scoring. Chapman proceeded to provide some light relief with a cameo 24. This was not a great series with the bat for Percy Chapman who averaged only 23.57. When Chapman fell, England were 201–3 with Hammond approaching a hundred.

Hammond, the immovable object, assumed the role of pseudo sheet anchor. Every shot played out as low risk, quiet, yet masterful, and irritating the hell out of the Melbourne faithful. As eyes drooped from booze the crowd grew soporific, awoken only by rifle shots as he stood erect and hammered the bad balls with powerful off drives.

Hendren, the chirpy cockney, small and stocky, rode his luck in the gathering gloom but he fell too, hitting out at Hendry the part-time seamer. As A'Beckett caught him, one presumes the 21-year-old seamer was probably stationed somewhere deepish, probably mid-on.

By this stage Hammond was as commanding as ever, playing the percentage game and picking off the bowlers with a broad bat. He drew applause for his handsome back-foot drives, the power of which sent the ball clattering to the boundary fence time and time again. Partnering Hammond now was none other than Douglas Jardine, a lean, jaw-jutting, ex-Winchester and Oxford right-hand bat, 28, who had just enjoyed successive seasons back home averaging around 90. Australians would grow to hate Jardine, the brains behind the 'Bodyline' crisis of 1932/33. He sported that Harlequin's cap and exuded the arrogance of an Edwardian colonial master.

Jardine was a difficult partner for the then convivial Hammond. Between overs they would do no more than nod to each other as they prodded the pitch, both so focussed on the job at hand. For Jardine there was no place for light-hearted comments, designed to ease tension. As history was to reveal, he took the game very seriously indeed.

Hammond spent a tea break, pads still on, sat next to the great playwright Ben Travers. Without as much as a word, he took Traver's binoculars and spent a quarter-of-an-hour scrutinising the ladies' enclosure. Then, a few minutes after the bell, he duly gathered up his bat and followed the umpires back on to the pitch.

At the close of a demoralising day for the home side, Hammond posted an imposing 169 not out, with Jardine neatly settled in on 74. England, at 312–4, were within site of Australia's first innings 397 with all advantage of winning the toss squandered. Journalists fired abuse at slack Australian fielding, unimaginative field placements, fielders fielding out of position and the huge errors of trying to save singles whilst leaving the boundaries exposed. That night, the Australians reflected on an abject performance. Tactics on how to contain Hammond were re-examined. A glance at his wagon wheel revealed the vast bulk of runs sent whistling through the offside. Hammond had to have a weak spot, so they tried his legs, and vowed to bowl there first thing the next day.

Fourth morning opening salvos speared into Hammond's legs as planned and to a bloated leg-side field. This time leg-side boundaries were covered and Hammond at last began to feel caged in, cramped, frustrated. The plan was to bore him out.

Hammond duly blocked the leg-side deliveries or nudged them into gaps. The running became frantic in an effort to push the score along. When he eventually reached his double century, the score stood at 363–4, a mere 34 behind. The Ashes, if not quite out of Australia's grasp, were slipping away towards the horizon. Then Jardine called for a quick single, a stupid one, and had the throw hit its target, he would have been run-out by yards but Blackie was not back at the stumps.

Immediately after that Hammond perished, tied up as though literally bound around arms and torso, shorn of his favourite gorging options. Trying to hit Blackie over mid-on, he toed the shot and A'Beckett took a splendid left-hand catch, falling over in the process.

This colossus had scored a shade under 60 % of the runs whilst at the crease – a noble effort lasting 398 minutes and including seventeen fours. He was the first Englishman to score back-to-back double centuries, a feat he was to repeat in the early part of 1933 in New Zealand. His knock here ensured a first innings lead. It had looked like being a daunting difference, but the lower order collapsed rapidly. The lead was only twenty.

The fighting spirit of the Australians came to the fore in their second innings. Harold Larwood managed to penetrate Richardson's defences before the Australians forged ahead. Centuries from the unbowlable Bill Woodfull and the young 20-year-old Don Bradman ensured a stiff target of 332 for England in the fourth innings of the game.

Hobbs and Sutcliffe again started with a century partnership, but then Blackie pinned Hobbs LBW for 49, a crucial, memorable knock for the 46-year-old. Hobbs had become a legend to Australians and they cheered him as their own. He reminded many of their childhood, for he had competed in Ashes arenas since way back in 1908, five tours in all.

This time Jardine was promoted above Hammond and, together with Sutcliffe, took the score to 199 before falling to Grimmett for 33. Enter Hammond, now the greatest batsman in the world. He sauntered to 32 before being run out with the team still 74 runs away from victory. Sutcliffe's 135, with a fine 45 from Hendren, took England to within fourteen of the target before both perished. The run-out of Tate maintained the intensity, whilst Geary and Duckworth knocked off the winning runs.

So England took an unassailable 3–0 lead in the series. The fourth was also won but by just twelve runs. Again Hammond's contribution was decisive – a score of 119 not out in the first innings was followed by 177 in the second. During the course of this, he shattered Sutcliffe's record series runs set in 1924/25.

It was also becoming noticeable how the England victories were becoming steadily less emphatic. Indeed, despite Hobbs scoring the last of his fifteen test centuries (142 and 65 in the match) in the fifth test, England lost by five wickets. The shoots of an Australian renaissance had already started to emerge, in the form of that 20-year-old, 5ft 7ins, slightly-built boy, Bradman. This rising star finished the series with notable scores of 79, 112, 40, 58 run out, 123, and 37 not out. Another colt, Archie Jackson fired off a memorable 164 on his debut and also showed vast potential.

England, with an over-mature 1930 side, simply could not contain Bradman who went on to eclipse all of Hammond's main batting records. Forever after, Hammond was to exist in the shadow of a much smaller physical specimen. Sadly Jackson's health began to fail him and he died at the tragic age of 24.

Hammond graced the fields of England throughout the 1930s and 1940s. He enjoyed a life as a carefree womaniser and was a fixture in high social circles. Often aloof in the dressing room, he isolated himself from team mates, travelled to games separately, and lambasted young team mates who not coming up to scratch. This great icon re-emerged after the Hitler war, but never truly shone again. A tour too many to Australia in 1946–7, saw over-the-hill Hammond out-played by the still prime Bradman.

Unwisely, Hammond, the faded star, went on to occasionally represent Gloucestershire right up until 1951. He was 48, portly, with deep wrinkles etched across his face. Failed businesses and gambling debts had taken their toll over the years. He died in 1965, aged 62, a pauper in South Africa. His 200 at Melbourne began in 1928 and finished in 1929. Without his unwavering concentration, remarkable power and impeccable defence, England would have been out-batted in these timeless tests. This third test lasted into the seventh day, so did the fourth test and the last test, eight days.

Australia 397 (Ryder 112, Kippax 100, Bradman 79, Geary 3–83, Larwood 3–127).
England 417 (Hammond 200, Jardine 62, Sutcliffe 58, Blackie 6–94).
Australia 351 (Bradman 112, Woodfull 107, J. C. White 5–107).
England 332–7 (Sutcliffe 135, Hobbs, 49, Hendren 45).
ENGLAND WON BY 3 WICKETS.

Innings Ranked Number 25
Dexter's 180 at Edgbaston 1961

Opponents: Australia.
At stake: Ashes.
Bowling attack: Davidson, Misson, Mackay, Benaud, Simpson: 33.13 runs per wicket.
Pitch: Fair.
Game situation: First Test, third innings, England 321 runs behind on the first innings.

Ted Dexter was one of 52,675,094 British people as declared by the 10 year national population census on the day before the first Ashes test match of the summer. Out of this figure he was, without doubt, the British subject with the finest off drive.

Australia held the Ashes after defeating a highly rated but complacent England 4–0 back in 1958–9, perhaps the most disappointing test series for England fans in the whole of the twentieth century.

In anger, England had thrashed India 5–0 the following summer, beaten the West Indies 1–0, in the West Indies, then hammered South Africa 3–0 in 1960. However, there was no winter tour so by 8 June 1961, England had not played any test cricket since the 23 August 1960

– a gap of 289 days, unimaginable in the twenty-first century.

One abject failure from the previous series was the then 23-year-old Ted Dexter. Dexter, a free scoring 6ft, right-hander with immaculate presentation and the looks of James Bond, had averaged only 4.25 in four innings in the two tests he played. Nonetheless, he was now a permanent fixture in England's line up with a cavalier touch about his batting.

Australia meanwhile had played the greatest-ever test series against the West Indies, and won. It is questionable whether Australia was still regarded as the world champions. They had beaten India and the West Indies, but not as convincingly as England.

England won the toss but slumped to a paltry 195, with the apparently innocuous medium pace of Mackay grabbing 4–57. When Australia countered, an England attack comprising the veterans Trueman, Statham and little else, bowled over 150 overs and still could not dismiss them. Australia's 516–9 declared left an embarrassing first innings deficit of 321.

Then the rain came and curtailed play during the third and fourth days. When the ground dried in the evening session of the fourth day, England had four sessions left of the test and settled weather. They fared better. Pullar and Subba Row took the score to 93 before Misson forced Pullar to edge behind.

Dexter had to face Alan Davidson, a superb left-arm quick who moved the ball into the right-hander through the air then moved it either way off the seam. Davidson was 32 and many thought he would be 'put down' before the series began, but that was wishful thinking on England's behalf. He was still close to the top of his powers, whether he would replicate the 33 wickets at 18.54 in the previous series remained to be seen.

Opening with Davidson was the honest, blond 23-year-old, Francis Misson, a right-arm medium pacer. First change was more of the same from 'slasher' Mackay, followed by Benaud's leg breaks and Bobby Simpson's own less famous ones. This was an awkward time and after a single to get off the mark, Dexter did well to edge a lethal Davidson leg cutter. The chance went begging. Dexter took his score to five from the last twenty-two minutes of play.

On the final day England had to bat through to survive, yet Dexter, despite the horrible moments in the evening session, looked a new man, flamboyant and imperious. It was such a shame that England's most-attacking batsman so often had to fight rearguards and rein himself in. Too much was at stake. His company was another fellow ex-Cambridge graduate, the tall, lean figure of left-hander Roman Subba Row. The crowd settled down, old men on cushions, many with sunhats.

Roman Subba Row had the fantastic quality of being able to rotate the strike at ease, and he did just that on a perfect morning. According to E. W. Swanton, Subba Row looked 'completely composed'. He scored predominantly on the on-side whilst Dexter drove the occasion loose bowl handsomely through the covers off both front and back foot. During the stand, Subba Row reached his century, the twelfth England player to score an Ashes century on his debut. Together the pair added 109, before Subba Row had his stumps castled by Misson for 112.

The captain, Colin Cowdrey, now joined Dexter. On his day Cowdrey could touch the ball to the boundary, all elegance and ease the portly Kent right-hander appeared to have so much time. He had touched the hearts of many England supporters ever since his brave 102, out of just 191, as a 22-year-old at Melbourne back in 1954/55.

Inexplicably, Mackay breached Cowdrey's defences to leave England 239-3 mid-way through the afternoon session and still 82 runs behind. Dexter decided to play each ball on its merits and hoped to build a lead and thereby force Australia to bat again. He glanced up at the clear skies and realised he had to just bat out time, but the weather closing in. Keep it orthodox, keep it simple.

Barrington, the stout Londoner, patted the turf between overs whilst swopping notes and theories about the bowling with Dexter. Both wore caps and had dark hair, but there the similarities as batsmen ended. Dexter batted in a free-flowing, buccaneering manner, standing tall and upright, classical in a Walter Hammond manner, whilst Barrington provided the grit, more in the style of today's Paul Collingwood.

Benaud was feeling the strain and was seriously handicapped from a shoulder injury. On this day he looked innocuous. Every Dexter boundary soothed the nerves of the home crowd, whilst the occasional square cut for four from Barrington was seen as a bonus. With the deficit ever-narrowing, Dexter merely speeded up and ran a mastery over the Australian attack to the delight of the nation.

With the game running out of time and little chance of a result, Dexter went into overdrive and lit up Edgbaston during the last session. England took the lead and all pressure eased; the crowd sat back and admired the craftsmanship, the like of which had not been seen since the days of Hammond. By the time he was finally dismissed, coming down the track to be stumped, England had forged ahead by almost 80 and barely five minutes remaining of the game. His partnership with Barrington realised 161, of which Barrington contributed 48. Dexter had batted for 344 minutes, through almost all of the final day, and hit 31 fours, a vast majority from the meat of the bat.

It was not a happy series for England. They lost 1–2 after seemingly coasting to victory in the deciding fourth test at Old Trafford. Chasing 255 to win, England raced to 150–1. Then Dexter, having made a sublime 76 in just 84 minutes, snicked behind off Benaud. There followed a collapse of such crushing disappointment that England lost her last nine wickets for 51 runs; Benaud, recovered from his shoulder, finished with 6–70 from 32 overs to guide Australia home by 41 runs.

Dexter ended his career prematurely, retiring in 1968 at the age of just 33. He had business interests to pursue. His era, the 1960s, saw a decline in interest in test cricket. During that decline, Dexter, more than any other Englishman except for perhaps Colin Milburn, reminded crowds of what thrilling top-class batting should be like. He scored 4,502 runs at an average of 47.89 in 62 test matches. No one since, apart from the ultra defensive Barrington, has completed a test career for England at a higher average, not even Boycott (47.72).

Some say that Dexter's 174 against Australia, fighting another rearguard in the 1964 series, was a better innings, but that the pitch was dead. Others point to his exquisite brace of 70s; the one at Old Trafford – which precipitated that collapse – provided an hour of cruel joy. In the other at Lord's against the 1963 West Indians – spearheaded by the fearsome Hall and Griffith – Dexter scored an outstanding 70. When he fell, England were just 102–3. If either had gone on to win the test …

Roman Subba Row, who scored 468 runs at 46.8 in this his first Ashes series, also suddenly retired from the game to pursue business interests – successfully too by all accounts.

It would be the series in Australia in 1970/71 before England regained the Ashes.

England 195 (Subba Row 59, Mackay 4–57).
Australia 516 (Harvey 114, O'Neill 82, Simpson 76, Mackay 64, Lawry

57, Statham 3–147).
England 401–4 (Dexter 180, Subba Row 112).
MATCH DRAWN.

Innings Ranked Number 24
Hussain's 207 at Edgbaston in 1997

Opponents: Australia.
At stake: Ashes.
Bowling attack: McGrath, Kasprowicz, Gillespie, Warne, Bevan, S.R. Waugh – 26.7.
Pitch: Some lateral movement early on the first day, but a fine pitch.

This was the dawn of New Labour and Tony Blair. The economy was in good-enough shape, but the country needed a change after eighteen years of Conservative rule. For England cricket supporters, drained by lack of success in a cruel world of high-class international bowling attacks, the summer had an expectant, if over-optimistic, tinge to it.

This was in the middle of arguably the greatest Australian cricketing era, ever. Their national side was slowly but surely evolving to even greater height,s with perhaps the 2001 Australians as the strongest, on paper, in the era. Only two test sides bare comparison; the 1948 Australians, led by Don Bradman, and the 1984 West Indians. Australia had taken the unofficial crown from the West Indies following the Caribbean series of 1995, when Steve Waugh famously told Curtley Ambrose to 'get back to your mark.'

Australia possessed genuine fire power in Jason Gillespie, fine seam back-up from Kasprowicz but it was the two greats Glenn McGrath and Shane Warne that gave Australia the 'go-to' bowlers whenever a break through was needed.

England, however, had her finest test team of the 1990s. A strong batting line up, comprising Butcher, Atherton, Stewart (as a wicket-keeper batsman at number 3), Nasser Hussain, Thorpe and Crawley, had all made runs in the championship, Ealham was no slouch at number seven, Robert Croft a useful off-spinner with all-rounder pretensions came in at eight, followed by a quite penetrative and fierce pace department of Gough, Caddick and Malcolm.

England had unusually swept the Australians to a 3–0 victory in the ODIs, so an air of expectancy filled the country. The toss at Edgbaston was won by Australia and they elected to bat. Lessons in schools were disrupted up and down the country as Ashes fever ignited on that first morning. At 54–8 the writing was on the wall. Australia recovered slightly to reach 118, thanks to Warne's 47 but Caddick (5–50), Gough (3–43) and Malcolm (2–25) completed the rout by the thirty-second over.

England started badly. Atherton edged McGrath behind for two, a dismissal that would continue through to Atherton's retirement. Then Butcher did the same to Kasprowicz, England 15–2. Out strode the man the Australians loved to sledge, Nasser Hussain.

When batting, Hussain always wore an intense face that delighted the cartoonists. Australians picked up on the impressive size of Hussain's nose in relation to the rest of his facial features. 'I want you just under Nasser's nose at cover point!' said the Australian skipper to his fielder, well in earshot of the Indian born public-school educated, Durham University graduate.

Hussain had grown up under immense pressure to perform, particularly from a cricket-loving father. Failure as a schoolboy ended with Hussain sulking in his bedroom. Low scores in school or representative cricket left an in-built hatred of failure. Now, at last, established in the England batting line up, he sought to stabilise the situation and grind out a first innings lead.

For once Warne and McGrath entered the series undercooked and their lines strayed. Stewart and Hussain began to steady the ship by putting away the bad balls and rotating the strike. As a comfort zone dawned, however, Stewart edged Gillespie to Elliott in the slips and England quivered on 50–3.

Back in 1993, Graham Thorpe and Nasser Hussain had saved the Trent Bridge test with an undefeated stand of 113. Thorpe, on his debut, scored 114 not out in the second innings, and Hussain 71 and not out 47. Whilst Thorpe became a mainstay whenever fit until his retirement just before the 2005 Ashes, Hussain was soon dropped for three years. It took a century against India in 1996 to cement his place. Now all England looked on desperate for success.

A massive cheer roared up from the bull ring at Edgbaston as first the 50 partnership came simultaneously with the 100 up for England. Hussain, shrewd cricketing brain, operated in a bubble of concentration, fierce determination and massive pride. He simply hated getting out.

Warne suffered a stiff shoulder which failed to give him the rip necessary, yet both the right-hander Hussain and the left-handed Thorpe never allowed him to settle. Here were two of young England's aggressive 'young guns' tearing apart the best bowlers in the world. McGrath for once bowled too short, too often, failing to adjust to the fuller length demanded in English conditions. Euphoria struck the crowd as Hussain cut with precision and power any time Warne bowled too short. Runs came at a fair lick. At anything full, Hussain strode forwards and drove handsomely through the covers. Kasprowicz was the pick of the bowlers yet by the end of that first day the pair had put on 150 in just 169 minutes to take England to 200–3 already a lead of 82 over the Australians.

For Dennis Amiss, Chairman of Warwickshire, the fall of thirteen wickets so soon into the game came as a grave concern. The Edgbaston wicket in 1995 and 1996 had seen low scores and an indifferent bounce. Any threat of a test match ban from another sub-standard wicket would lead to a great loss for the club and ground. Hussain and Thorpe's stand evaporated the fear before his eyes.

Next day the stand continued to take the game away from the shell-shocked Australians. Thorpe, if anything, played a greater array of strokes and was certainly Hussain's equal. Both were schoolboy friends who had played for the same representative teams.

The stand continued passed the third-wicket England record against Australia of 222 – Wally Hammond and Eddie Paynter, at Lord's in 1938 – and so represented the only time since the war that England had beaten one of the Ashes partnership records, a tremendous feat that planted a fog of euphoria.

Thorpe fell for 138, caught by Bevan off McGrath, with England 338–4, the partnership yielding 288. Crawley fell soon after, snicking Kasprowicz behind, but Mark Ealham, the Kent all-rounder, helped Hussain add a further 76 runs, becoming the first Englishman to register an Ashes double-century since Gower's scored on the same ground in 1985. At last, and with the score on 416, Hussain edged Warne, and Healy accepted the chance. In his 207 Hussain hit no fewer than 38 boundaries, all fours, and batted for a total of 337 deliveries and 440 minutes. *Wisden* describes his double century as batsmanship 'with a touch of genius'.

Australia fought back hard in their second innings, with centuries from Greg Blewett and Mark Taylor (the under-pressure skipper), but England knocked the 119 runs off to win by nine wickets.

Rain saved England at Lord's where they were skittled for 77 with McGrath taking 8–38. Too much time was lost, although England batted out the last day under calm skies.

The next three tests were lost heavily and in palate puckeringly disappointing circumstances, as Australia exerted her authority through Steve Waugh's excellent batting and Australia's more balanced attack.

Hussain batted for England through the next seven years, finishing on a high with a century to guide England to victory at Lord's in 2004. His legacy was the tough-leadership qualities he gave to ensure England became harder to beat.

Australia 118 (Caddick 5–50, Gough 3–43).
England 478–9 declared (Hussain 207, Thorpe 138, Ealham 53*, Kasprowicz 4–113).
Australia 477 (Taylor 129, Blewett 125, Elliott 66, Ealham 3–60, Gough 3–123, Croft 3–125).
England 119–1 (Atherton 57*, Stewart 40*).
ENGLAND WON BY 9 WICKETS.

Innings Ranked Number 23
Hutton's 145 at Lord's in 1953

Opponents: Australia.
At stake: Ashes.
Bowling attack: Lindwall, Miller, Johnston, Ring, Benaud, Davidson: 25.20.
Pitch: Fine.
Game situation: Australia won the toss and elected to bat first. They scored a respectable 368. Hutton and Kenyon opened the England innings soon after lunch on day two.

England had lost every Ashes series since the resumption of test cricket in 1946. Successive losses of 3–0 in 1946/47, 4–0 in 1948 and 4–1 in 1950/51 have been gauged on the lack of 26–32-year-olds. The post-war England teams relied too much on the pre-war young – all over 32 on the 1950/51 tour – and the post-war young of under 26.

In effect, Hitler had deprived England of the development of a generation of cricketers. Only the chirpy Godfrey Evans and Alec Bedser excelled as test cricketers from between these demographic age groups.

The 1953 side was still made up of a couple of pre-war youngsters in the form of Len Hutton and Denis Compton. Together with these two was another pre-war veteran who made his test debut as long ago as 1931, the burly, red-faced and jolly Freddie Brown, a durable bowling all-rounder. England had control in their attack with the 23-year-old Brian Statham and, still in his prime, the 35-year-old war horse, Alec Bedser. Trevor Bailey at 30 completed the fast-medium department. Wardle offered penetrative spin whilst old Freddie could use his cutters to keep the scoring down.

England's batting still had to rely on Len Hutton, who was now 37. Denis Compton at 35, still made useful contributions but a knee injury stifled his genius. For this test England brought in Willie Watson (33), and kept Don Kenyon (29) and Tom Graveney (27), despite their lack of runs in the first test. It ended in a rain-affected draw.

Hutton was in no doubt that a big innings was required. The sun shone for the whole test, five full days were forecast so there was no escaping the need for big runs. Also, Hutton had dropped two easy chances in the gully and a further harder chance; his thumb and pride both hurt, but there is nowhere to swallow you up with a capacity crowd in attendance. Coronation year meant streets across England now had access to the daily Ashes battle. For the first time, millions could view the proceedings on black and white TV screens, slightly 'grainy' by today's standards, but this series, this test match and Hutton's innings reached out to the growing populace.

Hutton glanced around at the typically attacking Lindwall field – fiveslips and gullies, two sort legs, a cover point and a mid on. No one guarded the boundary, Hutton made a mental note. A single from Hutton, reciprocated by Kenyon, then Hutton lent into a drive for three. A stroke for two from Kenyon completed seven off the first over.

Miller opening at the other end settled for the same field. In he burst, all macho and hostile. Hutton kept his concentration, allowing the game initially to flow around him. This was the passive phase of a big innings. Hutton knew the longer he spent at the wicket the more tired the bowlers would get, the older the ball and the more scoring opportunities that would become available. He winced as Kenyon fell to a leg slip in Lindwall's second over, fending off a short ball. Out came the 6ft, sun-tanned Tom Graveney to join his senior partner. Hutton carried double responsibilities. Not only was he the most prized wicket, he was also the captain – the number-one target for Miller and Lindwall.

In later years, Hutton admitted he feared facing such a probing and hostile opening attack. Long before the advent of helmets, Hutton wore a cloth cap, just like prep-school boys are allowed to wear when fielding. Nevertheless, a Miller half volley was pleasantly middled and sped to the long off-boundary. Graveney, very much the junior partner, glanced a Lindwall delivery also for four and gradually the tension eased. Hassett spread the field with Lindall removing slips to fill up the outfield and apply pressure that way.

Right from the first ball, Graveney began to lay into Johnston, the large lumbering left armer. Ring replaced Lindwall, and Hutton, the master technician, hit him contemptuously for four. All seemed well and the 30,000 crowd sat back to see 53 added in the first hour. Graveney kept pace with Hutton to rapturous applause. By tea time England had advanced nobly to 90–1, after exactly 100 minutes – Hutton 46, Graveney 38.

Soon after tea, Hutton reached his 50, then the 100 came up followed by the 100 partnership, to a great crackle of applause. The bowling throughout had been testing, initially fierce, well directed and hostile, yet Hutton's defence had held, secure and impermeable. Hutton had put the occasional bad ball away with consummate ease, his off-side shots straight from the coaching manual. Colin Cowdrey, a known fan of Hutton, reckoned that Hutton's defence could even have been more impenetrable than that of the great Jack Hobbs. Like the master batsman from a generation before, Hutton's concentration at the crease encouraged long innings.

Just like Hammond to Hutton back at the Oval in 1938, so Hutton on occasions walked down the wicket to advise his junior partner Graveney. Of the two, Graveney's shots reeked occasionally of recklessness. The junior partner quickly took heed of the advice and looked on and marvelled at the manner in which Hutton played every ball on its merits and continued to give a chanceless display, great on-the-spot education.

Miller returned and immediately set about roughing up Hutton who ducked under a bumper, then took two through the slips from a high full toss, followed by another bumper, under which he again ducked. Soon the partnership passed the 150 mark and England looked set for 600+. The pitch was, according to ex-Australian batsman and journalist Sidney Barnes, as 'docile as a lamb.' By the end of day two England had advanced to 177–1, Hutton on 83, Graveney 78.

A cooler, breezier third day still saw the ground packed, with thousands sat on the turf between the seats and the boundary rope. The gates were shut on the queues of people 45 minutes before the start, and both foot and mounted police had to keep order in the streets outside the ground.

With the new ball due, Lindwall went through some warm up deliveries in the first over still using the previous day's ball. He reasoned that this was necessary in order to maximise the chances of success when converting to the new ball. It was one of these exploratory early-morning deliveries that accounted for the hapless Graveney, yorked fourth ball without adding to his overnight score.

Compton arrived at the crease and at once Lindwall converted to the new ball. Hutton and Compton rarely enjoyed large partnerships together, surprisingly since both were true greats with the bat. Hutton typically grafted out long innings with care and attention, whilst Compton usually provided the dashing mements. Not so today. Before Compton had broken his duck, Hutton cut a three off Miller then hit Lindwall for a four, a two and a single all in the same over.

Compton sneaked a two through the slip cordon and streaked a boundary to fine leg. Nonetheless, a further couple of boundaries took Compton to fourteen, with the crowd now nervous in anticipation of a Hutton century. Lindwall ran in from the far end with Hutton on 96, eyes level, peaked-cap pointing towards the bowler. Gaining perfect rhythm, with an immaculate fast bowler's action, Lindwall unleashed a leg-stump half volley which Hutton instinctively glanced down to fine leg. Around came Johnston, not the most athletic on the field that day, and the ball trickled between his legs and over the boundary ropes. All England cheered and the whoops of joy mocked the poor Australian as he threw the ball back to the bowler with a pardon expressed with a raised hand.

Hutton required 132 at the start of his innings to reach 2,000 against Australia. This was Hutton's last Ashes century and technically the best. Throughout the bowling attack had been far more threatening than in the 1938 attack at the Oval. Here runs had to be earned through courage, technique and concentration.

The sun shone and Hassett gave his tiring openers a breather and on came Johnston, fresh from his humiliating fielding error. He proceeded to bowl raggedly and was soon taken off and replaced by Miller. Hutton struck a couple of resounding boundaries. According to Bruce Harris: 'Never had I seen him bat better than that day. The chances of him getting out seemed to be one in a thousand.'

Half an hour before lunch the 250 came up, and Hutton and Compton were now running some superb singles. It is often quoted of Compton, that he was a disaster between the wickets, not so on this day and the 100 partnership was sealed.

Even Hutton could not bat for ever and so it was that, on 145 princely runs, garnered in the heat of five-hours battle against the old enemy, he fenced off a rising delivery from Johnston to Hole at leg gully. He had hit sixteen fours and the score was 287–3 upon Hutton's dismissal, just 59 runs behind Australia's total, job done!

England collapsed following the loss of their leader, but thanks to a last-wicket partnership of 32 entertaining runs between Wardle and Statham, England took a slender first innings lead of 26.

Australia replied strongly through a century from Keith Miller and an 89 from Arthur Morris. England needed 343 for victory. At close on day four, disaster struck and England lost Kenyon, Hutton and Graveney and tottered on 12–3. Only another of England's 50 greatest-ever knocks brought about a fighting rearguard action to earn the draw.

England regained the Ashes with victory in the fifth test at the Oval. Hutton also captained the successful 1954/55 Ashes side before retiring.

Australia 346 (Hassett 104, Davidson 76, Harvey 59, Bedser 5–105, Wardle 4–77).
England 372 (Hutton 145, Graveney 78, Compton 57, Lindwall 5–66).
Australia 368 (Miller 109, Morris 89, Lindwall 50, Brown 4–82, Bedser 3–77).
England 282–7 (Watson 109, Bailey 71).
MATCH DRAWN.

Innings Ranked Number 22
Compton's 184 at Trent Bridge in 1948

Opponents: Australia.
At stake: Ashes.
Bowling attack: Miller, Johnston, Toshack, Johnson, Barnes: Bowling runs per wicket average 24.40.
Pitch: Fair.
Game situation: England with a first innings deficit of 344 are 39–2.

Don Bradman's 1948 Australians remain arguably the strongest team in cricket history. This was the first domestic Ashes test match for almost ten years, although in Australia eighteen months earlier England had been soundly beaten three tests to nil in a five-test series.

Around this time it was decreed that professional sport was to be played on weekends only to encourage a sound work ethic – cricket being the exception. For these reasons, the post-war, cash-strapped England supporters flocked to first-class games to cheer on new heroes.

The first Ashes test on home soil since the war was keenly awaited. England had been harder hit with regard to the development of new cricketers than Australia. The noted cricket writer, E. W. Swanton, stated that cricket had been played more or less to the full in Australia during the war years whilst in England, the game remained dormant, any shoots of emerging talent being shackled by the grim times. By 1945, the post-war Australians were ready and primed, England was not and was over reliant on pre-war youths.

In Ray Lindwall and Keith Miller, Australia had the fastest bowlers on the planet. Both were capable of 90 m.p.h. with outstandingly fluid actions; Lindwall slimmer and more probing, Miller more muscular. England pinned their hopes on a solid and experienced top four batting line-up comprising: Hutton, Washbrook, Edrich and Compton. Godfrey Evans was superb as a wicket-keeper and Alec Bedser, comfortably the best seamer in England, completed a sturdy backbone to the team.

England won the toss and elected to bat under full cloud cover.

After over-night rain the game was able to start just after mid-day. The hurricane pace of Lindwall and Millert quickly became obvious to the partisan supporters. For a quarter-of-an-hour they bowled at full throttle, with both Hutton and Washbrook experiencing discomfort. Miller tore in from the Pavilion End and unleashed a furious inswinger that cut in late and hurried off the pitch. Hutton's stumps shattered and the Trent Bridge crowd went silent. Shortly after at 13–1, play was suspended for rain.

That afternoon England collapsed in pitiful circumstances to reach 74–8, her much-vaunted line up that had so gorged themselves on South Africa's friendly offerings the summer before, now had a long summer to endure against a potent and confrontational line up.

Jim Laker and Alec Bedser salvaged some pride by more than doubling the score for the ninth wicket, however England made just 165. Australia finished the first day on seventeen for no wicket.

For most of the next two days Australia batted in finer weather and amassed 509 with centuries from the 40-year-old incomparable Bradman and Lindsay Hassett. Hutton and Washbrook went out to bat the second time with $2^1/2$ hours left of day three.

Washbrook fell early, glancing Miller to keeper Tallon. The score was 5–1 but four of the runs were from leg byes. Then Edrich hit a four, followed by another four from Hutton and immediately the crowd felt better. Soon Edrich groped at a ball to give Tallon a second catch, this time off Johnson, 39–2.

Hutton and Compton refused to lie down and the two great Englishmen fought fire with fire, both unleashing powerful drives through the off-side as statements of intent. Depression lifted like the mist. Keith Miller decided to pitch short and into the batsmen's body. There followed a 35-minute session before the close where Miller, bowling fast and furious, unleashed a spell of four bouncers an over.

The crowd grew angry. This was Nottingham, home of Harold Larwood. It was Larwood, the tearaway England quick, who answered Douglas Jardine's call for bodyline bowling in the 1932/33 series. He never played again for England, being effectively banned. Bradman, a victim of bodyline back then (modest average not injury) now seemed intent on re-employing it.

Compton had a quickness of eye that was almost superhuman in nature. During the bumper barrage, he ducked and weaved out of the way. From the corner of his eye he could see Bradman grinning at cover point. Hutton on the other hand took some body blows in a grim moment in Ashes history. The crowd became incensed, booing Miller angrily. By the end of play, Hutton and Compton remained, defiant on 121–2, still some 223 runs behind Australia, and with two days to go. As the Australian team filtered through the crowd by the pavilion, hundreds of hostile supporters glowered at Miller, who simply strode in with his sweater over his shoulder, smiling like some swashbuckling Hollywood legend. How he played the part of pantomime villain that day.

Sunday was a rest day. By Monday, the weather again became gloomy, the ground enveloped in thick, dark cloud with intermittent rainfall, most difficult to play cricket in and, with poor light and Miller in full bullying mode, it was particularly unpleasant for batting. The first four overs were just to use up overs before the next new ball (in 1948, the new ball came after only 55 overs). Hutton and Compton gratefully used these to get their eye in.

Then, racing in from the dark pavilion end, Miller pierced through Hutton's defences for the second time in the game, this time though for 74 priceless runs. Hardstaff replaced Hutton and immediately looked uncertain in the gathering gloom. The umpires offered the light to England's finest batsmen and the pair trudged off.

Half-an-hour later Compton and Hardstaff were forced back out, in light that had only marginally improved. Surprisingly, given the conditions and the score, both batsmen played freely and the score rattled along at a run a minute up to lunch and again in the hour beyond. Compton seemed content to push singles rather than blaze away and squander his wicket. Commentator John Arlott, there that day, wrote 'to every man who watched Compton on that dull June day his innings will remain a classic.' Hardstaff, then Barnett, both fell before bad light again stopped play. Compton, who had mastered all the bowlers that day, walked off on 97 not out.

Out again they came again. Miller had Compton dropped in the slips and Yardley batted doggedly for an hour before clipping Johnston back to himself for 22. In that time, Compton continued to chisel out some gallant runs. In came Godfrey Evans, the plucky Kent keeper, and both he and Compton added a further 24 runs before the close. England, on 345–6, were effectively one run ahead with four wickets left and one whole day of test cricket left. Compton, shining above all others, dined-out on an undefeated 154. It seemed that only Compton or the weather could save England.

Next day, events commenced on time with Evans in particular

strutting out with a military straight back full of purpose. Compton trailed his bat along the ground as though possession of it were an after thought. The first fifty minutes saw Johnston and Johnson bowl their full variety in an effort to out-fox the batsmen. Evans scored thirteen to Compton's nine and they had added 22 runs before a further stoppage for rain, this time for 40 minutes.

In deep gloom, play was resumed and matches used by pipe smokers in the stands flared up like tiny beacons. Compton added a further 21 runs and had caught up on Evans for the day. It started to drizzle as Miller took off his sweater to launch the third new ball. Compton added a further five whilst Evans made ten, including a disdainful drive through the covers off Johnston. Then rain once again stopped play. Ten minutes later, they were back out. Compton, batting with quiet certainty, had taken his score to 184, and England were 62 ahead. In short, poor Compton had to play himself in no fewer than nine times during the course of his innings.

Pause and consider the high esteem bestowed on Denis Compton at this precise moment. Before the eyes of the Nottingham public, he had taken England from a position of hopelessness into a slender lead, a land of hope. His innings had began with Hutton late on Saturday afternoon, when he had to cope with a bombardment of injury-threatening 90 m.p.h. missiles aimed at his head. He batted whenever possible without even a cap, let alone a helmet. He had batted throughout a rain-interrupted Monday and accumulated, through unnatural restraint, a further 118 runs. On the Tuesday morning, with two further interruptions, he had added another 30.

Compton was a batting genius at the very height of his powers. He had scored 100s in both innings against the Australians in the latter half of the 1946/47 series. He scored a further eighteen centuries in a run-glut 1947 County season in which he amassed 3,816 runs at an average in excess of 90. In short, he was a batting God who now had mastered the much-vaunted Australian attack. It is true that the injured Lindwall did not bowl in the innings, but the appalling light and deteriorating weather, coupled with the Miller onslaught, made conditions for batting as life threatening as at any time in the history of the game. Bodyline in Australia was performed in a hot, sunny Mediterranean style climate – conditions that were easier to the eye.

It was approaching lunch when Miller unleashed a leg-side bumper from the dark pavilion end under a steady drizzle. The ball reared up alarmingly on the fifth-day pitch. Compton at first shaped to pull, but approximately a tenth-of-a-second later, pulled out. Instinctively he ducked and in doing so moved across his wicket and pulled back his bat. On the slippery turf he fell, in comic tragedy, onto his wicket – a most miserable end to a truly heroic innings.

England were dismissed shortly after for 441, with Evans falling for a highly entertaining 50. Australia reached the target of 97 for the loss of Morris and Bradman, both to Alec Bedser. A dark cloudburst, which would have halted play for good, came just as the winning runs were scored, a further tragic fate for a remarkable innings of grit and determination. Just five minutes longer and Compton would have earned a draw against the greatest team in history.

Thereafter England were comprehensively beaten 4–0. The problem was the lack of penetrating bowlers. Bedser was a reliable warhorse seamer, dependable, accurate and with the gift of generating significant seam movement either way. Other than him, there was Norman Yardley who was more of an attritional bowler. The blame for England's shortfall in the bowling department goes to the curtailment of cricket during the war.

It took five years for England to develop a world-class attack. The fact was that England's batting in 1948 deserved to regain the Ashes, certainly it held firm in three of the tests. There were enough England runs at Nottingham and Headingley to forge victories, that is with an attack as potent as that of Australia. Whilst at Old Trafford, England were able to declare. The bowlers were just not up to scratch as a unit.

As for Compton, he went on to represent England for a majority of the tests played until early 1957. Despite declining fitness from a knee injury, that ended with the knee having to be taken out, he still featured nobly in tests and retired with a test average of 50.03. He goes down as one of the true great sporting entertainers, a once in a generation cricketer who defined his era: Grace, Hobbs, Compton, Botham and possibly Pieterson.

England 165 (Laker 63, Johnston 5–36, Miller 3–38).
Australia 509 (Bradman 138, Hassett 137, Barnes 62, Laker 4–138, Bedser 3–113).
England 441 (Compton 184, Hutton 74, Evans 50, Johnston 4–125, Miller 4–147).
Australia 98–2 (Barnes 64*).
AUSTRALIA WON BY 8 WICKETS.

Innings Ranked Number 21
Sutcliffe's 135 at Melbourne in 1929

Opponents: Australia.
At stake: Ashes.
Bowling attack: A'Beckett, Hendry, Grimmett, Oxenham, Blackie, Ryder: average runs per wicket: 42.52.
Pitch: Sticky wicket.
Game situation: England required 332 to win the test, the series and the Ashes. Although England were 2–0 up, 332 was a lot to chase on the fourth and fifth days when play had been interrupted because of rain on an uncovered wicket.

Herbert Sutcliffe was reputedly the finest hooker that Bradman ever saw. He possessed an exceptional batting average in test cricket of just over 60. When the benchmark for greatness is measured by a batting average of 50-plus, and considering only Don Bradman and George Headley of those who played over twenty tests, averaged over 60, one can see how difficult Sutcliffe was to dislodge.

Melbourne 1928/29 represents the end of the great England side of the mid 1920s. By 1930, England were too old or inexperienced to conquer Woodfull's outstanding batting line up; comprising Woodfull (overall test batting average of 46.00), Ponsford (48.22), Bradman (99.94), Kippax (36.12), Jackson (47.40) and McCabe (48.21).

The test match took a record attendance of 262,000 for the seven-day game. Sutcliffe rates his 135 in the third and, as it turned out decisive test of the 1928/29 series, as perhaps his finest. For the record, Australia were growing stronger throughout the series and England's margins of victory, huge and by 675 runs in the first test, tangibly narrowed.

On the first day of 1929 Australia were in a period of rebuilding. At the helm was veteran Jack Ryder, rising 40. His batting line up was a mix of old (himself 39, V. V. Richardson 34, Hendry 33, Kippax 31, Woodfull 31) and the very young (Bradman 20). In both innings Australia's transitional line up stood up impressively to Larwood, Tate and White. Bradman especially took the game away from England with scores of 79 and a 112 under huge pressure.

All of the tests had been designated 'timeless' and, as Bradman entered the arena in the second innings, Australia were only 123 in front with six wickets left. When Bradman departed for his first test hundred, 112, Australia had a lead of 325 with two wickets still to go. The Melbourne crowd gave Bradman a standing ovation. A contemporary Australian newspaper reported on Bradman reaching his 100:

> The crowd, scenting a definite Australian superiority for the first time in the match, was in raptures. Men who long ago waved and gesticulated, still making hoarse, throaty noises. Bradman and Oxenham were going after tired bowling.

With rain forecast overnight, England would have to bat on a sticky, drying wicket already five days old.

Sure enough, rain came to Australia's cause. Play started late on day six. The roller had to be stopped before the full seven minutes since the top was cracking under its weight. In short, it was a dusty nightmare. Australia gained four byes in front of 25,000, but White clean bowled both Oxenham (who had made a gritty 39 in an eighth wicket partnership of 92 with Bradman the day before) and Blackie for a duck. Australia set England 332.

There were only three overs for Hobbs and Sutcliffe to negotiate before lunch. They began a partnership that 'deserves to be inscribed in letters of gold in the annals of cricket.' By now the sun baked the crust of the wicket. Over lunch, Hugh Trumble, the old veteran turn-of-the-century off spinner, told Hobbs that '70 would be a good score.'

Immediately after lunch, the ball lifted awkwardly. Soon Hobbs gloved an off break from the 46-year-old Don Blackie that spat from a length, but Hendry at slip failed miserably to take the chance. Australia's heads went down, as Hobbs – same age as Blackie – weathered the storm with the 34-year-old Sutcliffe, both taking body blows as the ball spat, reared, hung, kicked and broke. If there were two players on the planet who could cope with the conditions it was Hobbs and Sutcliffe, the most successful opening pair in all of test history. Twice Hobbs was struck on the side of his face. Sutcliffe reckoned the wicket was worse than the Oval in 1926 and the bruises stayed for days afterwards. Three quarters of the Australian fielders huddled in a ring around the bat.

Ryder mixed his bowlers around but, to the intense frustration of the crowd, they, especially Balckie and Oxenham, bowled too short. Instead of bowling full to draw the batsmen forward, they had time to wait on the back foot and play the ball from the pitch. Quiet accumulators Hobbs and Sutcliffe took the score to 105 before Hobbs walked in front of a straight one from Blackie, but by now the pitch had eased.

Jardine arrived at the crease with his traditional Harlequin's hat and looked uncomfortable from the start although the wicket had eased slightly. By the close, none of Australia's bowlers had been sufficiently skilled to provide enough turn. Jardine survived on 21 whilst Sutcliffe, with his shiningly combed dark hair, walked off with a rock-like 83. On the final day England required 161 with eight wickets in hand, the pitch remained unrolled and had a scruffy appearance.

Blackie opened on the line of middle to leg rather than off stump and both batsmen helped themselves to early runs. Clarrie Grimmett came on with his leg breaks and wickets started to tumble. Jardine was bowled through his pads for 33. Hammond looked distinctly ill at ease with the wicket for one who had scored 200 in the first innings. Nonetheless, he added a useful 58 with Sutcliffe before being unluckily run out for 32.

Patsy Hendren, the short and stocky cockney, came out to join Sutcliffe. Hendren had already made big runs in the series after a magnificent 169, made at a healthy strike rate, to take the first test away from the Australians. Had Hendren been around in the 1970s or 80s, instead of the Hobbs/Sutcliffe/Hammond era, he could quite easily have become a legend.

Hendren hit four boundaries in rapid succession to ease the tension and take England beyond 300. He outscored the now tiring Sutcliffe, but kept the Yorkshireman entertained in between overs.

Finally Sutcliffe fell (with just fourteen required) LBW to Grimmett for 135 scored from 462 deliveries at a strike rate of just 29.22 over six hours of intense concentration, a rock for the England team to cling to and ultimately conquer. The score was 318 and Sutcliffe was only the fourth batsman to be dismissed.

Wisden has this to say about Sutcliffe's innings:

> Scarcely anything in the whole tour approached the long, drawn-out tension of the last innings before the winning hit was made... these runs had to be made on a rain-ruined wicket and anybody who knows the Melbourne ground will appreciate the stupendous effort required.

Jardine claimed that: 'without Hobbs and Sutcliffe, the remaining nine Englishmen could have been bowled out twice on such a wicket for half the runs.'

Hendren added eight with Chapman, England's amateur, 25-year-old skipper, before being bowled by Oxenham's medium pace just before tea. England 326–5.

Chapman aimed a mighty off drive to hit the winning runs but was caught at cover by Woodfull off Ryder, bowling admirably straight, 328–6. The Australians ran Tate out at the non-striker's end, scampering for a single, halting, turning and failing to get back, England 328–7. Thankfully Geary hit a boundary to seal the win and with it the Ashes retained.

England won the fourth test by just twelve runs with Bradman 40 and run out 58, again not trumping Hammond's 119 and 177. However by the fifth test Bradman had 123 and 37 not out, to Hammond's 38 and 16. Australia won by five wickets.

Australia 397 (Ryder 112, Kippax 100, Bradman 79, Geary 3–83, Larwood 3–127).
England 417 (Hammond 200, Jardine 62, Sutcliffe 58, Blackie 6–94).
Australia 351 (Bradman 112, Woodfull 107, J. C. White 5–107).
England 332–7 (Sutcliffe 135, Hobbs, 49, Hendren 45).
ENGLAND WON BY 3 WICKETS.

Innings Ranked Number 20
Hobb's 187 at Adelaide in 1912

Opponents: Australia.
At stake: Ashes.
Bowling attack: Cotter, Hordern, Armstrong, Minnett, Matthews, Kelleway: 27.45 runs per wicket.
Pitch: Fine.
Game situation: 1–1 in the Ashes of 1911–12.

Eighteen months without a test match seems a long time nowadays, but this was typical in Edwardian Britain. There were still only three test-playing nations (South Africa having joined in 1889). In fact

England's last series was a disappointing 3–2 loss to South Africa, where, out of the batsmen, only Jack Hobbs flourished with 539 runs at 67.4.

England brought in new blood for the first Ashes test and gave debuts to J. W. H. T. Douglas, F. R. Foster, J. W. Hearne, S. P. Kinneir and C. P. Mead. They retained Hobbs, Frank Woolley, Wilfred Rhodes and wicket-keeper H. Strudwick – those in their prime – and brought back S. F. Barnes and George Gunn.

The first test was lost by 146 runs. Dropped immediately was Kinneir, the unfit opener, replaced by a bowler, J. W. Hitch, who was to perform moderately in a stretched-out career. Then the batting was strengthened by replacing number eleven, Strudwick, with number nine, E. J. Smith, as wicket-keeper.

There ensued another tight game with England taking a lead of 81 in the first innings. Australia fared better, with Armstrong smiting 90. England required 219 to win. The rest is history but if the reader wonders when England's finest ever cricketing period was, from the inception of test cricket to the present day, it would not be 2005, or 1985, or 1981, or the great 1950s. The greatest-ever period of England dominance in world cricket started on 2 January 1912 and continued on until the outbreak of the Great War.

Jack Hobb's 126 not out has long been quoted as one of his finest ever innings and established him as the world's number-one ranked batsman. It is true that Hobbs never made a really big score for England, his highest was 211. However, in real terms, he did. This 126 not out added to his next innings comes to 313 which would have been a record at the time. Here is *Wisden's* account of the match winning 126:

> He scored his 126 not out in just under 3 hours and a half, and did not give a chance of any kind. His hits included eight 4s.

His innings was full of brilliant opportunistic cricket, stolen singles to the covers. Hobbs square and late cutting was powerful and precise. To the spinner Hordern, Hobbs 'hunted down the wicket' or rocked back and played him from the base of the stumps. England won by eight wickets, ushering in a run of sixteen tests, thirteen wins, three draws and no defeats against Australia and South Africa.

In Jack Hobbs England had the world's best batsman. In Wilfred Rhodes they had the premier all-rounder, and in Foster and Barnes their most penetrative pair of opening bowlers ever, with Barnes (ingrained into my head from an early age) being the greatest-ever bowler. England had a strong batting line up but Hobbs was in a class of his own.

England moved on to Adelaide, team unchanged. Australia won the toss and elected to bat. At 65–2, with Hordern and Armstrong seemingly established, Clem Hill sat back contented in the right and obvious decision. It was, apparently, a perfect wicket and the sun was out on a glorious day. Frank Foster, bowling very fast in-swingers to cramp the batsmen, had other ideas and took five for 36. Barnes supported and Australia stumbled to 133 all out.

Hobbs and Rhodes entered the arena with a strut in their step. Life was relatively easy with the best pair of opening bowlers in the world. A good start and Australia would soon feel the pressure. Calmly and with controlled circumspection, both openers remained at the close of play, Hobbs on 29 Rhodes 20.

A roasting second day started with Hobbs and Rhodes illuminating the ground with a blazing stand of 147, reliving their fruitful partnership first allowed to flourish back in South Africa eighteen months previously. Rhodes had started his test career in the previous century, at number eleven, and with W. G. Grace in the side. English cricket had come a long way since then.

Cotter and Hardern were met, discussed and seen off. Hill placed a ring of fielders on the off-side in a vain attempt to stem the flow of runs. Eventually, Rhodes fell LBW to Cotter but by now England were in front and in command.

Out strode G. Gunn, an absolute nutter and a spectator's delight. Down the wicket he hunted to both pace and spin, whilst Hobbs remained more orthodox. Gunn knocked the bowlers off their length and Hobbs feasted. Gunn and his rumbustious attempts to keep up with Hobbs led to his eventual downfall and he fell caught off Armstrong for 29. Nonetheless the pair added a further 59 and took the score passed the 200. J. W. Hearne helped to add 54, but Hobbs was by now demonstrating his status and dominated the partnership. Hearne fell for twelve. C. P. Mead was a quality left-hand batsman who would achieve a test average of 49.35 and score 153 centuries in his first-class career. His left handedness complimented the right-handed Hobbs, who was by now starting to wilt in the heat. On Hobbs batted, handing out chances as he weakened. With the score on 323 and a lead of 90, Hobbs gave a catch to Hordern off Minnett and retreated thankfully into the shade. He had quashed the obvious danger of Hordern, who had rampaged through England with twelve wickets in the first test.

For the rest of the series Australia were simply outplayed in all departments. This was not a classic innings and Hobbs played many more with greater freedom and less error. It lasted a mere $3^{1}/2$ hours but dominated the test match and once more took the lead away from Australia.

Australia were sunk, and had to concede a first-innings deficit of 368. They fought gamely and set England a target of 112 in the fourth innings. England won by seven wickets with Wilfred Rhodes 57 not out. Australia never recovered, with England taking the series 4–1.

England dominated the triangular series back home in the summer of 1912 with Barnes leaving his indelible mark as the greatest bowler of all time. He was up to fast medium in pace, but with subtle changes. Barnes had command of seam, pace and spin. Batsmen all too frequently could not decipher even the spin from the seam, such was the blurr as the ball was delivered. He stood straight backed and had immense stamina. Unusually, he played most of his cricket in minor counties though this did not stop him being selected for England, even at the age of 40.

As for Jack Hobbs, he set records which today – and despite Bradman, Tendulkar, Lara and Ponting – still exist and are likely to stand for ever, etched in the stained record books on distant museum shelves: 197 first class centuries and over 61,000 first class runs.

Australia 133 (F. R. Foster 5–36, S. F. Barnes 3–71).
England 501 (Hobbs 187, F. R. Foster 71, Rhodes 59, Cotter 4–125).
Australia 476 Hill 98, Carter 72, Bardsley 63, Matthews 53, Barnes 5–105).
England 112–3 (Rhodes 57*, Gunn 45).
ENGLAND WON BY 7 WICKETS.

Innings Ranked Number 19
A. G. Steele's 148 not out at Lord's in 1884

Opponents: Australia.
At stake: Ashes.
Bowling attack: Spofforth, Palmer, Giffen, Boyle, Bonnor, Midwinter: 21.21.
Pitch: Fine but slower than in 1946/47.
Situation: England were 90-3 in response to Australia's 229. This was the second of three tests with the first test drawn due to rain.

1884, a long time ago, even before the first car, was when Maxim invented the machine gun. Gladstone's Reform Act had extended the right to vote to people in the counties, increasing the number of voters from three million to five million. England's cricket team had still not recovered the 'Ashes' won by Australia in England in the solitary test of 1882. The series in Australia in 1882/83 ended 2–2.

Expectations rose during the summer of 1884 as England could field her strongest eleven. Australia still possessed a potent bowling combination in Spofforth, Palmer, Giffen, Boyle and Bonnor and England managed totals of just 95 and 180 in the first test on a wet wicket at Old Trafford where the first day was washed out. Australia did not have time to win.

Frederick Robert Spofforth has gone down in history as the first bowler to humble W.G. A fit, lean man who could run 100 yards in less than eleven seconds, he was essentially a fast-medium bowler. At 31 going into this test, he was still technically in his prime. His bowling feats around the country in the summer of 1884 testify to the great man's number-one ranking in the world at the time. Against a respectable 'Eleven of England' six weeks earlier he had taken 7–34 and an incredible 7–3, followed with match figures of 9–61 against Yorkshire. Crucially, against Liverpool & District, his reign of terror came to an end, and he took only 2–66. Athough Australia won that game by one wicket, he had met his match in A. G. Steele.

What infuriated Spofforth about Steele's batting was his technique, hunched over the bat as though short sighted and looking like a very ordinary fellow. Yet Steele had taken 72 and 29 against, not just Spofforth, but Palmer, Giffen, Boyle, the lot!

In this the first ever Lord's Test, Australia won the toss and elected to bat first. Edmund Peate recorded figures of 6–85 including the top five by bowling accurate, slow left arm deliveries. England responded steadily with W. G, Grace (his long, dark beard not yet greying) opening with A. P. Lucas, the latter, like Steele, an ex-Cambridge blue.

By now W.G. had become good friends with the Australian skipper Billy Murdoch, both being regarded as the best batsman in each hemisphere. W.G. fell first, though, at 37–1, caught Bonnor off Palmer, the fast, right-arm off-spinner. The crowd gasped in disappointment, the expectation every time W.G. arrived at the crease was for a repetition of his great 152 at the Oval four years earlier. W.G. was box office.

Lucas fell in identical fashion. Where did Bonnor field? Statistically the best chances were at slip. With the score on 56–2, at the wicket was George Ulyett, the hefty Yorkshire hitter, partnerung the 28-year-old right hander, and resolute defender, Arthur Shrewsbury. Shrewsbury settled in and George Ulyett blasted a few and together the score approached 100 before Shrewsbury stumbled out of his crease to be stumped off Giffen's accurate slow-medium, a frustrating moment for the Nottinghamshire batsman.

Steele awaited his turn, padded up with the fall of W.G. It was a typical July day, sunny intervals, cloudy with some wind blowing across the ground. Gentlemen in the crowd wore long, dark, extended bowler hats and almost all wore heavy moustaches. Pleasant surroundings, bit of a slope to the ground running square of the wicket, trees in full summer bloom in the middle distance.

Allan Steele was regarded as one of England's finest all-rounders, second only to the incomparable W. G. Grace. He had been a member of the Cambridge team that beat the Australians, including Fred 'The Demon' Spofforth, by an innings in 1878. He was a powerful driver of the ball, quick on his feet, a right hander.

Steele soaked up the atmosphere and allowed his eyes to get accustomed to the light. Then Shrewsbury fell and a great gasp came from the crowd, as though national honour was on the line. The crowd applauded the diminuative figure of the Lancastrian all rounder as he trotted onto the ground through the members' pavilion.

Steele had a moustache that was typical of the day, thick, bushy and spiked at the ends. An intense-looking man, he was 26, astute, technically correct, and occasionally flamboyant with bat in hand. He provided right-arm spin to help balance the side. He could turn the ball both ways on a length and took his wickets economically.

Spofforth and Palmer, sensing a critical stage in the game, were brought back by Murdoch and bowled in long spells. George Ulyett never liked being bogged down for too long, preferring to entertain, and had showed crowds hits as far as 130 yards back in his native Yorkshire. This time, George Palmer cleaned him up as Ulyett missed a straight one, 120–4. In came Lord Harris, England's captain, but Spofforth was simply too good again – 135–5.

Now with a score of twenty not out, and with the limited skills of Dick Barlow, a 'stonewaller' and magnificent purveyor of the forward defence, Steele, to the annoyance of the Australian bowlers, began to play splendidly well. He encouraged Barlow out of his shell, particularly as the ball was now older and doing less. The outfield had been cut to an impressively short length, so both batsmen gained full purchase for their shots.

Eventually Murdoch replaced his trusted pair of spearheads and turned to 6ft 6ins George Bonnor, the 'Australian Giant'. Bonnor rarely bowled, he was just this big, big hitter. He bowled tidily enough, his job was simply to contain before the second new ball.

Sure enough, with the England total having overtaken Australia's, Barlow fell, caught by Palmer off Bonnor, but his job had been done. It was now that Steele rammed home England's advantage dominating a stand of 38 with W. W. Read. History recalls Steele's handsome driving. The applause as he raised his bat for his second test century was richly deserved. Words such as 'brilliant' have been used to describe this innings.

The Rt Hon. Alfred Lyttelton, who now partnered Steele, could bat a bit with a first-class average close to 28. He had played in the 1878 Cambridge v. Australia game and could also play Spofforth. He owned a resolutely straight bat and, whenever possible, played the game on the front foot.

Steele finally fell for a breathtaking 148. England reached 379 and Spofforth, twenty wickets in his three previous test matches, took to bed the unflattering figures of 2–102. In his obituary of Steele, published in the 1915 *Wisden*, Allan Gibson wrote:

> As a batsman Steel was great in every sense of the word. He was a master of every kind of hit. The cut, drive, leg hit, and play off his legs

all were alike to Steel, and in addition his driving was equally good on both sides of the wicket. He had not exactly an attractive style as he was short in stature, and he was a trifle short-sighted, and seemed to stoop a little to get a sight of the ball. But he hit at every ball that was off the wicket, and a great many that were straight, and master as he was of every hit he was a very fast scorer, and few cricketers were less troubled by nerves ... Steel played a superb innings of 148 at Lord's with only one chance ... Among other batting gifts Steel was very quick-footed, not in the sense of habitually moving in front of the wicket – Steel was never guilty of that – but in jumping out and smothering the ball at the pitch. Spofforth used to bowl a slowish ball every now and then, but Steel constantly was out of his ground and driving any ball that he could get at. In 1884 one of the strongest elevens Australia ever had were playing MCC at Lord's, and the Club on winning the toss made 481 of which W. G. Grace, Steel, Barnes, and T. C. O'Brien made 412. Steel's share was 134. W. G. Grace said of this innings that he should never forget the unceremonious way Steel treated the Australian bowling directly he went in, and Spofforth, Giffen, Palmer, an Cooper had an unenviable time of it.

Australia never came close and succumbed for 145 to give England a win by an innings and five runs. This was the only test to achieve a successful outcome as the Oval wicket provided a featherbed and a mountain of runs. Again Australia won the toss and batted, and this time they reached a then record 551, with Murdock breaking the test highest score with 211. McDonnell and Scott also took centuries off England's attack. However a remarkable partnership of 151 between W. W. Read, batting at number ten, and Scotton, the opener, took England's score to 346. In the second innings, England reached 85–2 before time was called.

England, fortunately and perhaps only because of Steele's innings, regained the Ashes for the very first time. As for Spofforth, he continued to terrorise any teams that summer that did not have Steele shoring up the innings. Against Middlesex, a still angry Spofforth took 12–42; against the Players, a strong team, he recorded match figures of 14–96. Then, against England at the Oval, Spofforth took only 2–81 from 58 overs again without A. G. Steele's wicket.

Steele never toured with England, but led the 1886 team to a 3–0 clean sweep against the Australians. He last played, again as captain, in the first test of the 1888 series, but England lost, he made three and ten not out, took 1–4, and never played for England again. He retired from the game in 1895, with a respectable first class average of 29.25

with the bat, and an eye catching 13.5 with the ball, having captured 781 wickets. Across eighteen seasons, he only scored seven centuries in first class cricket. His 148 won the Ashes for England and there followed the most successful string of series wins for England against Australia ever.

In thirteen tests between 1880 and 1888 Steele's batting average (35.29) exceeded his bowling average (20.86) by 14.43, quite some feat! It seems that, glancing at Steele's vital test statistics, that he could feasibly have been chosen at his peak simply as a batsman or purely as a bowler, like Botham and Flintoff in their prime.

Australia 229 (Scott 75, Giffen 63, Peate 6–85).
England 379 (AG Steele 148, Palmer 6–111).
Australia 145 (Ulyett 7–36).
ENGLAND WON BY AN INNINGS AND 5 RUNS.

Innings Ranked Number 18
Hutton's 156 not out at Adelaide in 1951

Opponents: Australia.
At stake: National pride as the Ashes were already lost.
Bowling attack: Lindwall, Miller, Johnson, Iverson, Johnston, Burke: 19.90.
Pitch: Fine but slower than in 1946/47.
Situation: Australia scored 371, as Hutton opened with Washbrook.

England was still ravaged by the effects of the Second World War. A whole generation of cricketers had their formative years pole-axed by Hitler and the need to defeat Nazism. The make up of the England touring party relied all too heavily on the over 32-year-olds, players such as Hutton, Washbrook, Compton, Brown and Wright with pre-war test experience. Only Simpson and Evans were aged between 26 and 31, whilst the rest of the party comprised youthful potential rather than bedded-down talent.

Freddie Brown was 40 and chosen to captain the side because of one blistering innings in the Gentlemen v. Players fixture where he hit 122 out of 131 in 1 hour and 50 minutes. Up to the fourth test, aside from Hutton, Brown was the only Englishman to have achieved a score of 50 or over. It was no surprise to find England already 3–0 down, although two of the tests were lost narrowly.

Washbrook declined to tour at first and had to be persuaded. He endured a miserable series and averaged only seventeen. Denis Compton averaged 92 in the State games, but simply ran dry in the tests; his series has entered folk lore as an unparallel feat of failure for such a talented batsman. Across seven completed innings, Compton was to average a prep school 7.57.

What of Hutton? He of the famous one arm shorter than the other due to an accident in the gym during the war? England's batting relied so heavily on Len Hutton that it is hard to imagine in the history of English cricket a time when so much depended on one man. The closest comparison is probably Boycott in Pakistan and New Zealand around 1977–78 whilst Botham was still discovering himself.

At any rate, with only national pride and the reputation of the cricketers at stake, Australia won the toss – for the third time out of four in the series – and naturally elected to bat. Bedser, Wright and Tattersall shared the wickets, whilst Australia amassed 371, with Aurthor Morris batting 426 minutes for 206. Opening the innings Morris was also last out.

This was a fine Adelaide wicket, slow enough to kill the threat of a steep-rising delivery, yet sufficiently quick to allow full purchase across a fast outfield. In an otherwise slow-scoring series, the scoring rate throughout the Australian first innings touched four an over (in the days of eight ball overs, equivalent to three an over today). In statistical terms the Australian attack had the lowest runs per wicket total out of all the greatest 50 test-match innings recorded in this book – 19.9 runs per wicket. Such a low average was down to the mystery spinner, Doug Iverson who had entered test cricket at 35. Having experimented with a ping-pong ball, he had developed a new grip upon which to spin. With his index finger under the seam, he could bowl pronounced leg breaks and googlies at will. Though a proper jester with the bat, itself appearing as old as himself, and a significant liability in the field, Iverson's brief, but spectacular, test career amounted to a 15.23 bowling average.

The remainder of Australia's attack was the same as the 1948 'Invincibles' team and Lindwall, Miller, Johnston and Johnson need no further embellishment at this stage.

It was another hot day as Hutton strode out in the early-afternoon heat of day two. So one sided had the Ashes contests been in the immediate aftermath of the war that the expected happened again and England lost an early wicket. Washbrook played an injudicious shot off Lindwall that looped to Iverson, England 8–1.

Reg Simpson, at 31, was in his prime and his 49 runs at Sydney in the previous test had indicated potential if nothing else. Another right hander, he intended to stay and grind out a total alongside his senior partner.

Australian supporters are rarely generous in their praise of English cricketers. When so far ahead in the series though they are quick to point out and marvel at cricket artistry, even from the old enemy. The destiny of the series already decided, the Adelaide Oval crowd sat back and hoped for some fight back or grand batting masterpiece, most probably from Hutton or Compton.

Hutton, playing the percentages, steadily accumulated alongside Simpson and the England total passed 50. Pressure eased as the ball softened in the evening sun. Hassett turned to his fast-medium Bill Johnston, and at once Simpson succumbed, bowled by the change of angle, England 80–2.

Compton entered the arena, got off the mark and appeared to be settling in at last, then snicked Lindwall behind for five, 96–3. All Hutton could do was hold his end up, survive, graft, put away the bad ball and stay there hoping for a long partnership with someone, anyone.

Sheppard, a Cambridge blue, chosen for his powers of concentration, held an end for a while. The 22-year-old certainly had the potential, but this was a series too soon. In his young life Sheppard had never faced a spinner such as Iverson. Before he reached double figures, Iverson had conned him into playing down the wrong line, England 132–4 Sheppard bowled for nine.

Now the skipper came out to join Hutton. Big Freddie Brown had been a small revelation in the series to date. His big hitting grabbing crucial quick runs to prevent the middle order, shorn of Compton's genius, from stagnating. Brown blustered his way to sixteen, but just as he was about to get set, Miller bowled him a yorker that beat him through the air for pace, 161–5 and now England stared down the barrel of another large, first-innings deficit.

All the while Hutton remained secure in an almost faultless exhibition. It is true that Hutton was missed twice. There was a stumping chance that went begging when he was on 34 and, right at the end, he gave a sharp chance to mid-off. He struck eleven fours and batted for over six hours, whilst all around crumbled away. A sprightly last-wicket stand of 53 with Doug Wright took England to within 99 of the Australian total. In the heat, Hutton's exhaustion began to tell. It came as something of a relief to the crowd when Lindwall eventually pinned Wright in front of his stumps.

Hutton traipsed off dehydrated and suffering from heat exhaustion; his walk betrayed his physical condition, feet dragging upon the Adelaide outfield. Hutton had batted for 370 minutes in all and became the first Englishman to carry his bat for the second time in tests. That England were not totally out of the game at the half-way stage owed everything to the Yorkshire opener.

Australia batted on for just over 100 eight ball overs and declared at 403–8, setting England an impossible 502 to win.

Hutton and Washbrook set off in determined manner and posted 74 but, aside from Simpson's 61, England fell away to lose by 274 runs. Indeed the last five wickets fell for just seven runs. When Hutton was dismissed for 45, he had spent the first $23^1/_2$ hours of play on the pitch, a remarkable statistic. It is a shame that his great, lonely feat of stubbornness, his mastery of a potent attack, should be drowned out by the wafer-thin England batting resources and the complete failure of her other genius Denis Compton. Had Compton performed as Compton could, the series would have been far closer with honours more even.

So Hutton's great act of defiance coincided with a nadir in English cricket and his feat has been less pampered than perhaps it should. However, writing for the *Daily Telegraph* at the time, Swanton saw fit to describe Hutton's 156 not out thus:

> It was a superb illustration of the art and almost faultless, as was his judgement of length, the execution of his strokes and his unremitting concentration.

Like the first swallow of summer, the bursting bulb in early spring and the rising sun from a polar winter, the fifth test gave a glimpse of a brighter future ahead and England won by eight wickets. Hutton as ever provided reliable backbone in both innings with a firm 79 in the first and a fine accelerating 60 not out to guide England home in the second. It is fitting really that the great trump at the top of England's order bridged the $12^1/_2$ years between England's previous Ashes victory, back at the Oval in 1938, with the Melbourne victory of 1951, scoring significantly in both games.

Hutton's stock as a batsman was never higher and he finished the series with an average of 88.83. Odd too that England possessed easily the best batsman, as well as the most successful pace bowler in Bedser and the better keeper. So, despite having a stronger backbone, England still lost 1–4.

Australia 371 (Morris 206, Wright 4–99, Bedser 3–74).
England 272 (Hutton 156*, Lindwall 3–51, Johnston 3–58, Iverson 3–68).
Australia 403 (Burke 101*, Miller 99, Harvey 68).
England 228 (Simpson 61, Hutton 45, Sheppard 41, Johnston 4–73, Miller 3–27).
AUSTRALIA WON BY 274 RUNS.

Innings Ranked Number 17
Hammond's 240 at Lord's in 1938

Opponents: Australia.
At stake: Ashes, held by Australia.
Bowling attack:McCormick, McCabe, Fleetwood–Smith, O'Reilly, Chipperfield: 37.58.
Pitch: Superb.
Game situation: First innings, England 20–2 after winning the toss.
Attendance: 100,933.

Friday, 24 June 1938 saw the RAF launch a new recruitment campaign. By the end of the first day, there were 1,000 enquiries. Indeed, during the game, the British Government announced a doubling of the anti-aircraft defence force. Storm clouds gathered over Europe, Hitler had annexed Austria and all German children were forbidden to talk to Jewish children in schools across Germany. Elsewhere, in Asia, Japanese fighter planes had bombed the Chinese city of Canton, killing tens of thousands. At least world heavy-weight boxing champion Joe Louis's punching power had knocked down the only man to have beaten him, the German Max Schmeling.

Hammond liked to peruse the news over breakfast. Captaining England was a big honour and he had been a star for a decade. He rubbed shoulders with high society, yet tended to be rather aloof to his team mates, even more so now he was captain.

At this point Australia held the Ashes, having come from 0–2 down to win the previous 1936–7 series 3–2, an amazing turn around that centred on a return to form from Bradman.

This Lord's Test was only Hammond's second as captain after qualifying as an amateur. The first test at Trent Bridge had been a run glut with four England batsmen (Barnett, Hutton, Compton and a double from Paynter) scoring 100s. McCabe fought back with 232 for Australia, but England enforced the follow on. Australia batted out time thanks to centuries from Brown and Bradman.

Australia had a wild and fast opening bowler in Ernie McCormick who, steaming in off a 31-pace run up, had reduced England to 20–2, with the wickets of Len Hutton and Bill Edrich back in the hutch. Fierce and at top speed, McCormick, a tall and lean bowler, delivered the ball to the batsman at express pace. The 32-year-old was still in his prime.

A slammed door silenced members of the Long Room and the footsteps down the stairs turned everyone's heads. Hammond walked through the crowd of MCC folk with a jaw set so firm a member whispered: 'Good God. He'll score a century today.' His stride to the middle bore the hallmarks of a gladiator, broad-shouldered, square jawed, the 35-year-old captain fanned a mood of angry defiance, cap slanted slightly. Like all great champions, he took his time to study the field placements; three slips, two gullies, a leg slip for the leg-side bouncer and a forward short leg – standard fare.

A bouncer whistled passed Hammond's eyes as he swayed out of the way. He was too old and wise to go hooking at the short stuff, especially so early in the game. Next ball, McCormick attempted a yorker which bounced just before Hammond's toes, swinging in from the off. A crack of noise that was akin to a rifle shot resonated around the crowd as the ball sped towards the pavilion, all along the ground, then crashed into the railings. It was a false dawn for England though as another wicket fell – that of Charlie Barnett, trying to impress the crowd, caught Brown bowled McCormick.

England had slumped to 31–3 after having won the toss. Lord's was aloud with chatter as the jaunty Lancastrian veteran Eddie Paynter came out to join his captain. The 37-year-old left-hander encouraged the possibility of bowlers losing their lines. What is more, Paynter was the man in form, with 216 not out to his name in the Trent Bridge test.

Hammond soon blazed away at McCormick with regal authority, through the covers and back passed the bowler again. Anything short Hammond kept swaying out of the way. Bill 'Tiger' O'Reilly posed the main threat in this Australian attack – a tall, right-arm leg spin and googly bowler. He did not extract much turn, but every delivery seemed to bounce more than expected. O'Reilly was the Anil Kumble of his time. Bradman rated O'Reilly the greatest bowler of the 1930s. His 144 wickets came at a lower average than any leg spinner in history, 22.59.

The ball soon softened and runs came in abundance. Hammond cut and drove with exquisite precision, controlled power and great timing – a master craftsman, punishing all that Australia had to hurl at him. According to Cardus this was 'a red-carpetted innings' averaging 40 runs per hour.

After lunch Paynter too, found his touch. Unlike Hammond, he liked to hook, and he hooked well. The afternoon session ignited the crowd and the pair accumulated a 222-run stand to completely change the face of the game.

Paynter reached 99 (and an aggregate of 315 runs so far in the series) without being dismissed. Then O'Reilly pegged him back in front of the stumps. Australia, despite athletic fielding, leaked runs with wayward bowling.

The youthful Denis Compton joined Hammond, fresh from a 102 at Trent Bridge a fortnight earlier. Sadly for the crowd, the young genius was also undone by an O'Reilly arm ball, plumb in front for six Now the total stood at 271–5 with England, despite the record 222 run partnership, in danger of handing over the initiative.

Seeking total domination, Hammond savaged poor Fleetwood–Smith, a left-arm spinner, normally difficult to pick off. Onwards he accelerated, with the right-handed Kent wicket-keeper Leslie Ames for company. As a batsman/wicket-keeper, Ames was the finest England ever had, with career statistics surpassing even Alex Stewart's at the turn of the millenium. Ames watched as perhaps England's greatest batsman mauled Fleetwood–Smith in a leonine manner, as though latter had been an antelope brought to his knees by a predator at the apex of the cricketing pyramid.

Ames picked at the carcasses of the bowlers dismantled by Hammond and helped to complete the utter domination. When Hammond took on Chipperfield, he hammered the ball back at such velocity that the caught and bowled chance – inches above the ground – fractured the poor bowler's finger bones. It still crossed the rope.

By the end of day one, Hammond had thrashed a brilliant 210 not out with Ames also undefeated on 50. The score stood at 409–5. *Wisden* states that he offered no chance and every shot was executed to perfection, in so much as he was not beaten, rushed or uncomfortable for a moment. In a work of art on how to dominate and counter-attack hour after hour, this was the finest. The most famous off drive ever played at Lord's bounced half-way back to the middle from the railings under Old Father Time.

A crowd of 33,800 turned up on the second morning, the largest ever seen at Lord's. It was so large that spectators had to spill onto the outfield. The boundary ropes had to be taken in a few yards from the previous day, in theory benefiting the Australians. From 409–5 overnight Hammond, in partnership with Ames, added a further 30 imperious runs on the second morning. By now he nursed an elbow injury and a strained thigh. Eventually, with the score on 457, and 186 added with Ames, a simple straight delivery went through Hammond's tired defence. Despite soreness and fatigue, he must have felt soundly satisfied on his walk back to the pavilion, a standing ovation ensued, with applause extending well beyond the time he stepped off the field.

In all Hammond batted for 367 minutes and blasted 32 boundaries in an innings of extraordinary power and beauty. He never seemed ruffled and this innings, out of all of his 140 in tests, is the innings that writers and artists of the time wish they were present at. Hammond was 35 and gave a display so wonderfully authoritative as to be universally approved at the time as the greatest show of batting ever from an England blade.

England's last five wickets fell for just the addition of 37 runs, to end on 494. Australia countered with a double hundred from Bill Brown who carried his bat. Hedley Verity took four wickets, including Bradman's for eighteen, bowling his blend of slow left arm. With a lead of 72 on the first innings, England then declared on 242–8 with the 20-year-old Denis Compton 76 not out. In the four-day test, not enough time was allowed to bowl Australia out, but a defiant 102 not out from Bradman secured honours were shared in this, the second drawn test in the series.

It is not ranked as highly in statistical terms as the second of the back-to-back double hundreds in the 1928/29 series because

Hammond's 200 at Melbourne was the difference between the two teams and helped to win both the test and allow England to retain the Ashes.

His master class here warded off the threat of defeat. To be honest, statistics point to a comparatively impotent Australian attack. They had been caned for over 600 in the first test. There followed this colossal knock by Hammond. Later, during the fifth test at the Oval, in the absence of McCormick, Hutton, then a young 22-year-old Yorkshire batsman, camped out for over two days against the attack and returned with 364, the record highest score in test cricket for nineteen years.

This was Hammond's last great knock, although he made another three centuries against South Africa in the winter, and a final 138 against the West Indies in 1939. After that, there was a six-year break while the European countries tore each other apart.

It is really quite difficult to accurately rank Hammond's top innings. They all showed the pedigree of classical driving. They were all compiled from a percentage mindset that led to careful shot selection that erred towards accumulation in the comfort zone rather than extravagant flashes. It is likely that no one before him was a better driver. In later years, many, such as Ted Dexter, possessed the power of execution, but Hammond cut the path, raised the benchmark and provided the mountains for Bradman to conquer.

England 494 (Hammond 240, Paynter 99, Ames 83, O'Reilly 4–93, McCormick 4–101).
Australia 422 (Brown 206*, Hassett 56, Verity 4–103, Farnes 3–135).
England 242–8 declared (Compton 76*, Paynter 43, McCormick 3–72).
Australia 204–6 (Bradman 102*).
MATCH DRAWN.

Innings Ranked Number 16
Boycott's 191 at Headingley in 1977

Opponents: Australia.
At stake: Ashes.
Bowling attack: Thomson, Walker, Pascoe, Walters, Bright, Chappell: 29.96.
Pitch: Fine.
Game situation: England won the toss and elected to bat.

England had not regained the Ashes at home since 1953. This was the Queen's Silver Jubilee year and Virginia Wade had won Wimbledon six weeks earlier.

The first test at Lord's was rain affected and drawn. England won the second test by nine wickets at Old Trafford, set up by Woolmer's 137 and Underwood's 6–66. Geoffrey Boycott had spent three years on a self-imposed exile from test cricket, some said because the world had gotten all nasty from fearsome fast bowlers. Dennis Lillee, who had terrorised England (except Derek Randall) in the Centenary test at Melbourne that March, was unavailable for selection. At the start of the summer, Boycott announced that he was available for selection once again. Not wishing to pander to him the selectors ignored him for the first two tests in order to prolong Dennis Amiss's career. After 43 runs in three completed innings Amiss was discarded for the Trent Bridge test and Geoff Boycott reinstated to his rightful position, opening the innings.

The 'prodigal's' return promptly ran local hero Derek Randall out in a crisis, yet scored 107, his 98th first-class century. With another 80 not out in the second innings England took a 2–0 lead into the penultimate test at Headingley.

On the Saturday before the start, Boycott added his 99th hundred for Yorkshire against Warwickshire at Edgbaston. Now the scene was set for him to reach his 100th century in front of his adoring home crowd, in an Ashes test.

Boycott left the team dinner early the night before to get a good night's sleep. In the end he had but four hours and complained about this to his captain the next day before the start.

Mike Brearley won the toss and elected to bat. Out the pair strode, a couple of veteran professionals who had both been on the first-class circuit for a decade and a half. Brearley was worth his place as a captain, if not as a test standard batsman, whilst Boycott was the one supreme batsman in the team.

It was a hot, sunny day but poor Brearley edged Thomson behind for 0 without a run on the board. Max Walker bowled searchingly with a fine line and length, even getting decent swing. Woolmer joined Boycott and the pair batted reassuringly against quality swing bowling. Boycott played late and only if necessary. He had a knack of positioning himself quickly onto either the front or back foot and excelled in both front-footed and back-footed drives through the covers, his trade mark. Sometimes he had to jab down quickly as Walker caused him to hurry, otherwise this great run-making machine continued on serenely.

Partners came and went with regularity now, but each one providing useful supporting roles. Woolmer fell for 37, Randall an entertaining twenty in a partnership of twenty-three, and Tony Greig 43. The partnership of 96 with Greig was vital and began to take the game away from Australia.

The crowd gushed at Boycott's 50. Brearley states in his book *The Return of the Ashes,* that the crowd's exuberance '... on and off the field, reached West Indian proportions.'

Thomson and the metronomic Walker kept a tight control on preceedings, the former shattering Greig's stumps. Graham Roope, a curly-haired slip fielder from Surrey entered the fray at 201–4 (he had been at the other end when John Edrich reached his 100th century two months earlier). He chatted to Boycott between overs, reassuring him. Steadily another stand grew and Boycott was edging closer.

Towards the end of the day, Chappell put himself on as his four-pronged specialist attack began to tire. The longer you stay in, the easier it gets – simple as that. This adage holds true to a certain extent, then fatigue, or the second new ball, or bad light can change everything. With Boycott's concentration, fatigue was never an issue. Bright light and with a part-timer on, Boycott fancied his chances. The second new ball would be taken soon.

Chappell turned at his mark and started in. At such moments the nervous expectation of the crowd is like static electricity, buzzing with anticipation. Chappell releases the ball, about 70 m.p.h., it swings slightly through the air and lands as a nice half volley just outside the off stump. Feeling good Boycott picks his spot unusually through the onside and times a splendid on drive, back passed the bowler.

The crowd erupts for ten minutes. Various sectors of the crowd flood onto the pitch. It is the single, longest cheer in recorded history. The Ashes means everything to England cricket fans, the very pinnacle. Yet here in this crucial test match, that England needed to win to retain the Ashes before the last test, the Ashes themselves were temporarily forgotten as the nation cheered in wild adulation at the great, technically-blessed, opening batsman.

England reached 252–4 by the close, slow by modern standards. Think of England's 407 at Edgbaston in 2005 or the 364–6 at Lord's in 2009, but Boycott remained on 110 overnight.

After a few lusty blows, Roope fell early the next day for 34 to bring in Alan Knott, the impish Kent wicket-keeper. Both batsmen had enjoyed a record-equalling 215-run partnership in the last test, a precious stand beginning at 82–5 on the first day.

By now, hard though Australia tried, the game fell away and Knott and Boycott added a further 123. A Boycott cover drive off Ray Bright's slow left-arm spin was pure poetry. The front foot extended out to the pitch, left elbow high, the bat following a straight arc through 270°, finishing up like an extended forward defence, the ball scorching along the grass to the boundary. My father purred with awe, even better than the on drive the day before.

Bright regained some direction to have Knott LBW for 57 and then immediately the young 21-year-old Ian Botham bowled for 0. Batting with the tail for company Boycott began to force the issue.

'What better way to celebrate his 100th 100 than with a double century and carrying his bat!' my excited father announced. Pascoe hurtled in with the tail now exposed. Underwood kept Boycott company briefly whilst the score passed the 400 mark before Pascoe removed him. Boycott crept into the 180s with Hendrick alongside but Pascoe removed him too. Out came big Bob Willis, at this stage of his career a proper number eleven.

Boycott moved into the 190s, stealing the strike when he could. Then, on 191, and having batted for 629 minutes, Pascoe induced an edge from the legend's bat and Chappell grabbed the chance. So an unforgettable innings entered folk lore.

England's 436 provided the ideal platform to pressurise the beleaguered Australians. They were not a happy bunch. Hookes, the golden wonder-boy, who had lit up the Centenary test just months earlier, was a shadow of his former self, so was McCosker who two years earlier had enjoyed an outstanding series in England. The Australian camp was divided between those who had opted for higher wages playing for Kerry Packer's World Series cricket, and those who had not been chosen.

Botham ran through the Australians with 5–21, his second five-wicket haul in only his second test. Together with Hendrick, 4–41 and a magnificent run out of McCosker by Randall Australia subsided for 103. Following on Willis and Hendrick shared seven wickets and Australia, showing a distinct lack of fight, lost by an innings and 85 runs – funnily enough by the exact margin that England had been defeated by Australia at Edgbaston only two years previously.

The final test was drawn so England won, convincingly 3–0. This was Boycott's Ashes, much like 1981 was Botham's, 1985 Gower's and 2005 Flintoff's.

Geoff Boycott continued to play for England for much of the next five years, adding a further seven centuries, but his average dropped from over 50 at the end of the 1977 series to 47.72. Even so, his reputation as a quality batsman grew. Those who wrote him off as 'yellow' against fast bowling, were made to change their minds after a gutsy 100 not out to save a test against the brutal West Indies attack at the age of 40.

England's 1977 side was a good team that could take twenty wickets a game. Their seamers: Willis, Hendrick and Botham, supplied raw pace, metronomic accuracy and swing, whilst Underwood could be relied on to control the other end. Greig offered variations, so too Woolmer, and both took vital wickets during the series.

Similarly to 2009, the side included a first-rate test all-rounder (Greig/Flintoff) as well as the next in line (Botham/Broad), a transition watershed moment in English cricket like a handing over of the baton.

Greig soon followed the riches of World Series cricket and never played test cricket again for England, likewise Flintoff. In a test cricket world reduced in standard by many of the best players receiving bans, new shoots sprang up; amongst them Botham and Gower.

England 436 (Boycott 191, Knott 57, Pascoe 4–91, Thomson 4–113).
Australia 103 (Botham 5–21, Hendrick 4–41) and 248 (Marsh 63, Hendrick 4–54, Willis 3–32).
ENGLAND WON BY AN INNINGS AND 85 RUNS.

Innings Ranked Number 15
Butcher's 173 not out at Headingley in 2001

Opponents: Australia.
At stake: National pride, the ashes were already lost.
Bowling attack: McGrath, Gillespie, Lee, Warne: 25.63.
Pitch: Fine.
Situation: Australia, seeking the first Ashes whitewash over England since 1920/21, gave England the last day to score 315. Butcher came in with the score on 8–1.

The 2001 Australians were arguably as strong as any side to have ever visited these shores. They compare to Bradman's 1948 Invincibles and even to Clive Lloyd's 1984 Legends. Australia had two of the greatest bowlers ever to have graced the game, both destined to amass over 500 test wickets, one to go on to over 700. For series after series they mesmerised the best of the England batting. Too good for even Atherton to accrue a healthy average. McGrath's metronomic accuracy and the wizardry of Warne's leg break variations held a psychological edge over England that lasted over a decade, and in tandem across six series.

When relieved from their spells, McGrath would pass over to either Brett Lee, the fastest bowler in the world at the time, or Jason Gillespie, only a shade slower. If a partnership ensued, Steve Waugh, the gritty Australian captain, would pass the ball to either one or both of his legends who rarely ever let him down. Australia were top of the pile and had been since a clash of the titans saw Waugh's Australia defeat the declining West Indians in the Caribbean back in 1995. Australia's batting line-up was certainly the strongest of all time. Consider the number of legends, greats, and very good test-standard batsmen in the following top seven: Hayden, Langer, Ponting, M. Waugh, S. Waugh, Martyn, Gilchrist.

England, meanwhile, were ravaged by injuries from the start of the series, with both Michael Vaughan and Graham Thorpe sidelined, a devastating blow. England's bowling relied too much on the veterans Gough and Caddick, with precious little else for back up and certainly no spinner worthy of the name.

No surprises when England lost the first test at Birmingham by an innings, and the Lord's syndrome ensured a thumping defeat by eight wickets. With all to play for at Trent Bridge, England at last fought back and achieved first-innings parity, before submitting meekly to Warne. Australia romped home by seven wickets at $5^1/2$ an over, Caddick in particular thrashed to all parts.

As an England supporter, I purchased a ticket to the fourth test at Headingley – several months in advance of the series. This was done on the understanding that I would enjoy an all-day drinking binge with some fellow cricket followers, including school masters and police sergeants. Frankly I cannot remember much from what I believe was the second day. Australia had won the toss and chose to bat first. After the fall of a couple of early wickets, Ponting and Mark Waugh feasted for much of the rest of the day. Once again a test match against Australia assumed normal paths.

I sat back with my friends, supped beer on a hot day and watched Damian Martyn craft a beautiful century. At some stage my sober and younger cousin Robert, aged 24, joined me on the terraces and the banter from supporters started taking the normal pornographic and offensive route which so disturbs the traditional follower. To the tune of the Village People's *Go West* anthem, one supporter chanted out: 'Steward takes it up the a***!' This apparently was directed at the female steward, slightly podgy and about 45, who leant against one of the metal railings with her bottom pointing towards a large, drunken audience.

Australian wickets then fell with some regularity. In amongst five wickets for Gough, the Australians subsided from 263–2 to 447 all out. Then it was England's turn.

After Atheron and Trescothick had seen off the initial burst from McGrath and Gillespie, Lee took the ball and paced out his run from the Kirkstall Lane End. Another supporter chanted 'Brett Lee is a raving poof!' again to the tune of *Go West*. A glare from the young, express bowler towards the stand indicated that Lee had heard and was fuming. The first three overs were a mixture of fast, wide long hops as Lee vented his fury. Trescothick in particular cashed in with some thumping cuts and drives through the off side. Steve Waugh brought on Warne and brought back McGrath. Within twenty minutes both openers were back in the hutch, both snicking McGrath lifters to Gilchrist, same old same old.

On the third day England clambered up to 309 with Stewart left stranded on an enterprising 76 not out, one of his finest Ashes innings. All of the top order contributed but, Stewart aside, no one had reached 50. Once again England had been mown down by McGrath with 7–76 off 30.2 overs. Australia stretched their first innings lead of 138 to 314 for the fall of four wickets. With two days to go, Australia were firm favourites to go 4–0 up and romp towards a whitewash.

Then something welcome came England's way. It rained through much of the fourth day to deny the Australians from building a truly imposing total. Consumed with a desire to prove their greatness in the pantheon of great test teams, Gilchrist – acting as captain and on behalf of the injured Steve Waugh – declared to leave the Australians 86 overs to bowl England out. No one had yet scored a century for England in the series, with Mark Butcher's 83 in the Lord's debacle the highest to date.

Butcher had been recalled following the spate of injuries to England's batting line up. His first spell in tests had ended in the previous millennium with a modest average of 27 from 57 innings. Indeed, at the start of the season, Butcher was languishing in the Surrey 2nd XI. At Didsbury, against the Lancashire seconds, he failed for nought and walked off all at sea with his game and fed up, so low had his stock fallen.

His reincarnation had initially raised eyebrows but England were short of class. Nonetheless Butcher had established himself once again in the team. In seven innings he had outscored all of his contemporaries and though he had failed twice at Trent Bridge, so poor had England's batting been that he place was still secure.

In fact Butcher rather took things a bit too lightly during the third test and was reported to management for staying out beyond midnight during the game. The England management considered dropping him and asked Nasser Hussain the captain for his thoughts. Hussain asked the wise Michael Atherton and Butcher, owing to the desperate shortage of suitable other candidates, held on to his place by the thinnest of margins.

Atherton fell all too early in England's reply for eight after unleashing a couple of fine shots. Difficult to tell why it was that McGrath had such a hold over Atherton, but he kept getting him out. This time, all too familiarly gloving a McGrath lifter to Gilchrist, enter Butcher almost unnoticed.

Butcher bats in a beautiful manner, with elegance, timing, the closest to Gower since Gower. Immediately he hit the ball cleanly, everything seemed to hit the middle of the bat. At the other end Gillespie, bowling a yard fuller than any other opening bowler in the world, once again sent Trescothick back with a snick to slip. To bowlers pitching up Trescothick can sometimes have his feet stuck to the crease with minimal footwork. This was one such occasion. Enter skipper Hussain with England rocking on 33–2.

An intense man, Hussain grafted away just to survive the still new ball. From the other end Butcher creamed a drive through the covers on the front foot and pulled Lee effortlessly to the mid-wicket boundary. Hussain, tense at the other end, strove merely to keep his wicket intact.

Butcher lent into a straight drive off McGrath that screamed to the boundary. Despite the much cooler day, the sun shone and the wind blew strongly from the west across the ground. Hussain nudged and nurdled the ball through the gaps off Warne to rotate the strike nicely for Butcher.

Soon Butcher reached his 50, then England's hundred came up. In a season starved of success the Australians began to get rattled. Gilchrist juggled his bowlers around but without success. The shine went from the ball and the ball itself got softer. Butcher attacked and blazed away towards 100 with scintillating cuts, drives and pulls. His judgement of length was superb. In this mood Butcher climbed into full deliveries with assured front footwork. At last the maverick Surrey batsman had fulfilled his potential.

After a stand of 181, Hussain fell to Gillespie, caught behind but by now England and Butcher were purring along like a Rolls Royce engine, unstoppable and domineering. Ramprakash came in, another stalwart from the 1990s with still much to prove. He hung around, feeding the strike to Butcher.

Butcher passed 150, a significant total. In all of England's long test history, spreading across three different centuries, no one had yet scored an undefeated 150-plus fourth innings score to win a game. Ramprakash fell by the sword, energised and inspired from watching Butcher's finest hour. Together the Surrey pair added 75, Ramprakash's contribution being 32. Out came Afzaal, a fresh-faced, overwhelmed debutant from the first test who got dropped after one game then reinstated for this.

Butcher blew away the menace of Gillespie in spectacular fashion with a big sixteen runs in one over near the end. Racing towards a finishing line and ending up with thirteen overs to spare was a sensational a feeling and totally out of context with anything that had gone on before, a freak of the game, an episode of rare majesty. To beat the greatest team of Australians, indeed their strongest team in their strongest era, needed three factors to come together to make it possible. Steve Waugh was injured and Gilchrist was skipper and the young Simon Katich was brought in; it rained; Mark Butcher played an innings of such unusual splendour the startled Australians 'choked' in their own arrogance.

Mark Butcher went on to successfully hold down the number three position for the next three years, hitting five centuries. He lost his place through injury and was never able to reclaim it. Injury dogged his latter years and he retired in 2009.

Australia 447 (Ponting 144, Martyn 118, ME Waugh 72, Gough 5–103, Caddick 3–143).
England 309 (Stewart 76*, Butcher 47, McGrath 7–76).
Australia 176–4 declared (Ponting 72).
England 315–4 (Butcher 173*, Hussain 55).
ENGLAND WON BY 6 WICKETS.

Innings Ranked Number 14
Atherton's 185 not out at the Wanderers in 1995

Opponents: South Africa.
At stake: Series.
Bowling attack: Donald, Pringle, Pollack MacMillan, Eksteen: 40.30.
Pitch: Fine.
Game situation: England needed to bat out over five sessions to draw the test match or score the nominal 479 for victory.

The England team of the mid 1990s had just drawn a home series to the West Indies. Although the latter had lost their World Champion's crown to Australia, after two decades of dominance, for England to draw the series was a feat worth shouting about.

This was England's best era between 1987 and 2005. At the time of outstanding opening bowlers from Australia, South Africa and Pakistan, and a very useful one from India, England had the batsmen to eke out sufficient runs to stay competitive against everyone bar Australia.

With Gooch now recently retired after a twenty-year England career, the shackles of captaincy went to ex-Manchester Grammar and Cambridge blue, Michael Atherton – nicknamed 'FEC' (future England captain). Atherton had been at the helm for two years. It was his team now and he was blessed with the following qualities, all ticked at the right time: youth, experience, temperament, intelligence, physical flexibility and class. Since taking charge of the team, the extra responsibility brought out an even stronger desire to fight for his team and led to his being the number one target for opposition bowlers.

The first test of the 1995/96 series at Centurian Park was ruined by the weather, but England's solid looking top six of Atherton, Stewart, Ramprakash, Thorpe, Hick and Smith ensured a healthy total of 381-9 before declaring the only innings of the game. Atherton had underpinned the start with a typically defiant 79 and Hick had rescued the side with a wonderful 141. Question marks remained on Ramprakash's temperament, despite a County Championship average of 93 earlier in the year.

At the Wanderers, and although England won the toss, Atherton inserted the South Africans. Their total of 332 seemed neither good nor bad but Dominic Cork continued his golden first year in test cricket with 5-84 backed up by the thunderbolts from Devon Malcolm who took 4-62 at the other end.

In reply, England quickly lost Atherton who left a length ball from Donald, speared into the stumps from wide of the crease that clipped the off-stump bail – an absolute beauty, virtually unplayable. Only Robin Smith with a gutsy 52, Stewart with 45 and Thorpe with 34 offered any real resistance and after just 68.3 overs England fell short of South Africa by 132 runs on the first innings.

South Africa duly batted England out of the game after a couple of early scares, with all-rounder MacMillan finishing 100 not out. Cronje declared at 346-9, setting England the small matter of 479 to win in five sessions plus the awkward 30 minutes before lunch on the first day.

Atherton and Stewart walked across the grassy knoll, down the players' tunnel, a wire cage for protection against the obscenities yelled at by locals, and out into the formidable bull ring of Johannesburg. Atherton claims this to be the most hostile place on the planet outside India. The locals here had even got under the skin of

Merv Hughes and Shane Warne, both having been fined their match fees for verbal retaliation.

Now Atherton is the sort to do his homework with the thoroughness that an A–level schoolmaster would approve of. In his mind as he walked to the middle would be the bowlers and what to expect. Donald, all fire and brimstone would run in and deliver wide of the crease. There would be a lot of short stuff and yorkers. His first spell was usually his quickest.

Pringle was a modest, medium-paced, outswing bowler, easy to give your wicket away to with a sudden loss of concentration. Pollack, youthful and quick, will bowl straight. His first spell would inevitably be his quickest and his bouncer would be straight, always straight, so do not take him on. Macmillan, the large, first change all-rounder built as a number 8, would like to sledge. Do not get involved. Eksteen, the orthodox left-armer, did not spin it much but would be accurate. Play on merits.

Fidgeting now at the crease, Atherton went through the routine. He stretched, scratched the crease and looked around at the field. When partnering Stewart, Atherton always took the first ball. An outswinger from Pringle, nice and full outside off-stump, allowed Atherton to lean into a perfect cover drive for four, well timed and executed, complete with high left elbow. It was a fine shot and relaxed England's captain immediately. Both survived to lunch.

Atherton always felt reassured to be scrapping at the wicket with Alec Stewart. Stewart was a hard, experienced competitor, proud and patriotic. After lunch, Donald came back for a rapid spell. Atherton sensed the short ball coming. Twice Donald obliged and twice Atherton took him on. The wide outside the off-stump delivery was cut over point in defiance. The second bumper was straighter, but Atherton got on top neatly and pulled along the ground through wide mid-on. Donald stood nodding approval, a rare emotion but possibly liking the fact that Atherton wanted to take him on.

Sure enough, Pollack tested Atherton with his own style of bumpers that were straight and well directed. Atherton swayed out of the way, sticking to his game plan. Both were bowling quickly. Stewart got hit above the heart and winced in pain as a Pollack delivery reared up at him.

The kookaburra ball softened after fifteen overs and MacMillan was brought on. Stewart, having weathered the storm, drove over ambitiously at a straight delivery and was bowled, England 75–1.

Enter Ramprakash. Compared with Atherton, Ramprakash was the finer accumulator of runs, the more talented, and their first-class careers reveal a significant difference. In all first-class cricket – and as at October 2009 Ramprakash is still playing – in 75 more completed innings, he has scored exactly twice the number of hundreds as Atherton: 108 compared with 54. However, in tests, Atherton was to score eight times as many as Ramprakash. The obvious reason for the difference was temperament. Before the last 2009 Ashes test, the crucial series decider, a vacant number three position became available. Ramprakash, on his home ground was a firm favourite to regain his test place. Atherton, a Sky TV commentator was an outspoken critic, preferring the number three slot to go to Bell. Perhaps Atherton still had thoughts of Johannesburg 1995 on his mind.

McMillan thundered in, buoyed by an early scalp, a large imposing figure, like the head of a motorcycle gang, and bowled a quick, straight delivery that appeared to veer not one inch. Ramprakash executed a pitiful straight drive and in doing so played over the ball that subsequently shattered his stumps. As he traipsed off with thirteen runs in three innings, he knew his fate. It would be a while before he was ever selected again. Test cricket can be cruel, England 75–2.

Left hander Thorpe came in at number four. He was a revelation, a wonderful striker of the ball, particularly strong at cutting and pulling. In this innings he seemed unusually distracted. His head fell over to the off side, a bit too much noted Atherton at the time. Nonetheless, Atherton spoke to him in between overs to focus him and the pair put on 59, Atherton being the dominant partner. Then Thorpe fell too far away to the offside and Pringle pinned him in front, LBW for 17. England 134–3.

Donald came back an hour before the close and eliminated Hick for four, the batsman snicking to Richardson behind the stumps, England now in disarray at 145–4. The game was slipping away as last specialist batsman Robin Smith entered the fray.

Smith had a gladiatorial presence about him. A native South African, he spurned the chance to represent his mother country by moving to Britain some years earlier. A man of medium height with broad shoulders and mighty forearms, he was at his muscular best facing pace. He stayed with Atherton to the close, in a tightly fought contest. England slept on 167–4 although Atherton, 82 not out, slept not a wink.

Atherton had twice before been on or close to 100 overnight in his career. Both occasions his wicket came soon after the start of play next morning. A full day's play to go.

Sunshine and the prospect of a full day's play greeted a bleary-eyed Atherton as he opened the curtains. He had a few throw downs then walked into the arena with thoughts of a possible century.

Smith consumed vast amounts of energy between deliveries, jumping up and down, going through flexibility movements. 'Come on judgey,' he would shout, 'be strong!' Atherton bided his time, conserving energy and focussing only when the bowler was half way or more through his run up. Atherton reckoned the focus on each delivery lasts about seven seconds, from the run up to the execution of the shot, seven seconds. About 42 seconds of concentration every four or five minutes conserves energy. The in-between time is just relaxation, deep breaths, smiling politely, looking around at the open spaces, resting on the bat, thinking pleasant thoughts.

On 99, Donald fired in a short ball and Atherton, on his toes, played the ball into Kirsten's chest at short-leg only to see the fielder snatch at the ball and grass it. Somehow Atherton knew the next ball would be a bouncer, such was the intuition of having faced Donald on countless occasions before. Sure enough next ball was swift and short and Atherton swivelled round neatly and with perfect timing hooked the ball to the square leg advertising boards, 103 not out. Overcome with emotion Atherton gave his partner a hug, Smith recoiled at the smell – poor Atherton had the habit of not changing his clothes during a knock. Smith duly flashed at a wide one, top edged and held out to third man, an unlucky end, England 232–5.

There were four hours to go and the eccentric Gloucestershire wicket-keeper came out to join his skipper. 'Jack' Russell kept beautifully and was the one real class keeper in the country, even safer than Alec Stewart. It was only the absence of a Flintoff or a Botham that prevented Russell achieving 100 caps for England. Without a genuine all-rounder worth their place as both a batsman and bowler, England manufactured Stewart into a batsman/keeper. It is easier to turn a batsman into a decent wicket-keeper than a wicket-keeper into a test-class batsman. In another era he would have joined the elite band of England cricketers who played in 100 tests. There was no all-rounder and subsequently, in England's desire to have balance, Stewart took over the gloves within a year or two.

Russell was an obdurate batsman, totally unorthodox but effective, a stone waller. He played at nothing he did not need to. Meanwhile Atherton describes his mind set as being in 'the zone', a bubble of complete control where every shot was executed in the middle and where the batsman knew he would not get out.

By the end of the afternoon session the crowd quietened. From deafening the previous morning it was now becalmed, as though aware of the script. South Africa took the third new ball, but by now her bowlers were drained.

With Russell on 29 after four hours and Atherton on a career best 185, Hansie Cronje came over and shook Atherton's hand. The game was over and for almost eleven hours Atherton had withstood a fine pace attack, a feat of concentration that places this successful rearguard as one of the finest of its kind ever played by an England cricketer.

Atherton went on to play for another $5^{1}/2$ years, racking up over 7,700 test runs at an average of 37.7. The career average might seem a little low by comparison with say Bell's or Collingwood's of today, but Atherton faced a world full of altogether more hostile attacks. Indeed, had Atherton been transplanted to any other era of English cricket since 1895, he would have probably found life a lot easier.

South Africa 332 (Kirsten 110, Cullinan 69, Cork 5–84, Malcolm 4–62).
England 200 (R Smith 52, Stewart 45, Eksteen 3–12, Pollack 3–44).
South Africa 346 (MacMillan 100*, Cullinan 61, Rhodes 57, Cork 4–78, Fraser 3–84).
England 351–5 (Atherton 185*, R Smith 44, Russell 29*).
MATCH DRAWN.

Innings Ranked Number 13
Foster's 287 at Sydney in 1903

Opponents: Australia.
At stake: Ashes.
Bowling attack: Saunders, Laver, Howell, Noble, Armstrong, Hopkins, Trumper, Gregory. Runs per wicket: 27.92.
Pitch: Flat but recovering from overnight rain.
Game situation: Australia won the toss and elected to bat. They were bowled out for 285. Foster came in with England 73–3.

There was still much in the world to explore in December 1903. The Wright brothers had shown publicly their ability to get a piece of wood and a motor engine to fly through the air for twelve seconds. A woman, with the surname Pankhurst, had started a women's social and political movement apparently with the aim of giving women the vote. The UK's population was just a little over 32 million, about half that of today, and life expectancy for a live human birth was about 44. Cars were regarded as dangerous toys for the rich and England had picked an England footballer to bat at number five in the first Ashes test of the 1903/04 series.

R. E. Foster wore a moustache in typical Edwardian manner. He had dark hair, cut along the regimented short-back-and-sides style and heralded from Oxford University and Worcestershire. He batted in the manner of Ted Dexter, so at least one contemporary declared, erect, upright at the wicket with classical well-coached shots, particularly driving on front and back. He had made his reputation in the varsity match of 1900 with 171 and a few days later scored 100s in both innings of the Gentlemen v. Players match. Had England's batting in the 1902 series not been so strong on paper, with the likes of MacLaren, Hayward, J. T. Tyldesley, Braund, Foster, Fry and Ranjitsinhji, it is possible Foster could have played a part in the greatest of all series. Nonetheless his debut followed in the very next Ashes battle, the winter of 1903/04.

England's batting line up for the first test at Sydney looked rather thin on paper. Plum Warner captained the team and opened with Tom Hayward, followed by the reliable J. T. Tyldesley, then at four and five came two debutants: E. G. Arnold and R. E. Foster. After that England relied on the all-rounders Len Braund, George Hirst, followed by googly inventor Bernard Bosanquet, keeper Arthur Lilley, first change Albert Relf and the slow, left-arm Yorkshireman Wilfred Rhodes.

The problem with overseas tours right up until the 1950/51 series was that they took too long, often five months including six weeks travel by ship both to and from Australia. Not everyone wished to go. This time England had no Fry, Jackson, Ranjitsinhji or even Gilbert Jessop. Should they bother even going? Australia had defeated the strongest England XL over five tests just sixteen months earlier.

Australia won the toss and of course elected to bat. Ted Arnold, on debut, removed both openers swiftly, including Victor Trumper for one, to a very fine catch by Foster, and George Hirst induced Clem Hill to edge behind. In no time at all Australia were 12–3 and another classic Ashes series took shape. There ensued a recovery built around the rock like Monty Noble. The fine Australian allrounder, considered the finest in the Southern Hemisphere before Keith Miller, took his bat out for 133 and Australia finished the first day on 259–6.

Rain overnight turned the wicket into a drying 'sticky' and Australia succumbed after some risks to 285. Before a run had been earned, Plum Warner edged the medium-paced Frank Laver. Hayward and Tyldesley rebuilt in solid manner, defying the wickedness of the strip to add a crucial 49, until Hayward fell, bowled by an off cutter from Bill Howell for fifteen.

Tyldesley batted with great skill. His masterful 53 came at a time when the wicket was drying, cutting and turning. In the heat of the midday sun the wicket had dried out into a flat, obvious strip. In short, Tyldesley's 50 paved the way for Foster.

That afternoon over 12,000 viewed proceedings, but Tyldesley soon fell to expose Ted Arnold with the score on 73–3 and 'Tip' Foster. Arnold rode his luck in a brief cameo but it could not last, out having a swipe at Armstrong. England were now teetering at 117–4.

Out to join Foster strode Len Braund, an aggressive, right-handed all-rounder. Both men enjoyed high strike rates throughout their careers, although this is gleaned from contemporary perceptions rather than raw statistics. Together they took the score forwards, in Foster's case through powerful orthodox channels. Despite making this his debut innings, he played with no external indication of nerves. A tremendous athlete, Foster was used to playing in front of crowds. Perhaps he had no fear of failure, certainly he seemed unperturbed when dropped in the slips on 51.

By the close of the second day Foster and Braund remained and the England total fast approached that of Australia. With the overnight total on an imposing 243–4, England were just 42 runs short with six wickets in hand. Foster was not out 73, Braund not out 67.

Cricket writers at the time commented that day three saw the 'most brilliant and sensational cricket seen during the tour.' Not without luck, Foster escaped a strong LBW shout off Saunders then, to add insult to injury, struck Noble for ten runs in the next over. Foster and Braund took their stand passed the 150 mark at a healthy lick, using all possible avenues for run making. Braund drove powerfully through the gaps. Both batsmen reached their centuries then, soon after, and with the score on 309 Braund fell, bowled by Howell for 102, This started something of a collapse for shortly afterwards Howell bowled George Hirst for 0 and, at the other end, Monty Noble removed Bosanquet for two and Lilley for four. England's reply looked now to be stuttering to a halt at 332–8, a small advantage.

With Braund, the dominant partner gone, and the collapse of England's lower middle-order, Foster now began to move through the gears and accelerate. In the first half of his innings, he had allowed himself to treat each ball on its merits, now he sought to hit bowlers off their lengths.

With Relf the number ten for company, Foster assumed command and the lead increased rapidly. Relf, far too good for a number ten, played his share of attacking shots and the pair dominated the now flagging attack. The ninth wicket realised a full 115 runs. Then Jack Saunders began his cork-screw like run up starting from mid on, then obscured behind the umpire before his left arm came over with a vicious spinner delivered at medium pace. Relf flayed once too often and was caught by 'Big Ship' Warwick Armstrong, nine down for 447.

Of all the number elevens in test history, there can surely be no better batsman arriving in the middle than Wilfred Rhodes. Foster decided to throw the bat. His batting with Rhodes produced a record 130-run partnership. Through it Foster passed W. L. Murdoch's 211 that had stood for almost twenty years as the highest test score. *Wisden* describes Foster's record breaking innings thus: 'The latter part of his innings was described by all hands as something never surpassed.'

The last 130 runs came up in just 66 minutes. In all, Foster batted for just over seven hours and sprinkled his innings with no fewer than 45 boundaries. He had not only achieved the highest test score but had overcome the previous highest score by the greatest margin, in this case by a full 76 runs. Remember that this was Foster's very first test innings.

Australia rallied, as though inspired by watching such strokeplay, and in Victor Trumper they set England an awkward 194. Trumper arrived with Australia still over 100 runs away from an innings defeat and flayed the England attack for one of the greatest Australian innngs. He remained undefeated on 185. England knocked the 194 runs off for the loss of five wickets including Foster, stumped for nineteen. England won this first test, the second and the fourth to win 3–2 and regain the Ashes.

Foster's knock still remains as a record for a test debutant. There are few so lacking in nerves at the start of cricket's biggest challenge.

A sign of the times perhaps, but both Trumper and Foster were to die early. Foster was born a year after Trumper, but died of diabetes a year before him in 1914 aged just 36. Trumper departed this earth from Bright's disease, aged 38, and a nation mourned.

Australia 285 (Noble 133, Arnold 4–76).
England 577 (RE Foster 287, Braund 102, J. T. Tyldesley 53, Noble 3–99, Howell 3–111).
Australia 485 (Trumper 185*, Duff 84, Hill 51, Rhodes 5–94).
England 194–5 (Hayward 91, Hirst 60*).
ENGLAND WON BY 5 WICKETS.

Innings Ranked Number 12
Simpson's 156 not out at Melbourne in 1951

Opponents: Australia.
At stake: National pride as the Ashes were already lost.
Bowling attack: Lindwall, Miller, Johnston, Iverson, Johnson, Hole, Hassett: runs per wicket 22.98.
Pitch: Lively.
Game situation Australia won the loss and elected to bat. They scored only 217. Reg Simpson came in to bat with the fall of Washbrook caught behind off Miller with the score on 40–1.

A day before his 31st birthday, Reg Simpson, an athletic, lean six footer with short, black, curly hair, walked out to bat at the Melbourne Cricket Ground. The bowling attack was the second strongest in terms of potency – average runs per wicket in test cricket of the bowling attack weighted by the contributions of individual bowlers – of all the great innings in this book. The strongest incidentally was the attack that Hutton faced in the previous test.

England were staring at a whitewash, 4–0 down with one test to play. The problem was not so much in getting Australia out, but in securing enough runs against Miller, Lindwall, Johnston, Johnson (all present in Bradman's all conquering side of 1948) plus a mystery spinner in Jack Iverson.

Big Jack Iverson stood at 6ft 2ins and weighed fifteen stone, such a size stuck out more amongst the food-rationed populace of the time. Iverson was a peculiar threat. Stationed in New Guinea during the war years, he had wiled away his time developing an unusual bowling action by experimenting with a ping-pong ball. He gripped the ball between thumb and middle finger and bowled arm balls, leg breaks, off breaks and googlies, with no obvious change in action. Iverson first came to the selectors' attention with 46 wickets at 16.12 for Victoria in 1949/50, so he was rushed into the Australian team touring New Zealand. Here, Iverson captured an astonishing 75 wickets at 7.00 in all first-class cricket. What Australia lacked on the batting front in terms of the three Bs – Brown, Barnes and the incomparable Bradman – they now made up for in their outstanding bowling attack, with Iverson as their secret weapon.

Fortunately for Reg Simpson, the batsman at the other end was none other than the great Len Hutton, himself no stranger to brilliant batsmanship. Together the right handers steadied the England ship and proceeded on to a 131-run partnerhip before part-time bowler Graeme Hole claimed one of only three test wickets in his career, bowling of all people, Len Hutton for 79.

As many predicted, now that the great Hutton had gone, the evening session subsided. Compton arrived next in the middle but had endured the worst run of form of his life. Despite scoring runs in the state games, poor Compton could barely buy a run in the tests. He was to average just 7.57 for the series. After crawling into double figures, he fell to Lindwall for 11. The Rev. Shepherd, Freddie Brown and Godrey Evans fell like skittles and the close of play England were one run ahead, 218–6, with Simpson still there, playing cautiously but starting to stagnate on 80.

Day three started on time, with England desperate for a significant first innings lead to finally put pressure on Australia. The last test England had won against the old enemy was pre-war, at the Oval back in 1938. In Lindwall's third over, Bedser played on for eleven and should have gone forward to a full-length ball from Lindwall, then Iverson completely deceived Bailey who groped at the ball before spooning a catch up to short-leg. Doug Wright, the Kent spinner, joined Simpson for a brief stand before falling to Iverson's arm ball, LBW, offering no strike. England had a lead of 28 and had to bat last, when Roy Tattersall, a proper number eleven came out.

Simpson had spent 50 minutes of play clawing out runs at a drip, a single here and a single there, and had moved on to 92. Within sight of his first Ashes century, he now began to farm the strike, taking singles on the fourth, fifth and sixth deliveries, whilst trying to force boundaries in the early part of the over. Hassett placed as many as five fielders on the boundaries at the start of the overs to tempt him. A flick for four brought up Simpson's century, whilst Tattersall hung on grimly by planting his foot down the wicket to Iverson in forward defence.

Hassett grew impatient as Simpson hunted down the track to Iverson and lofted him nonchalantly over mid-on, then stepped back and cut him to the cover boundary. Journalists at the time remarked how strange it was to see a batsman obviously beaten earlier in the series now dominating the bowlers.

Miller and Lindwall returned to front up against a true purple patch in a batsman's career. Simpson took the fight to the bowlers in a grand manner, dancing down the wicket to the pair of them and driving, cutting and pulling with immense skill. Lunch came and Simspon had contributed 63 of the 85 runs taken from the morning's session. The afternoon began with Miller thundering, and at once Simpson cut him handsomely to the boundary. Eventually Tattersall fell, clean bowled by Miller.

In a last wicket partnership that lasted fully 65 minutes either side of lunch, Simpson and Tattersall added a priceless 74 of which Simpson's contribution was 64. He finished 156 not out, and England 320, a three-figure lead, just what Bedser and the rest of the bowlers had yearned for, proper pressure.

At the ground that day was E. W. Swanton, one of England's greatest cricket writers of the twentieth century, who wrote:

> I cannot praise Simpson more highly than to say that no batsman on either side, not even Hutton in his second innings at Brisbane, has looked more thoroughly in command of both himself and of the situation than Simpson today... latterly quite alone, he supported the whole England performance over a spell of more than five hours and a half.

Australia lost four wickets before reducing the deficit and Bedser took five wickets to make ten in the match and England were set 95 which, thanks to Hutton's imperious 60 not out, they managed by eight wickets.

So, thanks to a quite brilliant innings, a victory at the fag end of an Ashes series lifted the hopes and expectations of a nation. There followed the last great era of England dominance in the world arena. Until 1958/59, England did not lose another series to anyone.

As for Simpson, sandwiched between the Hutton/Compton and May/Cowdrey generations, he played another sixteen tests yet never again reached the heights. As at 8 April 8th 2010, aged 90, and with the recent passing of Alec Bedser, he is England's oldest surviving test cricketer.

Australia 217 (Hassett 92, Morris 50, Bedser 5–46, Brown 5–49).
England 320 (Simpson 156*, Hutton 79, Miller 4–76, Lindwall 3–77).
Australia 197 (Hole 63, Harvey 52, Bedser 5–59, Wright 3–56).
England 95–2 (Hutton 60*).
ENGLAND WON BY 8 WICKETS.

Innings Ranked Number 11
Watson's 109 at Lord's in 1953

Opponents: Australia.
At stake: Ashes.
Bowling attack: Lindwall, Miller, Johnston, Ring, Benaud, Davidson, Hole: Average runs per wicket: 26.91.
Pitch: Fair.
Game situation: England were 10–2 requiring 353 to win, or bat out over a day for a draw .

The Australians had held on to the Ashes since defeating England 3–2 back in 1936/37. It was now the end of June 1953, Coronation Year. Rain had prevented a result in the first Test that finished ten days earlier, but now it was sunny and stable climatic conditions were predicted throughout the test. In short, there was no getting away from it, no hiding behind stoppages staring blankly at rain.

Australia had hammered England in the three post-war series, a combined total of 11–1. Importantly, the one test victory to England came in the last test of the last series. Had the tide turned? Could England front up to the great enemy?

There were still three pre-war test youths in the England side. Len Hutton was still at the top of his powers and Denis Compton, although beginning to wane, was still worth his place. The other was the Chairman of Selectors, Freddie Brown, a 42-year-old who had toured with Douglas Jardine's 1932/33 Bodyline series. Bedser and Evans, who played against the 1948 Bradman side, could by now call themselves veterans. There was also certainly youth in Statham and Graveney, and an interesting pre-war youth in 33-year-old Willie Watson, a left-handed Yorkshireman. He did not make his test debut until 1951, but had played for Yorkshire in 1939 as a teenager. Bailey, a talented all-rounder, Wardle, an excellent off spinner, and Don Kenyon made up the team.

Sunny but cool, high summer, superb light, flat pitch and Australia won the toss. They chose quite sensibly to bat first.

Australia batted entertainingly and at the end of the first day were 263–5, match evenly poised. The second day saw England firmly in the driving seat. The bowlers, spearheaded by Alec Bedser, restricted Australia to 346. Bedser had 5–105 off 42.2 overs, a lion-hearted effort to go with his outstanding 14–99 in the first test. On this occasion he was supported most notably by Johnny Wardle, the tall Yorkshire off-spinner with 4–77. There was a superb 76 from 24-year-old, left-handed all rounder Alan Davidson, batting with the tail.

England however did loose Don Kenyan to Lindwall for just three to make the score 9–1. Hutton, and the stylish Tom Graveney, grafted away admirably and England were handsomely placed at 177–1.

The third day saw Australia fight back. Graveney had his stumps castled for 78 without any addition to his overnight score. Compton put on 102 with Hutton, without quite matching his buccaneering best of 1948, before edging Benaud. From there England lost their remaining wickets for 93. They took a slender lead of 26 but would have to bat last. Hutton's innings was an absolute classic, worthy of a chapter in this book. By the close, Australia had lost only Hassett, early doors, and slept well on 96–1.

The fourth day was easily the worst for England in the series to date. Australia pounded away their advantage with Keith Miller, the great Australian all-rounder scoring 109 and Morris 89. At one point, Australia had a lead of over 200 with eight wickets in hand. Then wickets tumbled around a whirlwind 50 from Lindwall. Bedser again chipped in with 3–77 and Freddie Brown 4–82. Wardle, despite 46 economical overs, only had Miller's wicket to show for his efforts.

England, set 343 to win, faced Miller and Lindwall with a tricky half-an-hour before stumps. Lindwall, fresh from his 50, raced in and removed both Kenyan for two and the great Hutton himself for five. When Graveney edged Johnston to Langley, England, at 12–3, had done enough to reduce fully-grown men to tears. Compton and Willie Watson dug in to the close, 20–3.

The Australians, according to former team mate Sidney Barnes, then partied into the night, safe in the knowledge that the test would most probably be won by lunch time the next day. They (the Australian team) celebrated their win. They went to see a show at the Coliseum and later attended a back-stage party before going on to the Café de Paris. It was a night of great celebration and carnival and they sauntered onto the field on Tuesday, physically tired and mentally fatigued.

The game was up. Only 5,000 spectators appeared for the start. The ones who turned up did so in morbid fascination to witness the final crumbling of England's hopes and dreams.

Watson and Compton batted within themselves against the starting bowlers Lindwall and Johnston. Compton, normally such a free-flowing swashbuckler, glanced a single off Lindwall but that was it from him for the first 25 minutes. Watson went ahead, standing up to the fast bowling as well as anybody. Once, Lindwall fetched him a painful blow in the chest, but Watson, a big, strong man, took it without even registering pain. What a fillip for England's supporters.

Benaud and Ring replaced the faster men. Compton immediately pounced and struck Benaud for three exquisite boundaries in the same over, a cut, a straight drive and a hallmark cover drive that raised a cheer amongst the sparse crowd. Then, when threatening to ignite the arena in a manner that only a genius could, Compton fell LBW playing forward to a 'creeper' from Johnson. Compton had scored 33 from a partnership of 61. England were 73–4. Enter Bailey, purposefully striding out in military manner, with a look of total concentration and mind-setting at the task which lay ahead.

Cricket scores are prone to misquotes and abuse of the facts when told by wily old men to impress on youngsters the characters of the day. One can tell much about a man by how accurately he recounts cricket statistics. Consider my cousin Robert. He and I played for a team called the Wasps in the early 1990s. Robert is an accomplished batsman at club level, but he was only a young teenager and claimed recently that his top score for the team was 40. It was in fact 33. By this I can estimate the young man's scope for exaggeration. These figures suggest by just under 20 %. This is nothing compared to a veteran

Latin teacher at the first school I taught at, Southend High School for Boys. Ted Read, a wonderful chap, told fantastic stories, like the time he middled a cricket ball and the game had to finish because the ball that Ted hit went 'miles' in the air, sailed over the boundary and eventually plopped down someone's chimney pot. I asked, and I cannot remember for what reason, whether he remembered the Watson–Bailey stand. Ted assured me that they batted for ever. When pressed for how long, Ted confirmed that the stand lasted for three days. The fact was that they batted for $5^1/2$ hours in what was the most pivotal point in the series, a day of destiny for English cricket. The stand was worth 163 in runs, but in the context of cricket history more like 500 runs.

Watson and Bailey were tasked with the job of maintaining the warm glow and feverish desire of a nation. Such was the impact that schoolmasters announced in the lunch hall that Watson and Bailey were still there at lunch with England 116–4. The pair started their famous partnership with a sparkling 27 runs in the first 20 minutes. It was before the new ball. The main threat would be Lindwall and Miller with the second new ball after lunch.

The crowd had doubled after lunch as word spread around town that England were putting up a fight. The hour after lunch Watson and Bailey batted steadily to take the score to 149. Then came the second new ball and a time of great vulnerability. This was an epic battle of survival with the two understated cricketers still together throughout the torrid, hostile spell from two of the finest exponents of extreme pace in the history of the game. By now, the run rate was a trickle, rearguards are often played out like this to wear bowlers down. As bowlers tire, they lose pace and accuracy. Hassett rotated his bowlers and even employed Hole as a seventh bowler in the innings but still the batsman remained, stone walling in their desperate attempt to save the game. By tea Watson had 84 and Bailey 39 with a partnership of 110.

By now the stand had captured the interest of the country, with millions hanging around the wireless or, if sufficiently rich, a black and white TV screen. Moments like these transcend the populace so that non-cricket enthusiasts, such as my lovely continental wife, become enthralled. In recent years the Hoggard/Giles stand of 2005 raised the game to a similarly high profile. Watson and Bailey's stand was long and drawn out, Hoggard and Giles's very much shorter, but the consequence of opening the game up to a wider audience was the same.

After tea England went beyond the highest fourth innings total at Lord's in tests. Then Watson reached his 100, not a memorable shot, but the moment generated a thunderous applause as the crowd registered the tribute to such a brave innings from the blonde Yorkshireman. At this stage Watson had batted for 330 minutes. Throughout his innings he met the ball with a measured straightness. With just 40 minutes of the game remaining, he fell, caught in the slips off Ring for 109. Watson had fought a rearguard battle for 346 minutes. Bailey fell soon after for 71, having batted with exemplary patience for 257 minutes. He was to turn the sobriquet 'Barnacle' Bailey.

England still had to bat out a further 30 minutes with only Brown, Evans and the tail. Brown batted boisterously and started smashing boundaries, whilst Evans looked like getting out any ball from the spinners. For 27 minutes these two made spectators clench knuckles, bite nails, chain smoke and count down the minutes to safety. This white-knuckle ride saw England close on 282-7. Brown fell for a belligerent 28 with only three minutes remaining.

England drew strength from this great escape and determined to win back the Ashes. This they achieved at the Oval ,with Laker and Lock taking nine wickets in the second innings. England's individually heroic performances, Bedser in the first test aside, all came from this drawn game at Lord's.

Australia 346 (Hassett 104, Davidson 76, Harvey 59, Bedser 5–105, Wardle 4–77).
England 372 (Hutton 145, Graveney 78, Compton 57, Lindwall 5–66).
Australia 368 (Miller 109, Morris 89, Lindwall 50, Brown 4–82, Bedser 3–77).
England 282-7 (Watson 109, Bailey 71).
MATCH DRAWN.

Innings Ranked Number 10
Trescothick's 180 at Johannesburg in 2005

Opponents: South Africa.
At stake: Chance to go 2–1 up with one test to play in the five-test series.
Bowling attack: Ntini, Steyn, Pollack, Kallis, Boje: 29.40.
Pitch: Fine.
Game situation: England were eight runs behind on the first innings when Trescothick came out to open the second innings with Andrew Strauss.

Twenty-nine-year-old Marcus Trescothick, the burly left-hander from Somerset, was at the height of his powers. He stood 6ft 2ins tall and battled a slight weight problem in his youth, apparently due to his fondness for sausages. He could hit the ball as hard as Botham and Flintoff on his day. Often accused of not moving his feet to the pitch of the ball, the fact was that, when he swung his blade and connected, the ball rocketed away to the boundary.

Trescothick made his reputation at test level in his debut series against the 2000 West Indies, but expectations rose spectacularly following his 219 at the Oval against South Africa, an innings which helped turn a test match around from a mid-afternoon score on the first day that read South Africa 290–1. England shared that series then went on to prosper 3–0 against the West Indies in the West Indies, followed by a 3–0 clean sweep of New Zealand at home, then a 4–0 clean sweep again against the West Indies at home.

With the South Africans rated as the number-two team on the planet behind Australia, it was vital for the psychological pre-Ashes build-up that England should defeat them in South Africa. One could argue that neither the West Indies nor New Zealand were top tier test sides, so England had it all to prove.

Nonetheless, England won the first test of the series with Strauss scoring 126 and 94*. The second test was drawn after England had been dismissed in the first innings for 138. Thankfully, Strauss and Trescothick knocked off the 191 run deficit with interest to put on 273.

South Africa came back strongly in the third test to level the series.

Vaughan won the toss and had no hesitation in batting first. 264–4 at the end of the first day pleased the England skipper who batted out the innings on the second day to be left high and dry on 82*. He had Strauss once again to thank for 147 and Key weighed in with a pugnacious 83.

South Africa replied with 419 to take a narrow first-innings lead of just eight. Herschelle Gibbs made a fluent 161, backed up by the classy Boucher with 64. England's most successful bowler was the gritty Yorkshireman Matthew Hoggard with 5–144 on an unresponsive wicket.

With almost five sessions of play remaining and most pundits sniffing a draw, Strauss and Trescothick walked out to start England's second innings. The 27-year-old Strauss had only broken into the England team the previous summer when Vaughan was injured, since then he had been quite prolific. However this time he lasted just four balls and England were 2–1.

During the afternoon session, Trescothick began to find his touch and together with Robert Key of Kent took the score to 51 before Key fell for 19. Vaughan entered the fray to join his former opening partner. Vaughan seemed hell bent on taking the attack to the enemy. Trescothick sensed controlled aggression was the order of the day. In between overs Vaughan repeated the need to get after the bad ball and put pressure on the opposition.

After tea England entered calm waters with a pleasing partnership that passed the 100 mark. In desperation, Smith posted a defensive field which merely served to milk runs. In the last 40 minutes Vaughan fell for 54 having hit eight boundaries. Then Thorpe fell for one, Flintoff hit a six and fell for seven, but Geraint Jones, the keeper-batsman, negotiated the remaining overs until the umpires curtailed play due to bad light; Dale Steyn's 93 m.p.h. thunderbolts aiding the decision. England, in command at 175–2, had limped to the close on 197–5, totally reliant on Marcus Trescothick, 101* overnight.

The fifth and final day of the fourth test match started with England only 189 runs ahead with five wickets remaining. As Trescothick walked to the wicket that morning so many thoughts were bombarding his mind. Should he attack from the start? What if he fell early, would that leave England too vulnerable? He watched from the non-striker's end as Steyn ran in to complete his over. First ball whistled from Jones's bat through the covers for four – just the start to settle nerves. Trescothick took guard again to face Pollack. The fourth delivery was full and straight, Trescothick leant into a forward defence and felt good.

Ntini replaced Steyn immediately and Jones thrashed him too through the covers for four.

Jones's twin boundaries had already lifted pressure from Trescothick's shoulders. He focussed now on Pollack, the classic and highly successful seamer, indeed the South African McGrath. Smith began the day as expected, placing trust in his experienced operators. He sought control. Pollack overpitched on the stumps and Terscothick dispatched him along the ground to the long on-boundary. Later in the over, as Pollack strayed wide of off stump, Trescothick leant into a crisp cover drive for a second boundary.

Next over Ntini raced in to Jones and sprayed a wide, long, hop outside the off stump which Jones latched onto with a vulgar cut which flew over point for four. Smith ran over to offer advice. The result was two fielders behind square on the leg side. Trap set, Ntini raced in and bowled a 90 m.p.h. bouncer which Jones hooked fatally to backward square. With England on 222–6, any result was still possible.

Ashley Giles joined Trescothick with the tone of slight panic in his voice. Trescothick digested the latest management take on events. 'Look' said Giles, 'We have to have a good partnership otherwise we'll be in the shit because we'll be in to the tail!'

Smith took Pollack off and replaced him with Steyn, his tearaway young quick. Steyn's job was simple, to rough up Giles and the tail. Giles had nailed down the England number eight slot for the last two years. It was his. He was England's premier spinner, which at the time was not in any way a great compliment, but he was a very useful number eight who could score 50s against anyone, and priceless 30s with impressive regularity.

Steyn delivered the bouncer to Giles's throat, compelling him to hook. Deep square-leg walked in too far and the ball just landed over the ropes for six. Had the fielder not walked in, Giles would certainly have been dismissed. Enjoying the luck of the day, Giles dominated the stand. Steyn kept up the bouncer war, but then overpitched and Giles smashed him through the covers for four. Kallis came on having taken just two wickets at 125 in the series, but he leaked runs. Eventually, after two further boundaries, Giles heaved at a wide long hop and cut the ball straight to cover. Another priceless 30 for the

England cause, the left armer walked off to rapturous applause from the Barmy Army. England had reached 272–7.

With Hoggard now for company, Trescothick vowed to bat as normal. He had faith in Hoggard's defence and knew that he could hang around as he had a history of it. But not today. From the fourth ball he faced Hoggard had his stumps shattered. Trescothick played a couple of nervous overs from Boje, South Africa's own left-arm spinner, and the turn from the rough startled him.

Over the drinks interval there ensued a mid-pitch discussion between Chris Read, ostensibly holding a pair of gloves, Harmison the number ten and Trescothick. The message was simple: 'Get as many runs as you can and quickly!'

Trescothick weighed up the situation. There were ten overs before the new ball. It was time to chance his arm and get after Boje. Next over from Boje, Trescothick defended a couple and then made up his mind to slog sweep the next delivery. Batsmen are often told not to do this. Boje delivered a ball too far outside the off stump, so Trescothick leant back and cut the ball through the covers for four. Next ball he released the slog sweep. It hit the toe of the bat and the ball hung in the air over the leg side.

'Get over! Get over!' shouted Trescothick. The ball obliged. Boje hurled a quicker ball outside the off stump. Trescothick glided it, using the pace, to the third man boundary – fourteen from the over.

Ntini came on for control. First ball glanced Harmison's thigh pad and the batsmen ran the leg bye. Trescothick hooked Ntini for four and strolled through for a single later in the over to farm the strike. Kallis replaced Boje, more control being sought by Smith. Trescothick took a two to deep mid-wicket then crashed Kallis back over his head for six, landing on the grass mound beyond the long on boundary. Smith drew a look of sour milk. Kallis gathered the ball and shined desperately on his trousers. England's 300 had come up at a roaring rate.

When Harmison scored his first single, the partnership had realised 45. Trescothick dabbed Kallis fine of first slip for four then flicked a length ball nonchanantly over mid wicket for a fourth six. When he fell for 180, off 248 balls, Trescothick had hit four sixes and twenty-four fours. Vaughan, standing and applauding from the players balcony, waved the batsmen in. Such had been the rate of scoring in that hectic 90 minutes, Vaughan had two sessions and two overs in which to attack South Africa.

This test match goes down as one of the more unlikely victories, given how much of it had still to be squeezed into the final day for a result, either way, to be possible. South Africa had a daunting batting line up, one of the more solid of the time. In the end, Matthew Hoggard sliced through the lineup and took England home with 8.3 overs to go. South Africa crumbled, despite Hershelle Gibbs coming within two runs of scoring a century in both innings of a test. G. C. Smith, suffering from concussion, was advised not to bat but defied the doctors to enter at number eight. In the event, Smith was left stranded on a defiant 67*, but morose in the knowledge his team had gone 1–2 down with just the final test to go.

Because of two phenomenal individual performances England grabbed the test and with it the series as the fifth test petered out into a draw. England now climbed to number two in the world test rankings, the highest position since the halcyon days of Boycott, Botham, Gower and Willis.

South Africa toughened England up still further and became the perfect finishing school before taking on the mighty Australian team fronted by legends such as Ponting, Hayden, Langer, Gilchrist, McGrath and Warne. Almost all of the personnel were in place. However there was to be one more change. Within weeks of the test series England lost heavily in the ODI series, but a new recruit, Kevin Pietersen, announced his introduction to the international stage with three hundreds.

By the time of the first Ashes test, England's veteran left-hander Graham Thorpe had to make way. The rest is history.

England 411 (Strauss 147, Key 83, Vaughan 82*, Ntini 4–111).
South Africa 419 (Gibbs 161, Boucher 64, Hoggard 5–144).
England 332–9 declared (Trescothick 180, Vaughan 54).
South Africa 247 (Gibbs 98, G. C. Smith 67*, Hoggard 7–61).
ENGLAND WON BY 77 RUNS.

Innings Ranked Number 9
Amiss's 262 not out at Sabina Park in 1974

Opponents: West Indies.
At stake: Test Series.
Bowling attack: Boyce, Julien, Gibbs, Sobers, Barrett, Fredericks, Lloyd, Kanhai, Rowe, Kallicharran: 39.58.
Pitch: Batsman's paradise.
Game situation: England, already 1–0 down in the series, had a 230-run deficit on the first innings and were required to bat out the last five sessions of play.

England had received a fearful thrashing at the hands of Garfield Sobers's West Indians the preceding English summer. At Lord's, the West Indies had so emphatically defeated England – by an innings and 226 runs – that her selectors had no option but to regime change and quickly. Out went Ray Illingworth as captain and in his place came a Scotsman, Mike Denness. England had problems in both the batting and bowling departments.

As a nation too, the UK appeared to be in a grip of electricity shortages with Edward Heath the Prime Minister calling for a three-day week for business and commerce as a means of reducing energy consumption. The television, a recent popular acquisition for most households (the wealthy had colour TVs), had been de-powered after 10.30p.m., again as an energy saving strategy, although this policy ended on 6 March. Miners were striking, no overtime was allowed and Heath called an election. The Tories lost, Labour came in with Harold Wilson returning as Prime Minister. It was a dark winter that year, the sun and heat of the West Indies seemed a million miles away after the domestic winter of discontent.

The first test of the winter series saw a convincing West Indian win by seven wickets, despite Dennis Amiss fighting for $6^{1}/2$ hours to accumulate 174. England capitulated from 326–1 to 393 all out.

There appeared no end to the gloom in the second test either. Despite winning the toss, and electing to bat on a featherbed, England mustered 353 but with Amiss out cheaply for 27, no England batsman amassed more than Boycott's 68.

In response, the West Indies batted for 196 overs yet strangely, for so talented a team, they never rattled along at more than three an over. Still England could not bowl the West Indies out, with Rohan Kanhai declaring on 583–9. Impotent at wicket taking the England bowling department might have been, but they did restrict the stroke makers admirably. Tony Greig bowled 49 overs for just 102. Underwood and Pocock provided miserly support. Nonetheless England had to bat for $9^1/2$ hours to save the game, no mean feat with only Boycott and Amiss in tangible form.

Dennis Amiss spent the first eight years of his first-class career scratching around before recording his first championship century. A square-jawed, powerful man, with forearms like the first rippling branches of a giant oak, he went through a patch so purple that no Englishman other than Walter Hammond has exceeded it.

Down the pavilion steps Amiss strode, with Boycott alongside for reassuring company. Still in the days before helmets, the sun out, a salad lining the stomach, Amiss took the non-striker's end. Keith Boyce bounded in with enthusiastic round the wicket bouncers from the off, supported by Brenden Julian, a left armer who could also bat a bit.

It was Amiss who took the attack to the bowlers, initially hooking with success, despite three fielders out for the shot. Boycott, never flourishing, fended off a Boyce bouncer only to be caught behind by Murray. England's best and most experienced batsman for once was to play only a minor role.

John Jameson, the Warwickshire opener, entered the fray and immediately batted as though he only had five minutes to live. First ball from Boyce was the expected bouncer, and Jameson – something of a compulsive hooker – flirted with danger. It is something to hit a six with the first ball, but this one skied over the slips from a top edge, short boundary. Next ball, Jameson hammered the bouncer with greater control for four. Forcing the pace took Jameson to seventeen in just a couple of overs so Kanhai cunningly introduced spin, knowing his fellow Warwickshire team-mate well.

Amiss now grew with confidence, cutting, straight driving and clipping leg stump half volleys with consummate ease. His 50 came up with the tenth four, but Jameson held out to slip off Barrett, bowling leggies. Hayes entered the arena, youthful and a century maker on debut the previous summer. Trouble was Hayes had only scored 67 runs in his last seven test innings. He must have been desperately nervous, stung from the original media hype and fighting for his place. In the event Amiss called Hayes for a suicidal single to Clive Lloyd, the best cover fielder on the planet at the time.

At this point England were stumbling at 107–3. Thankfully Mike Denness stayed long enough for Amiss to dismiss the run out from his thoughts and just get on with something he was becoming increasingly secure about, his batting.

At 176, Denness was given out – caught bat and pad – once again off Barrett and as he trudged off thoughts of impending failure resonated around the ground. Greig, the 6ft 7ins South African-born all-rounder ambled out and played a subdued innings, pushing tentatively against the spinners. Gibbs penetrated the large man's forward defence for fourteen. Underwood came out as nightwatchman to keep Amiss company until the close. England finished the day still twelve runs behind, with a whole uninterrupted day's play ahead. Amiss remained defiant on 123 and so there was hope.

The following morning, Amiss and Underwood fought on gallantly against a spate of short-pitched bowling. On just the third delivery Amiss poked a catch to Sobers at short leg, but the grand old man of the team dropped the chance. It was to be Amiss's only chance. Amiss took blows on the body from Boyce and Underwood rode the missiles as best he could for 90 priceless minutes, a remarkable effort. Fatally Underwood played an expansive drive and snicked behind.

What on earth happened next? Alan Knott, the impish Kent wicket-keeper and just the right man for the moment, reached six and started to feel-in the zone. Amiss pushed a full-toss into the covers, domain of the prowling Clive Lloyd, and inexplicably called Knott for the sharpest of sharp singles. Knott apparently missed the crease by inches. At any rate, Amiss now had the rest of the day, $4^1/_2$ hours, with only the specialist bowlers for company. Out strode Chris Old, a burly Yorkshire left-hander, who batted calmly through to lunch. Amiss ate another salad, 24 hours and 162 undefeated runs after the last. Exhaustion was upon him as team mates rushed around to cater to his needs. England had crept into a lead of 64, the next session would decide the game.

After lunch, Old continued his innings by opening up and playing a couple of handsome shots, Amiss too maintained his concentration and picked off the bad ball. When Old was bowled by Barrett there were still another $2^1/_2$ hours remaining with England just 113 runs ahead.

Pat Pocock had a first-class average of just over six He started by playing a couple of expansive drives outside the off stump that appeared to miss the ball by at least a foot on both occasions. England supporters, lobstered by the sun, shouted out the obvious in beer-fuelled annoyance. Pocock, by hook or by crook, remained at the crease whilst Amiss passed 200 for the first time in his life.

By tea time, the West Indies had all but given up. England's lead was 145 and there remained only one hour and twenty overs. In the age of fast-food style Twenty20 cricket, this would seem a doddle, not on this day. Amiss glugged a brandy, physically exhausted and mentally drained.

Kanhai's team walked back for the final session three minutes late which angered umpire Sang Hue. At last Amiss could relax and help himself to some easy runs. Kanhai bowled himself, Clive Lloyd's medium pacers, Frederick's chinamen and some gentle offerings from Kallicharran and Rowe.

Amiss and Willis played out time and the game was called to a halt half-an-hour before the scheduled close, with Amiss undefeated on 262. Christopher Martin-Jenkins who was there commented that this was

> ... one of the greatest of modern test innings ... a triumphant reward for iron-willed concentration and admirable batting technique.

England went on to draw the third test thanks to centuries from Tony Greig (148) in the first innings, and 129 not out from Keith Fletcher in the second. The fourth test was too rain-affected for a result, but Amiss again scored a century (118). In the fifth and final test Boycott (with 99 and 112) and Greig (with thirteen wickets for 156) ensured that England won to square the series narrowly by 26 runs.

This was to prove England's last test win against the West Indies for 24 matches and sixteen years, a time of West Indian domination in world cricket. For two decades a relentless flow of world-class West Indian pace bowlers lined up to form the most sustained, fearsome, four-pronged, fast-bowling battery in history. The combination began with Roberts, Holding, Holder and Daniel in 1976, to be replaced by Garner, Croft, Clarke, Marshall, Bishop, Ambrose and Walsh.

In England the following summer Dennis Amiss continued to pile up centuries against India (188 at Lord's) and Pakistan (183 at the Oval). In a period of twelve months he amassed 1,356 test runs. His purple patch faded rapidly against Lillee and Thompson, forcing critics to point out a weakness against the fastest bowling. Boycott at this stage had taken leave of England duty, some reckoned it was the fast bowling attacks that drove him away.

Amiss came back gloriously at the Oval in 1976 against the formidable Michael Holding, though his 203 failed to avoid defeat. He played his last game for England in the second Ashes test the following summer to make way for the prodigal return of Geoffrey Boycott. Soon after, Amiss joined Kerry Packer's cricket circus where he became England's most successful batsman. Despite others being recalled to the England team in the post-Packer era, players such as the Kent trio of Bob Woolmer, Derek Underwood and Alan Knott, there was to be no call up for Warwickshire's greatest opening batsman. Amiss ended his career in 1987. In total the stocky Birmingham family man scored 102 centuries.

England 353 (Boycott 68, Denness 67, Sobers 3–65, Barratt 3–86).
West Indies 583–9 declared (Rowe 120, Fredericks 94, Kallicharran. 93, Julien 66, Sobers 57, Willis 3–97, Greig 3–102).
England 432–9 (Amiss 262*, Barrett 3–87).
MATCH DRAWN.

Innings Ranked Number 8
Stoddart's 173 at Melbourne in 1894–95

Opponents:Australia.
At stake: Ashes.
Bowling attack: Coningham, Turner, Trumble, Giffen, Lyons, Trott, Bruce. Runs per wicket average: 25.46.
Pitch: Fair.
Game situation: England, 24–1 in their second innings, are still 24 runs behind Australia.

The period 1894–95 coincided with the spread of electricity into the homes of middle England. Its spread was significant, but not as quick as would have been the case had gas not become the 'in thing' for the middle classes. Between 1893 and 1896 households with access to gas for cooking in Britain rose from 20,000 to 300,000. Rapid improvements in communication, most notably long-distance cabling, allowed, for the first time, scores to be cabled across the world so that the British population could receive updates whilst the match was still in progress. This brought cricket into the households of both countries and ignited a flame of interest unsurpassed at the time.

David Frith, a noted cricket historian, wrote a book 100 years later entitled *The First Great Test Series*. Andrew Ernest Stoddart, a 31-year-old England international at both cricket and rugby union – in fact he led both teams, though not at the same time – was approached by the Melbourne Cricket Club early in 1894 to select and captain an England team to contest the Ashes that winter.

Drewy Stoddart had already enjoyed success in Australia and had a famous role model in W. G. Grace, fifteen years his senior. The two often opened together, including the famous stand at the Oval in 1893 which compiled 151.

1894/95 provided a classic series of Ashes matches that stand the test of time. The series result went down to the wire, to the very last day, just like 2005. Just like 1981, the 1894/95 series yielded a victory for England after having been forced to follow on.

Australia had a formidable bowling line up. Opening was Arthur Coningham, a useful all-rounder, and the great Charlie Turner. Turner was a stout, open-chested, fast medium-pacer who captured 992 first class victims at just 14.26, imagine the value of Charlie Turner in today's IPL! This included 101 test wickets at 16.53.

Lest the rest of the bowlers feel inadequate by comparison, first change was none other then Hugh Trumble, a 6ft fast off-break bowler who was to end with 141 test wickets at 21.

George Giffen, Australia's captain and their own version of W.G., bowled slow medium with superb accuracy which was backed up by some effective leg breaks from Harry Trott

Australia, 0–1 down after England had won the first test by ten runs following on, won the toss and inserted England. Melbourne was not the grand stadium of today. There was the two-tiered pavilion, another less impressive two-tiered stand on the square-leg boundary and a smaller enclosure just to the right of the pavilion, otherwise spectators ringed the boundary fence on plain benches one line thick. The rest of the spectators sat in an open space of ten yards or so beyond the boundary ring benches. Considering the high temperatures, it is surprising to the naked eye how many spectators were dressed in jackets, trousers and ties. It seems even the Australians had Victorian modesty about their dress. Everyone wore hats as a concession to the sun, no one in shorts though.

Ward scored 30 in an England first innings of 75, Turner and Trumble between them took 8–47. Coningham, making his sole test appearance, took the wicket of Archie MacLaren with the first ball of the game.

During the interval awaiting Australia's first innings, a policeman stood by the pitch whilst the groundsmen hovered around him repainting the creases. It looked as though the policeman was suspiciously regarding the pitch as the centre of a crime scene.

Australia fared only a little better, yet the 48-run difference appeared significant at the time. England had Tom Richardson, the fastest bowler on the planet, approaching his prime. He took 5–57. A rest day on the Sunday allowed time for the pitch to be rolled again and dry out. Batting should be easier second time round.

New Year's Eve, the second day of the match, saw Melbourne fill up once again. In the second innings MacLaren and Ward put on 24, before Charlie Turner ripped a ball through MacLaren's defences and uprooted his off stump for fifteen. A poor test for MacLaren who had achieved only 39 runs from four innings in the series to date.

Enter 'Stoddy' the England skipper. Stoddart had not the strongest English batting line up available. In those days, the late Victorian era, travelling to Australia took a small matter of two months. Time away from families or careers prevented the likes of W. G. Grace and the honourable F. S. Jackson from touring. This was very much England's second eleven batting line-up. There was also no Shrewsbury or W. Gunn or R. Abel. A lot depended on A. E. Stoddart, a dominating right-hand batsman, who once scored the then highest ever in all known cricket, 485 for Hampstead against the Stoics in 1886. This time the attack was altogether better and the pressure far more intense.

Taking guard, Stoddart, along with many of his contemporaries, sported a bristling moustache. Dark hair, kempt and combed along a side parting, he represented the aristocracy of English batting talent. The previous tour in 1891/92 had taught him the benefits of building an innings. He saw in A. C. Bannerman the temperament required to minimise the throwing away of one's wicket. So it was that he set off in unusually cautious mood, settling for firm defence at anything straight, yet ready to cash in on anything wide. Out of the blue, and totally against the run of play, he launched into a length ball from Turner and dismissed it to the asphalt in front of the pavilion for five. Giffen posted a long on immediately after. Lunch came and England were 78–1, a lead of 30.

Soon into the bright and sunny afternoon session, England posted the 100, but soon after Turner bowled a vicious off break that spat into Ward's pads and onto his stumps. Out came Jack Brown, the gritty Yorkshireman, to up the tempo. Between the pair of right handers runs came at a fair lick. Stoddart was the main attraction but Brown was not to be out done. Ninety runs were added in just over an hour as Giffen rotated his bowlers. The crowd grew subdued until left-armer Bruce induced a snick from Brown to the keeper, 191–3.

Archie MacLaren, pads off and back in the hutch, watched and marvelled at the Stoddart innings that day on 31 December 1894, and he had this to say:

> It was one of those days when he convinced you from the commencement of his innings that nothing could get past his bat, that there was no ball that could not be hit to the exact spot he selected.'

It was during Stoddart's great knock that the umpire no balled Coningham and, rather than accept this with good grace, Coningham quite deliberately threw the next delivery at Stoddart out of annoyance and frustration.

Bill Brockwell made a rapid 21 in a stand of 31 with Stoddart. He attacked the loose ball, especially off the back foot, until he played on to Turner. Now England were 222–4, 174 runs ahead. They had benefited from the heavy roller between innings which seemed to have flattened the pitch out nicely. Most people believed the pitch would have more runs the second time around as a result, and they were right. At the close of the third day England stood on 287–4, with Stoddart 151 not out closing in on W.G.'s England record of the highest score in tests of 170. With Stoddart for the last 78 minutes was Bobby Peel, a useful bat but famous for his left-arm spin. Stoddart urged his partner to preserve his wicket and Peel, not wishing a rebuke from his skipper, behaved to plan.

Over 20,000 descended on Melbourne on New Year's Day, the fourth day. For the first time, news bulletins delivered running scores to England via long-distance cable. Even Queen Victoria wanted to be kept up to date on precedings.

Out came Stoddart and Peel. How long could the former carry on for? Giffen and Turner opened proceedings and strained every last sinew for the break-through. Only 33 were added in the first 50 minutes, but Stoddart unwrapped a couple of boundaries to move past W.G.'s record England score, and raised his bat to the acclaim.

His end, after a hitherto chanceless innings, surprised everyone not least himself. Giffen hurled down a much faster off break and Stoddart could only get an inside edge to it and play the ball onto his stumps. He walked back to the pavilion amid a generous standing ovation, his legend secure in Ashes history. Stoddart's 173 stood the test of time as the highest England captain's score in Australia until Mike Denness's 188 eighty years later.

After a thoughtful half century, and without the moderating influence of Stoddy, Bobby Peel danced down the track to Giffen, missed and Jarvis duly stumped the eccentric.

England eventually totalled 475 with everyone down to number eleven reaching double figures for the first time in test cricket. Australia took a while to be dismissed reaching 333, a shortfall of 94, to give England a 2–0 lead in the series after two tests.

Australia managed to win both of the next tests as England's batting floundered on the rocks with successive scores of 124, 143, then 65 and 72 at Sydney.

Finally in the test of the century, England's batting came good against the odds and momentum shift. In chasing 294 to win, England won by six wickets after a record stand of 210 between Jack Brown, 140, and Albert Ward, 93.

This was the greatest test series involving England for some considerable time. 1902 was spectacular, so too 1981 and 2005. The series of 1894/95 must rank up there.

Sadly, Stoddart was to shoot himself in the head, a deliberate act borne out of frustration at both deteriorating health and finances. Many of the cricketers who played in the test died a relatively young age, seven before the age of 60. Interestingly, the median age at which the English cricketers died was the same as the Australians, 64. The last survivor was Australian Len Darling, an attacking left-handed batsman, who died in 1946.

England 75 (Turner 5–32, Trumble 3–15).
Australia 123 (Richardson 5–57).
England 475 (Stoddart 173, Peel 53, Giffen 6–155, Turner 3–99).
Australia 333 (G. H. S. Trott 95, Iredale 68, Bruce 54, Peel 4–77, Brockwell 3–33).
ENGLAND WON BY 94 RUNS.

Innings Ranked Number 7
Jessop's 104 at the Oval in 1902

Opponents: Australia.
At stake: Personal pride, the Australians had already won the ashes and were 2–0 up in the series.
Bowling attack: Trumble, Saunders, Noble and Armstrong: 23.09.
Pitch: Fair.
Game situation: England were 48–5 in pursuit of 262 to win on the third and final day.

The 1902 series takes pride of place in the pantheon of Ashes battles. Its arrival was the most keenly anticipated series to date. Britain had just had the twin satisfactions of witnessing the final victory over the Boers just ten weeks earlier, and a couple of days before the start of this final test at the Oval, a new monarch had been crowned. King Edward VII, a 59-year-old, recovering from appendicitis, had just spent £30,000 paying for 456,000 poor Londoners to eat like a king in an evening of great joy. Britain was therefore a place of laughter and celebration, despite going in to the fifth test 2–0 down in the most entertaining series to date.

In times like those, cricket metamorphosed into quite brilliant entertainment. Coming off the back of a 4–1 thrashing in Australia earlier in the year, it was felt that England, on home turf and with a pick of all talent available, would put up a great fight against a supremely talented Australian side.

England totally dominated the first test. An innings of 138 from J. T. Tyldesley helped England reach 376–9 before declaring. The Australians were then destroyed by Wilfred Rhodes, who took 7–17 as Australia were blown away for 36. Rain ensured a draw. Only 38 overs were possible in the Lord's test.

By the third test the Australians, and in particular Clem Hill, Monty Noble, Hugh Trumble and John Saunders, were better prepared and swept England away by 143 runs.

At Old Trafford, an absolute thriller saw England lose by just three runs. Astonishingly, the selectors chose to omit Gilbert Jessop, the most exciting English batsman of his generation, and George Hirst, the legendary Yorkshire all-rounder, who had helped to bowl Australia out for 36 in the first test, and 23 against Yorkshire. Rarely, perhaps even more astonishingly than the omissions of Gower in 1993 and Hoggard in 2008, have England selectors made such ridiculous blunders.

For the Old Trafford test, England brought in Fred Tate and L. C. H. Palairet. Tate probably played the worst game ever for England. He bowled a wicketless 11 overs for 44 in the first innings, scored five not out in England's first innings, took the prize scalp of S. E. Gregory and Trumble in the second to complete match figures of 16–4–51–2. On paper, his bowling looked fine. But he dropped a crucial catch at deep square leg, where McLaren had placed him as he was regarded as a close to the wicket specialist. The batsman, Darling, then scored a priceless 37 in an Australian total of 86. England needed just 123 runs in the last innings. They collapsed. When Tate arrived at the crease, England, with only one wicket in hand, required eight to win. There was a break for rain then, on resumption, Tate inside edged for four and with only four needed to win. A shooter from Saunders bowled the poor batsman's off stump. In the dressing room, Tate wept inconsolably.

For the final test, the selectors brought back both Jessop and Hirst. Aside from Tate, they also dropped Kumar Ranjitsinjhi (who had also had a wretched series) and Bobby Abel. None of the three cricketers ever played for England again.

At the Oval for the final test, Australia won the toss on a good wicket. They started well (47–0), stuttered a bit (126–5) but recovered to 324 all out. George Hirst illustrated his credentials with 5–77 that included the first five to fall, bowling fast-medium left-armers, full of optimism, despite the lack of pace and bounce on the dry, flat wicket.

England replied with 183 all out with no one reaching 50, but George Hirst top-scored with 43. It was a damp wicket, very much drying out in the sun, lethal, and Hirst played exceptionally well to help England avoid the follow-on. Hugh Trumble, bowling medium-paced off breaks, took 8–65. On the drying sticky, he extracted the necessary bounce from his high arm. Imposingly, Australia took a first innings lead of 141.

Then it was Australia's turn to suffer and they collapsed to 114–8 at the close of day two. England gave thanks, mainly to rough diamond and boozer Bill Lockward, who went on to finish with 5–45.

Heavy rain descended on London in the early hours and Gilbert Jessop, realising the hopelessness of England's situation, took bets from fellow amateurs over a convivial dinner. He placed odds for him scoring a 50 at 10 to 1, and on 100 at 20 to 1.

The last two Australian wickets added just seven. England needed 263 to win and restore some pride. The team was close to being the greatest batting line-up in England's history to date, but the wicket was going to be a mine field.

Then the pendulum determining the direction of the day swung disastrously towards Australia. In the first hour, England collapsed to 10–3. A partial recovery saw the score advance to 48–5. The casualties, with no further hand to play, included the skipper, Archie McLaren (the writer Neville Cardus's favourite boyhood hero), Lionel Palairet (who never played again after debuting at Old Trafford), J. T. Tyldesley (England regular for a decade), T. W. Hayward (the future Jack Hobbs's first famous opening partner and scorer of 104 hundreds), and the all-rounder L. C. Braund.

Enter Gilbert Laird Jessop, a 28-year-old flash-in-the-pan batsman. Jessop only batted one way, equivalent to today's Twenty20 format. Reliable estimates suggest that, over a twenty-year career, Jessop averaged 80 runs per hour. To this end, of the 53 first-class centuries he scored, only two lasted longer than three hours and only a further ten for more than two hours. Jessop played as a useful bits and pieces cricketer; a good fielder and reliable medium-paced bowler completed the package. What attracted the general public and made Jessop a household name, was his electrifying batting.

Arriving at the crease Jessop met up with none other than the Hon. F. S. Jackson, a veteran from the recent Boer War. In the 45 minutes to lunch both batsman consolidated, trying to preserve their wickets. After lunch Jessop decided to launch himself at the bowling. He was particularly savage on Saunders the left armer, hitting him for four fours and a single off consecutive balls. Jackson maintained his pre-lunch tempo and prepared to ride out the hurricane knock taking shape at the other end.

Trumble operated from the pavilion end for the entire duration of both innings. Jessop looked to advancing down the track towards Trumble and hoisting him through the covers or back over his head. He chose to pull Saunders over mid-wicket, respecting him even less. By now, Saunders was tiring and his length was awry and he panicked, bowling long hops and full tosses. He should have been taken off sooner.

Then, after contributing eighteen in a stand of 109, Jackson patted back to Trumble and was caught and bowled. At this point, with still 106 needed for victory, England were six down. Jessop then rose in one final, majestic, demolition job, this time turning his attention towards Trumble to see just how far he could hit him. Twice he hoisted the ball into the pavilion, every delivery was being thrashed as if he had a thousand runs to squander in his trouser pockets. He and George Hirst put on 30 in eight fabulous minutes before tamely, and in a remarkably anti-climactic manner, he spooned a catch to short leg and departed. Kelly, the Australian keeper, gave Jessop a pat on the back and the entire Australian team applauded him all the way back into the pavilion. For a long time this knock was regarded as perhaps the greatest and most famous test-match innings in the history of the game. Jessop had recorded the fastest hundred in test cricket; his 104 took only 75 minutes and 80 deliveries. Perhaps in the public eye his knock is more famous than that made by J. T. Brown back in 1895, but then Brown's knock was 12,000 miles away from the main throng of British reporters.

With 76 still needed Lockwood, in a subservient role, joined forces with Hirst. The score edged passed 200 with Hirst dominating the stand, but playing sensibly and within himself. Lockwood contributed just two in a stand of 27 before Trumble got him LBW.

Lilley, the keeper, settled down to add a priceless 32 to take the score to 248 before Darling, the skipper, caught him for sixteen. Now, with England nine down for 248, and with fifteen still needed, in came the greatest number eleven batsman England has ever had, Wilfred Rhodes.

Rhodes not only captured 4,187 wickets, more than any other player in the first-class game ever, he also went on to score a fraction less than 40,000 runs, including 58 centuries.

Legend has it that both the Yorkshire all-rounders, Hirst and Rhodes, agreed to get the runs in singles. Both disproved this in later years, it was a Neville Cardus mis-quote. At 259, still four runs short, Trumble pinned Hirst back in line with the stumps and appealed loudly. For the rest of his life Trumble swore that Hirst was plumb, but the umpire remained unmoved.

Rhodes ended the torment by pushing the ball wide of mid-on and the batsmen scampered the winning runs, then rushed off towards the pavilion. A heroic England victory, one of the most famous, built on the foundations of an innings of rare quality and drama from Jessop, ensured a warm glow of satisfaction at the end of a monumental series.

England went on to defeat Australia 3–2 in the next series in Australia, though Jessop did not make the tour.

Australia 324 (Trumble 64*, Noble 52, Hirst 5–77).
England 183 (Trumble 8–65).
Australia 121 (Lockwood 5–45).
England 263–9 (Jessop 104, Hirst 58*, FS Jackson 49, Saunders 4–105, Trumble 4–108).
ENGLAND WON BY 1 WICKET.

Innings Ranked Number 6
Herbert Sutcliffe's 161 at the Oval in 1926

Opponents: Australia.
At stake: Ashes, lost by England in 1921.
Bowling attack: Gregory, Macartney, Mailey, Grimmett, Richardson: 31.95.
Pitch: 'Unplayable' after a thunderstorm on the third evening.
Game situation: The start of England's second innings, 22 runs in arrears in a timeless test with rain forecast.
Attendance: over 30,000 squashed in to the Oval.

Australia had been the undisputed world champions from the time of the cease fire on the Western Front to 17 August 1926. They had defeated England 5–0 in 1920/21, then further bullied them under Warwick Armstrong to win 3–0 in England the following summer. This was followed by a 4–1 defeat for England in 1924/25. Ten of the victorious 1921 side made the trip in 1926, among them veterans such as 40-year-olds Clarie Grimmett and Charles Macartney, as well as the 43-year-old Warren Bardsley.

The first four tests of the 1926 series were all drawn. The first was almost totally washed out, with Jack Hobbs and Herbert Sutcliffe left stranded on 32–0. The second test at Lord's saw England gaining the better of the draw, with Hobbs and Sutcliffe putting on 182 (this record Ashes opening stand for England at the headquarters of cricket stood until the 196 put on by Strauss and Cook in 2009). The Australians enjoyed the upper hand in the drawn third test, Hobbs and Sutcliffe putting on 156 in the second innings to ward off defeat after following on. Manchester's weather then ensured another draw, with honours about even, in the fourth test.

For the fifth test the England selectors appointed Percy Chapman as captain at the tender age of 25. They recalled the 48-year-old slow left-armer Wilfred Rhodes (who had first played test cricket in W. G. Grace's last test, way back in 1899) and brought in a young tearaway fast bowler from the depths of Nottinghamshire's mines by the name of Harold Larwood. Australia brought back H. L. Collins to captain the side and left J. Ryder out.

To add a further element of anticipation, this final test was to be timeless. England won the toss and elected to bat. They were duly dismissed for 280, with Sutcliffe's contribution a typically solid 76. In reply, Australia totalled 302, grafting out a small first innings lead of 22.

The crowd grew anxious as Hobbs and Sutcliffe walked down the pavilion steps to bat out the last hour of day two. The pitch was fine at this stage, but an impending thunderstorm lent an air of intolerable tension. The partisan crowd sensed that this final hour of day two would be the period that would ultimately decide the match. Surely Hobbs and Sutcliffe could not do it again. The law of averages stated that one or both was sure to fail. Collins selected many different bowling combinations; he opened with Gregory and Grimmett, only to switch to Arther Mailey, then Macartney. With quiet confidence the runs started to flow and, by the close of play, England had gained a slight numerical advantage. At 49–0 England were 27 ahead with all their second innings wickets intact, in what had now amounted to a one innings game.

Just over 30,000 spectators, from the youngest boy to the oldest Victorian veteran, left the ground at the end of day two with memories of an immense day's play etched into their minds for good. According to Warner, the youngest individual will remember it when his hair is white with the sands of time.

Overnight, disaster struck. A thunderstorm raged over the Oval and in the darkness lightening illuminated the empty tiers of the stands. Then torrential rain deluged the ground. By morning the pitch had turned black from the cloudburst, whilst the growing warmth of the day drew moisture out into a steaming blanket over the ground.

Play began on time, with Chapman ordering the heavy roller to draw moisture from the pitch so as to deaden it before the sun came out to bake it into a minefield. There would be time to play oneself in, but when the sun emerged, England would be lucky to club together another 70.

Hobbs wearing his cap and the hatless Sutcliffe began day three by facing Australia's meanest bowlers at the time: Grimmett's leg breaks and Macartney's left arm. It was Hobbs who took the attack to Australia and in the first 40 minutes he scored all 26 runs from the bat. Running between the wickets was quick and instinctive as befits all great opening partners. However, Macartney's first nine overs of the day brought only two runs. Eventually, Sutcliffe opened his account for the day with successive cuts for two and then three off Grimmett, to take the total to 80 without loss. Then the sun came out.

Grabbing the chance to attack, Collins substituted Macartney for Richardson's off breaks and brought in three short legs. First ball was too short and Hobbs lifted it over the infield for four to bring up his fifty. It was obvious to spectators behind the bowler's arm how much the ball was spitting and rearing off a length; any more runs now would be a bonus. Hobbs and Sutcliffe moved past the century stand. Collins attacked further with two more short on the leg side so that five fielders nestled in together in an arc from leg slip to silly mid-on. Now the ball spat and skidded alarmingly, some turned at right angles, some shot straight on, with Richardson landing the ball on a six pence. His spell of ten overs cost just a single. The umpire Frank Chester reported that he had never seen such a sticky wicket. Hobbs took the brunt, laying a dead bat for over after over. At the end of each maiden, applause resounded out from the stands. According to Sutcliffe:

> I found myself longing to have a go at him (Richardson), but I knew I could not afford the risk. My business was to stay there until the wicket became easier. Eventually, I scored the run that took Hobbs to Richardson's end, and there he was tied down, just as I had been, by Richardson's 'leg theory' attack. We surmounted our difficulties.

At lunch both batsmen remained to 'garden' the wicket for a few minutes whilst the umpires and Australians walked off. In a mammoth 150 minutes of batting, under the most unpleasant conditions, an hour of which being unplayable, Hobbs and Sutcliffe added 112 priceless runs to bring England up to 161–0, a lead of 139.

As they walked off, the applause was sustained, raucous and could be heard as far away as Westminster. The Prince of Wales in person congratulated both batsmen in the luncheon interval and as they ate, the wicket dried out into a deader, more benign surface.

In the afternoon Hobbs fell for exactly 100, the score 172–1. Frank Woolley began with a four through mid wicket, but fell for 27 just as he was looking good. The second wicket added 48 and the third wicket between Sutcliffe and Hendren 57, although Hendren was devoid of form. Chapman was clean bowled with the score on 316–4, then Stevens looked comfortable before perishing with a wild slash to cover-point.

In the last over of the day Sutcliffe finally fell to Mailey. His 161 had taken seven hours and fifteen minutes, he scored fifteen boundaries and his judgement in a chanceless innings was as remarkable as his stamina and skill. Sutcliffe's best strokes were his cuts and drives through mid off. Grimmett, in particular, had bowled well all day without proper reward and the Australian fielding was superb. England finished the day on 375–6.

On day four England reached 436 thanks to a belligerent undefeated 33 from Maurice Tate, then set Australia the tall target of 415 to win. In the end they did not come close. Harold Larwood, fast and raw, blasted out Woodfull, Macartney and Andrews, whilst Wilfred Rhodes, the 48-year-old bowling genius, took 4–44 including Bardsley – who had carried his bat for 193 not out at Lord's – Ponsford, Collins himself and off-spinner A. J. Richardson. The end proved an anticlimax, such was the collapse in Australia's second innings. It was as though the Australians had conceded defeat.

At five past six on Wednesday afternoon the Ashes came back to England and the era of Australian supremacy that stretched back to the Great War passed into the annals of cricket history. Euphoria spread around London as news broke via the scoreboard outside the *Morning Post* building. Thousands came to cheer and savour the moment.

Hobbs and Sutcliffe became the most prolific opening pair in history based on an average opening partnership in excess of 80. As for the Australians, the 1926 side had a good but overly mature bowling attack. The spinners, Mailey and Grimmett, both bore expensive series analyses and Macartney operating as a 40-year-old new ball bowler had not quite the spirit of earlier years. Gregory too was a shadow of his former 1921 self. Nonetheless, Sutcliffe's innings scored highly in terms of its value to the team, helping to win both the test match and the series, executed for the most part under unplayable conditions in front of over 30,000 expectant fans.

Sutcliffe went on to have a long life, playing 54 times for England over an eleven-year period up to 1935. During this time he secured a healthier test average than any other Englishman in the history of the game: 60.73. He died, aged 83, in 1978, but not before sitting in a wheelchair alongside Len Hutton and Geoffrey Boycott, after the latters 100th 100 at Headingley. It was fitting that the three greatest Yorkshire batsmen should squeeze into the same photo frame.

England 280 (Sutcliffe 76, Mailey 6–138).
Australia 302 (Gregory 73, Collins 61, Tate 3–40, Larwood 3–82).
England 436 (Sutcliffe 161, Hobbs 100, Grimmett 3–108, Mailey 3–128).
Australia 125 (Rhodes 4–44, Larwood 3–34).
ENGLAND WON BY 289 RUNS.

Innings Ranked Number 5
May's 285 not out at Edgbaston in 1957

Opponents: West Indies.
At stake: First test.
Bowling attack: Worrell, Gilchrist, Ramadhin, Atkinson, Sobers, Smith, Goddard: 31.58.
Pitch: Fine.
Game situation: England are 65–2 in the second innings having conceded 286 runs on the first innings.

The 1950s were an exciting time in world cricket. A new generation of players emerged from the shadow of world war, too young to have played first-class cricket during the years of conflict. England were now the undisputed world champions, especially due to the all-round balance and potency of the bowling attack. At no other time in history could England call upon an attack which comprised Trueman and Statham in the pace department, backed up by accuracy and swing from Bailey followed by England's greatest ever off-break bowler in Laker coupled with his Surrey colleague, the slow left-armer Lock.

The batting had been stripped of all the pre-war greats, especially Hutton and Edrich (1955), then Washbrook and Compton the following year. Now a new generation of swords, the sharpest being Peter May from Cambridge University and Colin Cowdrey from Oxford. The batting, however, looked weak on paper. Richardson and Close opened, followed by Insole at number three, none were to average 40 in their test careers and Close and Insole not even 30. A lot rested on the Oxbridge pair.

England had retained the Ashes the previous year to make three successive series wins against the old enemy. They drew 2–2 in South Africa over the winter, but somehow the press felt as though England would once again struggle against the spin threat from Ramadhin. Some reckoned England were the underdogs, after all they had not beaten the West Indies since before the war, although they had returned from 2–0 down to square the series in 1953/54.

England batted but on the first day were caught in Ramadhin's web. Not knowing how to read Ramadhin's varied bag of tricks England capitulated to 186 all out, the bowler returning 31–16–49–7.

West Indies had the more impressive batting line up with the famous 'Three Ws': Weekes, Worrell and Walcott, as well as Kanhai, O. G. Smith, and a youthful Garfield Sobers. Despite England's world-class bowlers West Indies clocked up 474, a lead of 289.

Richardson and Close strode to the wicket with a mountain to climb. Gilchrist hurled missiles at speed for a while but without success and England breathed a sigh of relief as the 50 came up. Ramadhin, opening the bowling in place of the injured Worrell, now started what became the longest, single spell of bowling in cricket history. Warming up, and buoyed by his startling success first time around, he first dismissed Richardson then, shortly after, bowled the hapless Insole. Out came May and he and Brian Close held out to the end of day three with Goddard rotating his other bowlers around Ramadhin.

May was famous for allowing his batsmen to work out their own techniques for dealing with bowlers. Seeing how his side had capitulated in the first innings, he broke his tradition and on Saturday evening called a team meeting to discuss how best to combat Ramadhin who bowled from a swift wrist action and front of the hand release. He was sharper than normal spinners and, as the ball was released, its path to the wicket seemed blurred. At any rate, no batsman could decipher the more usual off break from the leg break, despite the freakish front of the hand release.

May stressed the importance of treating each delivery as an off break, unless it was straight. If Ramadhin delivered the leg break, it would spin passed the outside edge and out of harm's way. Cowdrey listened to the theory and made mental notes.

Day four, and still over almost 200 runs behind, with eight wickets in hand, May and Close resumed. Goddard called on Gilchrist and Close edged to slip, leaving England tottering on 113–3, still requiring 176 more runs just to make the West Indies bat again. Out walked Colin Cowdrey, always cheerful and very polite. It was not yet high noon on day 4 so $5^{1}/_{2}$ sessions remained, with England's last pair of specialist batsmen at the crease, only all-rounder Bailey, keeper Evans and the tail left.

May and Cowdrey had similar upbringings. May heralded from Charterhouse and went on to Cambridge, whereas Cowdrey left Tonbridge for Oxford – two ex-public school boys, well trained in the art of classical techniques. Soon Ramadhin shouted an appeal for LBW, then another, and another, but each time the umpire turned away disinterested. May and Cowdrey vowed to play with their pads in defence. The umpire felt that with the front pad far down the track, there was too much doubt to give the batsman out. Indeed, the author Michael Manley, providing the West Indian viewpoint, claims Ramadhin appealed at least 50 times through the innings.

Because Ramadhin bowled such tight lines, when he pitched straight it meant the ball went straight on, easy, just get in line. If the bowl pitched outside off, both played for the off break. Any leg breaks would turn and pass the edge of the bat.

May reached 50 and lunch came. Shortly before tea, he reached 100 and Cowdrey 50, all the while whittling the arrears away, slowly, gradually, deflating the bowling attack. On Ramadhin bowled.

Asked to write a foreword for Cowdrey's autobiography twenty years later, Peter May stated:

> I must mention briefly our memorable stand at Edgbaston, in particular his steadying influence on me when I was charging down the wicket and trying to hit everyone into the car park. I recall that he calmed me down and said that occupation of the crease was the vital requirement!

May dominated the partnership, yet ruled out any shots off Ramadhin wide of mid on for fear of the repurcussions should the ball straighten. Coming off the back of just one fifty in the last fourteen test innings, May felt a huge load lift from his captain's shoulders. He noticed a pattern whereby when he took runs off Ramadhin, the bowler would aim to repeat the delivery with greater pace. How awful for one of the world's deadliest spinners to be so comprehensively out thought.

May and Cowdrey batted on throughout the rest of the day. Despite the over-use of their pads and the injustice of so many LBW appeals turned down, England added 276 runs for the day. At the close May had 193 to his name, with Cowdrey just the 78. The lead was now 90 and English hopes had brightened. Still England needed to at least bat out the morning session with their specialists together to ward off the prospect of defeat. May was all too aware of the threat from the West Indies batting line up.

Ramadhin continued on unchanged to lunch and still May and Cowdrey remained, Cowdrey now had passed 100 and May 200. The stand was reaching record-breaking potential. On through the afternoon the partnership grew, breaking Hutton and Leyland's stand of 382 at the Oval. Cowdrey's 150 came, then May's 250. When the partnership had reached 411 Cowdrey hoisted a Collie Smith off break to the long on boundary to be caught by the substitue, N. S. Asgarali. England were 236 ahead and still May batted on.

Out strode the purky Kent wicket-keeper Godfrey Evans who soon pushed his captain hard for a second run. Peter May in his typically polite manner called Evans for a mid-pitch discussion. 'I admire you for the way you took my words to heart about scoring runs quickly, but please remember I have been batting for over eight hours!'

Slightly embarrassed at his lack of thought, Evans helped his captain slap a merry 59 runs between them before May called a halt and declared. England had reached the imposing score of 583 for four. Sonny Ramadhin's analysis for the innings read a miserable 98–35–179–2 and he was never again quite the force of old. Before May's innings he had taken 120 wickets at 27.00, afterwards he would only take another 38 wickets at 35.24. England comfortably won the series 3–0 with all victories by an innings.

May's knock, especially his tactics of using the pad, brought about a change in the understanding of the LBW law. The partnership still remains the highest for any fourth wicket in test history, and the single largest stand for England.

Peter May retired from test cricket after the 1961 series at the youthful age of 32, whilst the durable Cowdrey went on until middle age, being called out at the age of 42 to shore up a battered England line up against Lillee and Thomson.

England 186 (Ramadhin 7–49).
West Indies 474 (O. G. Smith 161, Walcott 90, Worrell 81, Sobers 53, Laker 4–119, Statham 3–114).
England 583–4 declared (May 285*, Cowdrey 154).
West Indies 72–7 (Lock 3–31).
MATCH DRAWN.

Innings Ranked Number 4
Pietersen's 158 at the Oval in 2005

Opponents: Australia.
At stake: Ashes.
Bowling attack: McGrath, Lee, Tait, Warne, Clarke: 27.0.
Pitch: Excellent fast paced Oval track.
Game situation: England needed to bat out at least 60 overs of the last day in order to secure a draw and regain the Ashes for the first time since 1986.

England had only won one Ashes test with the Ashes still at stake in a test series since 1986. An entire generation of English cricketers had come and gone without the warm glow of an Ashes series win. Consider a team comprising the following: Atherton, Stewart, Hick, Hussain, Robin Smith, Thorpe, Cork, Caddick, Gough, Fraser, Malcolm. All had to retire without an Ashes series win. Thorpe indeed feeling pressurised into retiring just before the Ashes series – someone had to make way for a new South African-born attacking batsman who had just blasted three centuries in defiance in South Africa the previous winter.

Gradually, from a position at the foot of world test cricket following a home defeat against New Zealand in 1999, England, under Duncan Fletcher as coach, began to develop a team of worthy individuals, each with a specific task. Opening the 2005 series was Trescothick and Strauss, both left handers with Trescothick a more adventurous thrasher and Strauss the percentage accumulator.

Michael Vaughan captained with intelligence and batted first wicket down. Young Ian Bell, a diminutive, right-handed 23-year-old, batted at four. At number five, playing in his first test series, was a newcomer born and bred in South Africa. A tall, lean and powerful man with a shock of dark hair, tainted by an outrageous motorway of white, dyed hair that scorched its way on the wave of hair gel along a skull of prickly hair, Kevin Pietersen exuded box-office appeal. Shane Warne, a team-mate at Hampshire, knew Pietersen all too well. 'He can hurt you!' he commented. After Pietersen came an even more powerful man, equally tall and the finest fast-bowling, all-round sensation since Botham, Andrew Flintoff. Geraint Jones and Ashley Giles provided support at seven and eight in the batting line-up, with Geraint the keeper and Giles the side's token spinner, a miserly slow left-armer at that. Numbers nine ten and Jack were, along with Flintoff, chiefly responsible for working through the Australian line up that summer. Harmisan, Simon Jones and the dependable Matthew Hoggard each added a further variation of right-arm pace. Hoggard provided the early swing against Harmisan's 'Ambrose Thunderbolts' from the other end. Second change came Simon Jones, equally hostile, but with significant reverse swing in his tail. Finally, skipper Vaughan would turn to Flintoff, the talesman who hurled a heavy ball down at 94 m.p.h.

Collectively, England had never fielded a more threatening four-paced attack. With Giles closing down one end, Vaughan was able to rotate his pace men so they all felt fresh at the start of their spells. Only one enforced change was made to the England line up, with Simon Jones injured, England opted for Paul Collingwood instead of James Anderson.

The Australians were the world champions at the time and fielded one of their greatest-ever teams, many of whom, on mere test statistics, would command a place in the greatest Australian XI of all time: Warne, McGrath, Ponting, Hayden and Gilchrist. They also had the fastest bowler on the planet in Brett Lee.

The roller-coaster ride through the six week spectacle made the Ashes series of 2005 every bit as memorable as that of 1981, although in 1981 the Australians were not the undisputed world champions, the West Indies had that claim. For run rates and close finishes it eclipsed the 1953 series. 1948 was memorable, but too one-sided to Australia and 1956 likewise to England. The only truly comparable home series were 1902 (but even then England went into the last test already 2–0 down), and the Hobbs and Sutcliffe vintage of 1926.

At any rate, England had played the more aggressive cricket since their defeat way back in the first test at Lord's. Pietersen on debut threatened with a pair of swashbuckling 50s, but he had only made one other 50 in the rest of the series so now had a point to prove.

Looking more rock star than world-class athlete, Pietersen wore £50,000 ear rings that glittered, a sponsorship deal. All England had to do to ward off the might of Australia was bat out the last day. For all the gargantuan efforts over 24 days of heated battle, the whole outcome depended on the last few hours. There were to be 98 overs and England started on 34–1, a lead of 40, with Strauss the centurion in the first innings, out the evening before to Warne. The weather was fine, sunny even, but it was September and the days were drawing in.

Pietersen had slept well. He saw Vaughan and Trescothick bat in positive fashion for the first 40 minutes and then a double strike in two successive deliveries from McGrath sent Vaughan and Bell back to the pavilion.

Out Pietersen strode to meet his day of destiny, with the whole country watching the climax of the series. McGrath ran in as he tapped his right foot in anticipation. It was a throat ball that rose alarmingly from just short of a length. It whistled passed his glove, smacked into his upper arm and ballooned to the slips. The entire close cordon of Australians appealed in unison. Umpire Billy Bowden remained unperturbed, and technology supported a hairline decision. Still flustered, Gilchrist dropped Pietersen before he had scored off Warne, though it was a hard chance.

With Trescothick for company, Pietersen played himself in. Becoming more comfortable with his surroundings, he unleashed a cover drive to a delivery from Brett Lee that took the edge and landed invitingly right in Warne's lap at second slip. Incredibly, Warne dropped the regulation chance and all England could breath again.

Business around London took a nose dive and schools across the country had classrooms linked to the electronically communicated score via white boards and projectors tuned into the internet. It was going to be a long day.

Warne began to settle in and weave a magical spell. Trescothick edged to slip and Flintoff played back to be caught and bowled. England lunched on 126–5, looking shaken and vulnerable.

Ponting chewed over his lunch and informed Lee that he was to blast Pietersen off the pitch. Lee began proceedings from the pavilion end in what was to become the crucial phase of the afternoon. It was entirely plausible that, at the last hurdle, England would succumb to the wiles of Warne at one end and the shear speed of Lee at the other.

Astonishingly, and with reckless abandon, Pietersen launched an assault at Lee probably on the basis that the best form of defence was attack. A missile aimed at Pietersen's upper body was swotted for six over fine leg, just out of reach of a diving Tait. Lee walked back to his mark with fury etched on his flushed, red face. In he stormed, this time just short of a length and too full to hook. Pietersen, with the destiny of the Ashes at his fingertips, thrashed the ball like a double-handed, forearm tennis smash back passed the bowler at astonishing speed for four. With a huge pulled six into the crowd, Lee was taken off. What was left in Ponting's armoury? Tait, just raw and fast, McGrath now tiring and the ever available Warne sensing 40 wickets in the series.

Collingwood's presence was barely felt for the first 70 minutes, he had crawled along just nurdling the odd single here and there. At last Warne offered him a long hop and he gleefully pulled it for four to the mid-wicket boundary amidst a huge cheer. Next ball, Collingwood edged to Ponting. The score was 186–6 and, though he only scored ten, it was the most valuable ten in Ashes history and fully justified Collingwood's promotion to the team for this final test. Aside from Collingwood for the injured Simon Jones, England featured the same players for all five tests, a unique occurence.

When Geraint Jones fell for one, bowled by Tate, Pietersen was approaching his maiden test century. For company he had the perennially underrated Ashley Giles, a reliable number eight who never achieved the fluency of his successor, Stuart Broad.

It was still theoretically possible for this mighty Australian team to chase 206 in the time left, but time arrives for everyone at some stage, even such a team of decade-long world conquerors. The last chance boiled down to two great gladiators, Shane Warne, rated as one of the five greatest cricketers of the twentieth century and the new rising star with all that bling and glamour.

In the final throw of the dice, Warne tried to winkle his Hampshire team mate into error. Rising to the bait, Pietersen hoisted Warne over mid-wicket for six and then repeated the shot with equal conviction. Remember Warne stating that Pietersen could hurt? The batsman then bounded down the pitch to lift Warne twice over long on and the game was up. From then on, Giles and Pietersen shared a record eighth wicket partnership at the Oval of 109. Finally Pietersen hit across a good length ball from McGrath for 158 off just 187 balls with an Ashes record of seven sixes as well as fifteen fours, almost all of which were struck off the sweetest middle.

An unforgettable day saw the final test end in a draw. Foreigners wonder how a game that lasts for five days and ends in a draw can be so exciting. Pietersen's knock was indeed breathtaking. Time and time again in the immediate overs after lunch, during his macho ambush on Lee, Pietersen could have gifted his wicket away. Such a talented bowling line up would surely then have pounded away at the tail and chased down 200. The reasons Australia failed to do this was, with the greatest respect for Freddie Flintoff's heroics to date, Pietersen's quite extraordinary innings, played at a tempo and level of courage not seen by an Englishman since Ian Botham's prime.

These England players never played again as a team; injuries, retirements and loss of form saw to that. For a moment, a brief moment, England supporters felt the thrill of being world champions. The last time that an England team had in fact beaten the official world champions in a full test series was 1953. The Ashes-winning England team of 1970/71 would probably not have defeated the banned South Africans at the time.

Pietersen remains today the most gifted England batsman of his generation. Whether he will be rated as highly as pre-war legends Hobbs, Sutcliffe and Hammond, or indeed Compton and Hutton, time will tell. In my life time only Boycott, and briefly David Gower and Robin Smith, averaged over 50 at some stage in their test careers. Pietersen could yet become the greatest English batsmen of all time.

England 373 (Strauss 129, Flintoff 72, Warne 6–122).
Australia 367 (Hayden 138, Langer 105, Flintoff 5–78, Hoggard 4–97).
England 335 (Pietersen 158, Giles 59, Vaughan 45, Warne 6–124).
Australia 4–0.
MATCH DRAWN.

Innings Ranked Number 3
Jack Brown's 140 at Melbourne in 1895

Opponents: Australia.
At stake: Ashes.
Bowling attack: Giffen, H. Trott, A.E. Trott, Mckibbin, Bruce, Lyons.
Average runs per wicket: 28.21.
Pitch: Perfect.
Game situation: The sensational series that coined the phrase, 'test cricket'. England had to score 297 to regain the Ashes. Jack Brown entered the arena at 28–2.

The Blackpool Tower had just been built and Oscar Wilde was facing two years in jail for sodomy when England, under Drewy Stoddart, took the ship to Australia in the hope of retaining the Ashes during a 33-week-long tour with just thirteen men.

This was the series that coined the phrase, 'test cricket'. It had been the most sensational in the short history of the game. England, without W. G. Grace, R. Abel, W. Gunn and the Hon F. S. Jackson did not seem to have the batting to bring home the Ashes. Nevertheless they began by winning the first two tests.

England won the first test at Sydney after following on. It would take another 87 years before that rare feat was repeated. They won again in the second test after A. E. Stoddart's outstanding innings. Both the third and fourth tests were lost, both by colossal margins: 382 runs, then an innings and 147.

In the deciding fifth test, billed as the 'match of the century', it was said that even Queen Victoria took an interest in the outcome. Australia batted first and reached a mountainous 414. England completely reshuffled their batting order in bizarre manner. All eleven from the fourth test that lost so badly by an innings, were restored once again for the fifth test although no-one batted in the same position, the closest being A. Ward (who batted at number two for the fourth test and number one this time). Was this a deliberate act based on superstition? We can only guess.

Nonetheless England batted much better and almost achieved

more runs – 384 – than their previous four innings combined (404). Archie MacLaren scored 120 before treading on his stumps trying to hook a ball from Harry Trott. He was ably supported with 50s from Stoddart and Peel who helped pull England back almost to parity on the first innings. In Peel's case, his 73 gave him immense satisfaction, coming off the back of successive pairs in the preceding two tests.

Australia took the slender lead of 29 and built on it as best they could. Trying to prevent Australia setting too daunting a target was Tom Richardson, the greatest fast bowler in the world at the time. He bowled his heart out to claim 6–104.

England were required to get 297 for a series win, huge stakes. They needed a good, solid start. Albert Ward played out a maiden save for a no ball from Giffen. Not long to go until stumps, Stoddart had preached the importance of preserving one's wicket at the change of innings. Brockwell drilled his first ball from Harry Trott firmly to the boundary, a show of intent. Angered, Trott sent down a bouncer which Brockwell swivelled around and pulled. The top edge ballooned upwards and Giffen barely had to move, England 5–1 with Stoddart, captain and hero of the second test, now required to negotiate the last twenty minutes with nothing much to gain and everything to lose.

Brockwell had scored 182 runs for his ten completed innings in the series, a disappointment. As England had taken only thirteen men for the entire tour Brockwell could not really be dropped, especially as the two men who were not playing were the reserve wicket keeper, Leslie Gay, and the last in the line of genuine underhand lob bowlers, the cheerful, grey-haired, 45-year-old Walter Humphries. Stoddart and Ward hung on, the former just about, despite some tense moments against Trott. England closed on 28–1.

So to the final day of the series. Rain had fallen overnight, but the heavy roller flattened out the cracks. The ground filled with the expectant chatter of the day's events. Brown had a few throw downs, unfiltered cigarette dangling from his mouth. With ten minutes to the start he returned to the pavilion, sat in his chair and watched Stoddart and Ward follow the Australians out. The overnight rain had long gone and the pitch dried quickly. As an opener for Yorkshire, Brown at least knew when he would bat. At number four he just did not know; it could be next ball, it might not be for hours. It was at these moments that Brown chain smoked. He lit another cigarette and coughed from a damaged chest. Moustached, sporting the trendy dark-coloured belt to contrast with his whites, he drew in a deep drag as Harry Trott started the day's play with a straight top spinner. Stoddart played to leg, missed and a loud appeal went up. The umpire agreed and, as Brown exhaled, a roar from the 20,000 drowned out the good luck messages from his team.

As he strode out Brown knew the score. He already had 203 runs this series which, aside from Stoddart and Albert Ward, was the highest total in the team. He felt confident, as though he had already earned his rightful place in the team. Today he intended to express himself. Win or lose, right from the off, he decided to play by the sword.

First ball Brown square drove to the boundary. Next ball he hooked for four. He rode his luck, thrashing away at full-length balls and hitting in the air and just over the infield. When he miscued, the ball landed in the vacant areas. Albert Ward played his part with a glorious square cut that left the spectators applauding as though he were one of them. In less than half-an-hour, the Yorkshireman had raced to fifty – the fastest in tests. By lunch, after just 80 minutes of play, Brown was not out 80, Ward 41. Taking scant regard for the pressure induced by this pivotal point in the series, Brown simply continued onwards to play the first truly attacking innings in England's history.

Albert Trott returned to the attack but the umpire rejected a catch behind to the keeper because Trott followed through in the direct line of vision. Luck was certainly with England. A snick off Brown's blade shot along the grounds through the slips for another four. Brown, realising he was in for some sort of quick century record, now started to lay into Harry Trott's leg spin. A four to the ropes, followed by a cut took Brown to his century, 95 minutes since taking guard. He lifted his bat to soak up the applause, mopped his brow, and noticed the entire Australian team had joined in.

Albert Ward reminded the 20,000 crowd of his presence by smiting Giffen for a mighty five straight back over this head (a five in 1895 is a six today). On they continued, with Brown dropped on the mid-wicket boundary by Jarvis. The 200 partnership came up with England hurtling towards the finishing line. Finally Brown fell, snicking McGibbon to slip where Giffen took a left-handed catch. The pair had put on what was then an Ashes record stand of 210. In all, Brown batted 145 minutes for 140, a quite astonishing rate and equivalent to a Botham and Pietersen knock of many generations ahead. Ward fell for 93, but England won by the impressive margin of six wickets. The Ashes, which could have gone either way on the last day, were secured by J. T. Brown's marvellous series-swinging innings.

Brown was to earn a further two caps against Australia in England during the 1896 series. He failed to make a score above 36 in four innings and was dropped. He did return for the third test at Headingley in 1899 and had the honour of going in first. The mighty W. G. Grace had just vacated the Number One spot two tests earlier. C. B. Fry had failed in the second test and so Brown was tried. He scored 27 and not out 14 in a drawn game, but never represented England again. England was in the process of bedding down a strong batting line-up made out of the likes of A. C. Maclaren, Ranjitsinhji, F. S. Jackson, T. Hayward, J. T. Tyldsley, G. L. Jessop and L. C. Braund.

Tragically, Jack Brown, a heavy smoker and drinker until he became a tee-total, died in 1904 at the age of 35 from 'congestion of the brain'. Lord Hawke of Yorkshire commented that whilst Brown had obvious ability with the bat, with his solitary test hundred, sensational as it undoubtedly was, he grew a little boastful of this innings, often played for his figures and tended to hog the strike. Playing an innings ranked third by this author, he had every reason to boast and without his contribution England may very well have sunk.

Australia 414 (Darling 74, Gregory 70, Giffen 57, Lyons 55, Peel 4–114, Richardson 3–138).
England 385 (MacLaren 120, Peel 73, Stoddart 68, Trott 4– 71, Giffen 4–130).
Australia 267 (Giffen 51, Darling 50, Richardson 6–104, Peel 3–89).
England 298–4 (Brown 140, Ward 93).
ENGLAND WON BY 6 WICKETS.

Innings Ranked Number 2
Gooch's 154 not out at Headingley in 1991

Opponents: West Indies.
At stake: Series.
Bowling attack: Ambrose, Patterson, Walsh, Marshal, Hooper, Richards: 25.53.
Pitch: Irregular bounce, movement of the seam, permanent cloud cover, ball swinging.
Game situation: England take a narrow first innings lead of 25 in a low scoring encounter.

West Indies were still the world champions but had been stunned by the tough cricket played by England in the Caribbean fifteen months earlier when England had seized the first test and shocked the world by winning their first test against the West Indies since April 1974. England drew the second test on account of an appalling West Indies over rate, but lost the series 2–1. Graham Gooch missed the rest of the series after being injured during England's run chase in the second test.

Now Gooch was back to bolster the top six. On paper England's top six batsmen at Headingley in 1991 looked assuredly strong. In fact Gooch (172), Atherton (68), Hick (176), Lamb (108), Ramprakash (125 and counting) and Smith (88) eventually combined to score no fewer than 737 hundreds between them in all first-class cricket, test and one day, international and county matches. Scrutinising old cricket books, I wondered whether any England top six order had scored more hundreds in their careers? The answer is not for many a year. In fact one has to go back before the Second World War and to the England team of the mid to late 1920s. The record for the most number of first class 100s compiled in a career for any England top six batting line up was England's fifth test-match side against South Africa in 1924; the top six then were Hobbs (197), Sutcliffe (149) Hearne (96), Woolley (145), Sandham (107) and Hendren (170) – no fewer than 862 hundreds.

The trouble with skipper Gooch's top-six order in 1991 was experience. Too many were young and hopeful. Atherton was 22, Ramprakash, playing in his first test, was only 21. Hick also made his debut here after a lengthy qualifying period, yet he was only 25 and the placid, soporific atmosphere at New Road, Worcestershire is nothing like the cauldron of test cricket. The world knew Hick was a flat-track bully, but could he dominate the West Indies pace attack? Aside from the new and the old, Gooch had a couple of tough South African's in Allan Lamb and Robin Smith, both of whom had excellent records against pace.

The Headingley wicket looked rather green on the overcast first morning, but Viv Richards won the toss and inserted England in to take advantage of any variable bounce and seize the upper hand. With luck, his fast-bowling armoury would remove five by lunch and the game would be all over.

England duly capitulated on a day truncated by rain and, although Robin Smith hit out for 54 and Ramprakash stayed in long enough to eke out 27, they closed on a wretched 174–7, all the front line batsmen gone. Smith was unfortunate. In the time before third umpires, it looked as though Smith was mighty close to making his ground. Such a tough call was cruel to England's chances. As he traipsed off, a look of disappointment etched all over his craggy face. England was foundering.

Conditions suited the raw and varied thunderbolts from opening bowler Patterson, but there was nothing raw about the more refined skills of Ambrose, Walsh and Marshall. Ambrose dug it in from a great height (6ft 7ins), Walsh hurled it in from wide of the crease – but occasionally got one to hold its line – whilst Marshall's pace was skiddy and deadly accurate. There was little respite.

On day two England limped to 198. This was now the seventh occasion that England had failed to reach 200 in just nine innings against the West Indies, a poor record and further testimony to the potency of the bowlers. Yet England's bowlers dug in and, although Devon Malcolm was expensive, DeFreitas, Watkin (also on debut) and Pringle bowled England back into the game. With more stops for rain, West Indies closed on 166–8 with Viv Richards leading the resistance with a typically flamboyant 73 not out. But Richards, in full flow, took the offer of bad light. This was uncharacteristically defensive for such an attacking legend. Even though it rained soon after, Richards taking the light gave renewed confidence to the England cause.

Third ball of the third day Richards fell, caught by Lamb off

Pringle, as the West Indies handed England a 25-run advantage. Down the steps came Gooch and Atherton, heavy cloud cover and the threat of rain all around. Drizzle was the worst weather variable to encounter. It kept the teams out there, the ball getting wet and the oldfield slow. At least heavy rain earns a break.

Once at the crease Gooch surveyed the field. He wore a thick white England sweater with the three lions emblazoned on the sternum. His helmet, white, as was the fashion in those days. He never shaved during tests, not towards the end of his career, and his three days of black stubble could be seen from beyond the boundary.

As Ambrose ran in, Gooch stood quite erect at the crease, eyes level, always level, knees slightly bent and bat quivering behind his back. Gooch had been on the test circuit since the Lillee and Thompson days of 1975. He had made a positive 34 in the first innings and a mountain of runs against India in England the previous year.

Ambrose hit a rhythm immediately and proved the most awkward to score off. Gooch waited for the bad ball but concentrated on survival. He knew that soon enough an unplayable ball would come along, so the need to be alert was paramount. Luckily Patterson laid on a four ball an over to get the score flowing. Gooch felt and looked good, but Atherton was subdued.

Gooch concentrated on what he as a player could do for England's cause. From the non-striker's end he looked on grimly as first Atherton was prized out (unfortunate how his partner kept getting unplayable deliveries), then Hick failed for the second time on debut, a real blow. Gooch hoped Hick was not shot to pieces by his first taste of the big time. All this while Gooch climbed into the twenties and square cut, first Patterson and then Marshall, for fours. Gooch felt good, but Ambrose had his tail up. Lamb provided Gooch with some experience as he came out to bat. A rising lifter, just short of a length, jagged wickedly and the South African was good enough and classy enough to get an edge. England, at 38–3, now had a lead of 63. Ramprakash joined Gooch, but was followed soon after by the rain.

Rain breaks infuriated Gooch; each time he had to play himself in again and the bowlers enjoyed a break. Steadily though, he gained an ally with the 21-year-old. Ramprakash had a superb technique and there is no doubt that his defence held up against some searching questions. At the other end, the junior witnessed his skipper unfurling some classic back foot off drives, more square cuts and a glorious on drive for four off Walsh. The total climbed upwards and the West Indies started to get agitated.

Ambrose came back and again demonstrated his class. After another valiant 27 Ramprakash edged Ambrose to Dujon to end a crucial stand of 78. England were still only 116–4. Robin Smith took guard, then Ambrose pinned him in front, to be on a hat trick twice in the same innings, a bitter blow for England, now 116–5, and only 141 ahead. For company Gooch now had his reliable and experienced Essex colleague, Derek Pringle.

As far back as 1982 Pringle had been the first to be hailed as the new Botham. The first England cricketer to wear an ear ring, he had provided glimpses of true all-rounder status down the years and with Botham injured, he defended with Gooch for as long as possible. Ambrose strained for a further breakthrough that night, but the Essex combination survived to add 25. Gooch was undefeated on 82, with Pringle on ten, England 143–6, 168 ahead. It was still anyone's game but one could not help thinking that the West Indies, with Dujon at seven, were still in the driving seat.

Next day, Gooch continued exactly where he left off – trying to squeeze out every last run. His running with Pringle was spot on and kept the scoreboard ticking over, to the great frustration of his West Indian counterpart, Richards.

The ball softened and the pitch eased. Gooch noticed how the West Indians strained every last sinew to extract as much from the pitch as possible. He noticed their growing frustration and this helped him stay focussed. The 200 lead was clapped, as was the 200 itself. Richards brought himself and Carl Hooper on to give his bowlers a longer break. The move proved futile in terms of breaking the stand, but the eight combined overs only went for 16.

With the lead on 247, Pringle fell for 27, caught behind off Marshall. With Gooch, he had added 98 – huge in the context of the game. But still Gooch was not through. Particularly severe on a tiring Marshall and feeling entirely comfortable at the crease, Gooch continued to thrive in conditions few humans could.

DeFreitas fell shortly for three, followed by Watkin for a duck. With Malcolm at the crease, Gooch tried to farm the strike and gather the last few runs. Eventually Marshall clean bowled Malcolm for four, leaving Gooch stranded on 154 not out.

This was only the second occasion where an England batsman has carried his bat in an innings in England, Hutton being the other. For $7^1/_2$ hours Gooch defied the odds to change the course of the test match. He did so when confronted by a fearsome quartet of quick bowlers, in favourable seam and swing conditions and on a pitch where no other batsman had scored more than 73. Gooch struck eighteen fours: two off Ambrose who was the pick, four off Patterson, five off Walsh and six off Marshall. Throughout his innings he did not give one obvious chance to the West Indies bowlers. There was precious little to drive off the front foot and he failed to score a single run between point and long on, when facing bowlers from the Main Stand End. His wagon-wheel points heavily to runs off his legs, a favourite strategy of test-class batsmen – leave alone outside the off stump and wait for the bowler to drift onto your legs. Gooch's strike rate was 46.5 – a touch slow, yet this again provides evidence of the general accuracy and spite of the attack. There must have been an urge to get after Hooper and Richards, but Gooch chose not to take the bait. His innings was a classic for a very good batsman, playing the percentages game. Time was of no importance, even with weather a constant threat throughout the test, the pitch was such that a result felt inevitable.

England's bowlers continued the good work, especially DeFreitas with another four-wicket haul. The margin of victory, 115 runs, shows the difference that Gooch had made. Because of his stubborn resistance, the innings lasted for 106 overs, almost as long as both West Indian innings put together.

Robin Smith's 148 not out saved the Lord's Test and eventually the series was all squared at 2–2, with Botham making an emotional return and hitting the winning runs at the Oval. In the end, Atherton, Hick and Lamb were dropped before the series was out. Ramprakash scored consistently in the twenties, valuable runs that kept hinting at greater things. Of England's much heralded top six, however, only Gooch and Smith scored 50s or more all through the series – a sober assessment of those who could and those who could not.

Graham Gooch continued to play for England until 1995. In all types of cricket, one day as well as the longer format, he scored over 65,000 runs, more than any other person in history. Only Graeme Hick (176) and Jack Hobbs (197) scored more hundreds than him. He will, however, be best remembered for his boundary count, usually high and more a blaster than a nudger. Like Jack Hobbs, and to a lesser extent W. G. Grace, Gooch proved a reliable and prolific run-getter well into his 40s. He kept himself fit and demanded total commitment from his players.

England 198 (R Smith 54, Marshall 3–46, Patterson 3–67).
West Indies 173 (Richards 73, DeFreitas 4–34).
England 252 (Gooch 154*, Ambrose 6–52, Marshall 3–58).
West Indies 162 (Richardson 68, DeFreitas 4–59, Watkin 3–38).
ENGLAND WON BY 115 RUNS.

Innings Ranked Number 1
Botham's 149 not out at Headingley in 1981

Opponents: Australia.
At stake: Ashes.
Bowling attack: Lillee, Alderman, Lawson, Bright: 28.33.
Pitch: Uneven bounce.
Game situation: England are 122 runs behind with five wickets left as Botham walks out to join Boycott.

The Royal Wedding summer, marred by unemployment figures of almost three million, needed a boost. The melancholy mood echoed the haunting script of the number one in the charts, *Ghost Town* by the Specials, a sign of the times in a hitherto summer of discontent.

The England cricket team was also at a low ebb. They had not won a single test for over a year that spanned twelve matches. Botham, the 24-year-old England captain had presided over flattering 1–0 and 2–0 defeats in successive series against the undisputed world champions, the West Indies. He had not scored a 50 since his first innings as captain thirteen months earlier and had taken no five-wicket innings hauls since the thirteen wickets in the Bombay test of 1980, his last before being handed the captaincy.

England had few batsmen of note. Only four had scored any meaningful runs in the Caribbean a few months earlier: Boycott, Gooch, Gower and Willey. What is more, Botham had resigned the captaincy after bagging a pair in the Lord's Test and Willis was said to be over the hill and bowling with little rhythm. How could such an experienced campaigner bowl 32 no balls at Lord's?

The Australians emerged as a very good test team, spearheaded by the legendary Dennis Lillee, as well as the unknown quantity of Terry Alderman, and backed up by the pace of Geoff Lawson. England's batsmen had failed against these Australian quicks. Although Lillee had suffered from pneumonia, he had still taken eleven wickets in 2 tests at 24, Lawson 8 at 19 and Alderman 11 at 23. Alderman had been a revelation – team mates claiming he had put on a yard of pace since debuting at Trent Bridge. Ray Bright gave solid assistance with orthodox left-arm spin.

England lost the first test by four wickets and the weather ensured a drawn second test. For the third test, Mike Brearley was brought back as captain and replaced Bob Woolmer. Botham kept his place, just. Since Lord's, Willis had only played in a county 2nd XI game to try to find form.

In the end, Brearley and the England selectors opted to choose a four-pronged seam attack to take the game from the Australians. Willis and Dilley were to provide the pace, with Botham and Chris Old as first and second change. Gooch and Boycott opened, Brearley himself was to fill the nightmare number-three slot, followed by Gower, Gatting and Willey. Botham would enter at number seven. Whilst England's bowlers had, by and large, kept a lid on the Australian batsmen to date, her batsmen had struggled against Lillee, Alderman and Lawson, and the tail had been blown away every time.

At such a crucial stage in the six test series, if Australia won they would be 2–0 up with three tests to play and well on the way to regaining the Ashes. The cracks on the pitch were obvious from two days before the game. 'Win the toss, win the test' thought umpire Barrie Meyer.

On the Wednesday, the England team turned up for their usual net session followed by a team talk in the evening. According to Peter Willey, team talks were often ruined by Botham, who claimed he would '...tell us how he was going to bowl everybody out, slog a hundred, then he'd throw a few bread rolls around and that was it – we were off to bed.'

Brearley slept fitfully that night, deliberating in his mind whether to go for the four seamers plus Peter Willey's off spin, or include Emburey and three seamers. Were Willis and Dilley too much of an expensive luxury? Would the side be stronger with Old in place of Emburey? Woodcock predicted in the *Times* that 'No one will benefit from Brearley's presence more than Botham. If either side wins it will, I believe, be England.'

Australia won the toss and elected to bat. A new electronic scoreboard had been neatly installed to clock the first digital information at the ground. Viewing the scoreboard on the first day ended up like Chinese water torture for England supporters.

The first day started off in a howling wind and, after two overs, bad light stopped proceedings as a dark cloud hung over the ground. Back on in no time, an hour saw dour defence but far too many wide balls which the batsmen just left alone – a waste of the new ball.

As the 50 was posted Brearley turned to Botham as second change. Soon a vicious inswinger trapped Wood in front and the Somerset hero leapt into the air with relief. At 12.25 rain came and play was adjourned until three o'clock.

The next 90 minutes saw a pitiful England display. Botham, Willis and Dilley were clearly having issues with line and length. With the ball spitting here and there, the need for accuracy was vital and three out of four seamers were below par. Catches went down in the slips, first Gower, out of position, spilt a catch off Botham at third slip, then Botham dropped two, a straight-forward chance off Bob Willis and later, in the gully, a thick, fast edge from Dyson's would-be cover drive. At this stage the crowd, now two-thirds full, started to taunt the former skipper. At tea, Australia were 97–1 and afterwards Dyson, first with Trevor Chappell and then Kim Hughes, took the game away from England.

Dyson brought up his first test century before the close, in fact his first score above 50, but was yorked right at the close by Dilley for 103. Australia finished on 203–3. Australian critics gave widespread acclaim to Dyson's knock on such a spiteful wicket. That Australia now enjoyed the upper hand on a poor wicket, which Brearley reckoned a good side could struggle to make 90 on, owed as much to wayward seam bowling, with the locals' favourite Chris Old the notable exception.

On day two, Australia battled on in the face of a crumbling wicket that now had an even more irregular bounce. More catches went begging in the slip cordon, an easy one off Botham, when Hughes was 66, then a hard chance to Brearley off Old, when Yallop was 22. The crowd despaired. The weather matched the miserable mood of the partisan crowd. It was windy, slightly milder than the previous day, but rain again curtailed play. Twenty-five minutes were lost before lunch and another 70 in the afternoon session. Tea was taken with Australia on an imposing 309–4. Up until tea Botham had only bowled nine overs. Now Brearley gave him a pep talk and brought him on. Botham bounded in with a brisk step not seen for a while. A

huge delivery stride and massive swinging arms hurtled the ball through at pace and at once the nature of the game changed.

Botham rapped Hughes on the groin and the Australian skipper huddled up in pain. Enjoying the moment, Botham walked to his mark and ran in with renewed purpose. Next ball, Hughes flimsily played to leg and gifted a top-edged return catch to Botham. In an inspired spell of 5–35, Botham also removed Border, leg before, caused Yallop to edge to Taylor behind, then bounced out Lawson and yorked Marsh. The crowd now cheered him and the sound must have felt like the singing of angels to him. In fact his response on taking the sixth wicket was rather half-hearted, as though he knew his efforts came probably too late to save the test.

Now England had to counter Lillee and Alderman. That evening both Boycott and Gooch survived an over a-piece.

On the third day, England scratched around and lunched on 78–3. Lillee had bowled poorly, perhaps not fully recovered from pneumonia, and sprayed the ball down both the leg and off side. Alderman was far more penetrative, bowling straight wicket to wicket with a little late swing under perfect conditions. Gooch fell for two, LBW to Alderman. Brearley batted painfully slowly and, after two leg before shouts, an inside edge to square leg got him off the mark. On ten Brearley edged Alderman for the simplest of catches to Marsh and Lawson bowled Boycott for a painstaking twelve from 90 minutes at the crease. The ball pitched short of a length and broke back, hit the front pad and clipped the leg stump bail – a frightening delivery, unplayable, out of the blue, and cruel luck.

Gower settled awkwardly, but on drove Alderman for four to break the silence, the first boundary of the innings. Later in the same over, Gower leaned into a flowing cover drive for four and soon after caressed Lawson through the off side. The sun shone for the first time as Gower and Gatting lunched with all England's hopes resting on their young shoulders.

Within minutes of resumption, both batsmen fell to leave Botham walking to the wicket on 90–5 with the crowd still cheering him. He soon settled to thrash Lillee twice through the covers for four. After a stand worth 22 with Willey, a Lawson yorker thudded onto Willey's back foot, the intense physical pain doubled with the umpire's verdict, 112–6.

In came Taylor to block for all he was worth. Meanwhile, Botham continued to ride his luck with fours hit off Lillee to light up the entertainment in an otherwise dour cause. So freely did Botham bat that he scored two-thirds of the runs whilst at the wicket. Taylor took 35 minutes to get off the mark, then struck Lillee beautifully straight for four before edging to Marsh. Botham fell soon after for a run a ball 50, handing Marsh the test wicket-keeping record. England finished on 174 all out and was asked immediately to follow on. That evening Gooch fell just before the bad light was offered to leave England precariously placed 219 runs adrift with nine second innings wickets left.

Sunday was a rest day, so Hughes's exhausted bowlers could now enjoy some relaxation. Saturday evening, Botham invited the whole England and Australian teams for a barbeque. The drinking lasted well into the early hours. Next day Willis remembers a couple of pints in the local, a roast lunch and an afternoon nap. The test was not much discussed, although everyone was unanimous that by the end of Monday the game would be lost.

Monday came and under another gloomy sky barely 2,000 spectators turned up, many clad in anoraks. There were acres of space on the Western Terraces. For once Brearley looked secure in the initial stages, but edged behind after fifteen minutes. Gower took over half-an-hour to get off the mark, then helped himself to nine from a Lillee over. Soon, the gifted left-hander received a jaffer from Alderman and edged to slip. When Gatting fell LBW, hitting across the line, England had slumped to 41-4.

Peter Willey entered the fray under the realisation that this might be his last test. Certainly, despite his two hundreds against the West Indies and the usefulness of his spin, he lacked consistency. All the while, the cricketing public could not believe such an open-chested stance from an England batsman.

Willey scored freely and he and Boycott put on the highest England stand in the match to date by passing the 42 put on by Gower and Gatting in the first innings. Willey leg glanced Lillee, and then cut him over gulley for successive fours. Next over Lillee put in a fly slip and deliberately fed Willey's uppercut. The ball seamed in and cramped Willey who was now committed to the shot. The edge flew straight to Dyson, at fly slip. Willey traipsed off into the international wilderness. Lillee now claimed the record Ashes wicket haul of 142 beating turn of the century Hugh Trumble.

In a nonchalant manner, Botham hurridly picked up one of Gooch's bats that still had not been fully knocked in and strode out to bat with a big grin on his face, as though planning some naughty school-boy prank. Christopher Martin-Jenkins's commentating remarked 'What a triumph it would be for him, if he could still be batting at 6 o'clock this evening.'

Botham played himself in. His first four from a rash slash flew over the slips. Watchful defence and a further brace of boundaries took Botham's score to 22 from 31 balls and the stand with Boycott worth 28. Talk around the crowd had willed Boycott to the 95 required to overtake Cowdrey's record – the England test haul of 7,624 runs. The crowd had swollen to 5,000 in anticipation of their local hero at least raising a cheer. Then Alderman unleashed another full-length straight delivery that snapped into Boycott's left leg. To this day, Boycott complains about the decision, but the scorebook does not lie, England 133–6. When Taylor fell, poking Alderman into the hands of short leg for one, the mood of the crowd changed. Now the game had gone, the result inevitable, anxiety evaporated and the Yorkshire faithful sat back, supped their pints and watched the last rights.

The sun came out and the Australians relaxed, content with the task of taking the final three wickets. England were 135–7, 92 runs behind with only three second innings wickets left. At the time this was a meaningless statement but within 24 hours it would become the most magical sounding equation of all time.

Botham told left-handed Dilley, blonde locks flowing out from under the blue helmet, 'Lets give it some humpety!' Dilley decided to swing at anything full but, for the first few times, failed to connect. Botham, helmetless and shirt collar sticking rakishly upwards over the sweater, leaned on his bat from the non-strikers' end and grinned. When Dilley connected and the ball sped to the boundary, Botham roared out his approval. Somehow the match had reached a humorous ending, a farcical phase like a comedy sketch in a Shakespeare play. Thrash at the ball without a care in the world, what a fine way to go.

Dilley scored 22 of the 27 runs before tea. Botham played a hard sledge-hammer cut, a difficult chance to Bright. Soon after, a mix up saw Dilley and Botham at the same end. Trevor Chappell seized on the ball and hurled it at the stumps. No mid-wicket could stop the ball and how the audience guffawed with the gifted four overthrows. More laughter, and at tea England walked off 51 behind with three wickets left. Twenty minutes later Dick Maddock, producer of *Test Match Special*, announced: 'Tea is over. I return you, for the last time I suspect, to Headingley.'

'At least Botham, whatever happens now, has enjoyed a very good test!' I said, sat on a chair in the living room of the new Luxmoore. Nicholas, an anti-England cricket fan, remarked that nothing Botham had achieved matched the 7–81 that Lawson took at Lord's. I sometimes wondered about my brother, but before a retort could be made, Dilley continued to defy logic and smashed another couple of fours through the covers like Garfield Sobers. Botham also defied the odds and blasted away from the start. In the hectic 30 minutes after tea the pair scored at two runs a minute, astonishing in the context of the game, but nonetheless entertaining. Botham raced to his second 50 in the game off 57 balls, then immediately slashed the next ball through a vacant third man area for four more. England had now taken the lead, a point I mentioned to my brother.

'Yes but its not going to affect the result Andrew!' was his reply.

Dilley was not to be outdone and knelt down on one knee to strike Lillee through cover for four. Furious, Lillee stormed back to his mark only for his next delivery to be slashed even more violently and a little squarer, through the covers. Astonishingly, Dilley repeatedly thrashed out at anything just outside off stump and collected another couple of boundaries. All the while, at the other end, Botham pulled the short balls, cut thunderously, mishit a couple that fell into vacant areas and, in amongst this carnage, deftly played a late cut for four. All the while, both batsmen grinned like Cheshire cats.

The Australians at first smiled and laughed at these ridiculous shots, safe in the knowledge that sooner or later the ball would spill into the air – comedy sketch over. But the laughter got louder. Border sensed the crowd mocking the team, in fact the whole team grew aware that thousands of supporters were laughing at them. This was disconcerting to say the least. Every further boundary brought with it a needle of pain.

Botham's pulling took on a fantastical edge. One such ended up flying over mid-off. Another hit the splice, but still had the legs to end up a one bounce, four over mid on. To complete the package, Botham charged Alderman and met a full-length delivery in the meat of the bat. The ball powered over the long-on boundary and further onwards into a confectionary stall, and out again. How the crowd cheered, as though sudden lottery winners, then roared with laughter.

Dilley flayed Lillee once more through the covers to bring up his 50. Alderman switched to round the wicket, changed his angle and slanted the ball into Dilley's stumps. Dilley swung and missed with the ball clipping the bails. He had made 56 from 75 balls and added 117 in 80 breathless minutes. In just fourteen overs the pair had put on 100. By now Alderman and Lillee were exhausted, but England were 25 runs ahead with only two wickets remaining. In his search for Botham's wicket, Hughes ignored the tailenders and focussed on bringing Botham down. Get Botham, win the test. He cajoled Lillee and Alderman into bowling a long spell when both were shattered.

Chris Old, another left hander like Dilley, came out to join Botham. Old was certainly no slouch with the bat. Seven first-class centuries to his name meant that he also had pretensions of being a batsman. He played himself in. Meanwhile Botham, on 95, creamed successive boundaries off Lawson; one cut bisected the fielders perfectly, the next carved wide of gully – pandemonium broke out. Botham hoisted his bat in the air for the jubilant crowd. His second 50 had taken just 30 balls and 40 minutes. His 103 came from 87 balls and resulted in Hughes posting seven fielders on the boundary. Brearley gesticulated from the pavilion balcony, pointing at Botham to stay there. Botham winked, gave him a 'v-sign' and enjoyed the moment.

Soon Old picked off the bad ball to hit and began to keep pace with Botham. Old looked around to see no fewer than four Australians barking out field placements to confused team mates. There was general disarray. The stand passed 50 and, at last, with the score on 309–8, Bright was brought into the attack. In hindsight, this was a vast tactical error by Hughes. The last time Bright had bowled to Botham was the dismissal in the second innings at Lord's, for 0. First ball Botham swung at Bright, missed, so did Marsh and four byes were added. The look of sheer disappointment on the faces of Bright and Marsh, spoke volumes for how quickly the game had changed.

Now the England supporters' thoughts turned to not losing the test and they marvelled at Botham's watchful defence and new-found grit in amongst the immense hits. One gloved hook looped over Marsh's outstretched hands for four a half chance no more. With the lead approaching 100, Old made room for himself against Lawson who cleverly fired in a slow yorker which hit the leg stump. Old had scored 29 from 33 balls and hit six fours. The 67-run partnership angered the Australians who began to see the rich entertainment in a new light – one with England directly challenging their supremacy in the game.

Hughes had enjoyed a cheerful rapport with his bowlers all day. Now he frequently ran up to each in turn to make suggestions. Lillee, in particular, walked away scowling with irritation.

The crowd held its breath for the last 30 minutes as Botham and Willis played out time. Botham batted like Hammond of old, driving imperiously through the covers. Willis held an end up as best he could as Botham farmed the strike. Off the last ball of the day Botham called Willis for a quick single to mid on. After a hesitation Willis ran through safely and both batsmen ran for the safety of the Pavilion steps as the crowd rushed onto the pitch. The lead was 124 and still there was the prospect of some runs next morning. As the Australians weaved this way and that through the home supporters they all, to a man, held stunned expressions on their faces. The evening session had yielded 175 runs in two hours, Botham scoring 106 in just 27 overs.

Twenty minutes after the end of play, Bob Taylor popped into the Australian dressing room with some bats for them to sign, but was told in no uncertain terms to 'f*** off with your f****** bats!' He reported back that the Australians appeared beaten, the psychological balance had tipped England's way. Botham sat down in the changing room a national hero once again. He lit a cigar and grinned a large, smug smile. Outside the crowd gathered and sung 'For he's a jolly good fellow – and so say all of us!'

On the fifth day, Botham crashed another boundary through the covers for four but Willis fell to give the persevering Alderman a six-wicket haul. Botham walked off with 149 not out.

The rest is history. This book is about a batsman's glory. A time when innings were played that were so special they were one of the 50 greatest ever played by Englishmen in tests. In the context of an Ashes series, Botham's 149 not out ranks as the greatest ever knock played by an Englishman. The innings shifted the balance of power in just two hours.

Botham also took the first wicket in Australia's first innings before Willis claimed 8–43 to win against the most impossible odds. The new electronic scoreboard had at one time indicated odds of 500–1 against an England win. This was only the second time England had won a test match after following on. The last occasion was through Jack Brown's 140 back in 1894.

As those Australian wickets tumbled after lunch on the last day, a mysterious look descended on my brother's face. Nicholas eventually went into the church and today holds a post as a Welsh Methodist Minister. Ask him today whether he has ever witnessed a miracle and he will probably smile and say 'Just the one.'

Willis's spell no doubt added the varnish to Botham's achievement.

Botham's knock was of a rare nature, starting with a huge grin on his face. He rode his luck with outrageous shots until at last locating the middle of the bat. Yet he overcame his lust for a laugh and buckled down to add that precious 37 for the last wicket with Willis.

Of Botham's 149 not out I finish on a quote from Bob Bee:

'No shift in the balance of a test series has ever been greater based on the performance of a single innings. For this reason it has to rank as the greatest innings ever played by an Englishman.'

Botham stayed at the top for a while and within a year was one of the three top batsmen in the world. In terms of pure theatre, a Botham hundred ranks as the finest spectacle I have witnessed in 35 years as an England supporter – swashbuckling, heroic, barn-storming stuff.

Australia 401 (Dyson 102, Hughes 89, Yallop 58, Botham 6–92).

England 174 (Botham 50, Lillee 4–49, Lawson 3–32, Alderman 3–59) and 356 (Botham 149*, Dilley 56, Boycott 46, Alderman 6–135, Lillee 3–94).

Australia 111 (Willis 8–43).

ENGLAND WON BY 18 RUNS.

The Statistical Analysis

Stage	Criteria
1	*Proportion of runs in the innings*

The higher the proportion of runs in the innings, the greater the innings. Thus Colin Cowdrey's 102 out of 191 in the 1954/55 Ashes series must be given greater weighting than, say, a score of 102 out of 750 for 5. A percentage is calculated.

2   *Number of runs scored*
The percentage total is then multiplied by the number of runs scored.

3   *Number of wickets to fall in the innings*
Innings are penalised if not all of the team was dismissed because this indicates easy conditions. For every wicket that does not fall, the score is divided by 1.1 for 9 down, 1.2 for 8 down, 1.3 for 7 down etc.

4   *Pitch and conditions*
Featherbeds are wickets which yield a score of over 500. Because conditions are easy, the total is multiplied by 0.75. If pitch conditions are reported in *Wisdon* as having uneven bounce: x by 1.25. If there are many breaks for rain: x. 1.25. If conditions are treacherous or sticky: x 1.50

5   *Influence on the result*
Innings is multiplied by 1.25 if the innings ensured a draw and 1.5 if the innings helped to win the game.

6   *Influence on the series*
Innings is multiplied by 1.25 if it ensured a drawn series or by 1.5 if it won the series.

7   *Drama*
Multiply by 1.25 if the innings is scored at around a run a ball or if breaking a record; multiply by 1.30 if the strike rate is greater than 110; multiply by 1.40 if the strike rate is greater than 120; multiply by 1.5 if the batsman comes from a sick bed (Payntor), or is floored by a Lindwall bumper

(Compton), or is making a come back after 5 years as a 42 year old (Washbrook), or if considered the greatest sporting occasion in history by 1.25.

8   *Chanceless*
If *Wisdon* states the innings was chanceless the score is multiplied by 1.1.

9   *Against the world champions*
Multiply by 1.25

10 *Not out*
Multiply by 1.1

11 *Standard of the bowling*
The points tally is now divided by the average number of runs per wicket of the bowling attack, weighted by their contribution to the innings and based upon the career averages of each bowler. Important to note that a ceiling figure is put at 100 runs per wicket. Thus Waite who only took 1 wicket for 170 in his career is given a runs per wicket average of 100 to allow Hutton's 364 at the Oval in 1938 to make the final 50.

12 *Innings of the test match.*
To consider the natural deterioration of a wicket over the course of the game: 2nd innings is multiplied by 1.1, 3rd innings by 1.3 and 4th innings by 1.5.

13 *Rearguard value*
Rearguard Value: all 'wickets penalty' in stage 3 get removed if the rearguard is successful, plus 10 pts per hour are added in the 3rd innings, 20 pts an hour in the 4th innings.

14 *State of play at the start of the innings*
Multiply by 1.5 if hopeless, odds of 100–1 against; 1.3 if well behind, 1.1 if just behind, 1 if evens.

Bibliography

D. R. Allen: E. W. Swanton – *A Celebration of his Life and Work*, Metro, 1996.
J. Arlott: *Cricket: The Great Ones*, 1967.
P. Arnold and P. Wynne-Thomas: *An Ashes Anthology*, Helm, 1989.
J. Arlott: *Two Summers at the Tests*, The Pavilion Library, 1986.
M. Atherton: *Opening Up*, Hodder & Stoughton 2002.
J. Bannister: *The Innings of My Life*, Leukaemia Research Fund, Headline, 1993.
R. Barker: *Ten Great Innings*, Chatto & Windus, 1964.
N. Barrett: *The Daily Telegraph Chronicle of Cricket*, Guinness, 1994.
S. Barnes: *Eyes on the Ashes*, William Kimber, 1953.
M. Brearley: *The Return of the Ashes*, Pelham Books, 1978.
N. Cardus: *Play Resumed With Cardus*, Souvenir Press, 1979.
D. Compton: *Playing for England*, Sampson Low, Marston & Co, 3rd Edition, 1951.
C. Cowdrey: *MCC The Autobiography of a Cricketer*, Hodder & Stoughton, 1976.
P. Cox: *Sixty Summers*, Labatie Books, 2006.
P. Eagar: *Caught in the Frame–150 years of Cricket Photography*, National Power, 1992.
G. Evans: *Action in Cricket*, Hodder & Stoughton, 1956.
D. Foot: *Wally Hammond, The Reasons Why*, 1998.
B. Frindall: *Wisden Book of Test Cricket 1877–1984*, Guild Publishing, 1984.
B. Frindall: *Wisden Book of Test Cricket Volume II 1977–1994*, Headline, 1994.
D. Frith: *England versus Australia A Pictorial History of the Test Matches Since 1877*, Lutterworth Press & Richard Smart Publishing, 1977.
D. Frith: *Stoddy's Mission, The First Great Test Series 1894/95*, Queen Anne Press, 1994.
N. Giller: *The World's Greatest Cricket Matches*, Octopus Books, 1989.
D. Gower: *Gower, The Autobiography*, Harper Collins, 1992.

W. Hammond: *Cricket My Destiny*, Stanley Paul & Co, circa 1939.
B. Harris: *Cricket Triumph 1953*, Hutchinson, 1953.
N. Hoult: *The Daily Telegraph Book of Cricket*, Aurum Press, 2007.
L. Hutton: *Fifty Years in Cricket*, Stanley Paul & Co. Ltd, 1984.
D. Lemmon: *Benson & Hedges Cricket Year Book*, Bloomsbury, 1999.
C. Martin-Jenkins: *In Defence of the Ashes*, MacDonalds & Jane's, 1979.
C. Martin-Jenkins: *Testing Time MCC in the West Indies 1974*, Reader's Union, 1975.
C. Martin-Jenkins: *The Complete Who's Who of Test Cricketers*, 3rd Edition, Guild Publishing, London, 1987.
R. Mason: *Jack Hobbs A Biography*, Pavilion Library, 1960.
M. A. Noble: *The Fight for the Ashes 1928–29*, Harrap, 1929.
I. Peebles: *Woolley The Pride of Kent*, Hutchinson & Co, 1969.
K. Pietersen: *Crossing the Boundary*, Ebury Press, 2006.
K. S. Ranjitsinji: *The Jubilee Book of Cricket*, Nelson & Sons, circa 1897.
J. Rice: *One Hundred Lord's Tests*, Methuen, 2001.
J. Rivers: *England versus Australia Complete Test Match Records*, Boardman & Company.
E. L. Roberts: *Test Cricket Cavalcade*, Arnold, 1947.
I. Stafford: *Ashes Fever How England Won the Greatest Ever Test Series*, Mainstream Publishing, 2005.
D. Steer: *Cricket the Golden Age*, Cassell Illustrated, 2003.
H. Sutcliffe: *For England and Yorkshire*, Edward Arnold & Co, 1935.
E. W. Swanton: *Back Page Cricket*, MacDonald Queen Anne Press, 1987.
E. W. Swanton: *Swanton in Australia with the MCC, 1946–1975*, Collins, 1975.
A. A. Thompson: *Cricketers of My Times*, Stanley Paul, 1967.
M. Vaughan: *Calling the Shots*, Hodder & Stoughton, 2005.
P. Warner: *The Fight for the Ashes in 1926*, Harrap, 1926.
R. Webber: *The Phoenix History of Cricket*, Phoenix Sports Books, 1960.
Wisden Cricketers Almanac, 1881 to 2006.
Wisden Book of Test Cricket, Volume II, 1977–1994.
P. Wynne Thomas: *The Complete History of Cricket Tours At Home and Abroad*, Hamlyn, 1989.